The Spiritual Jurisdiction in Reformation Scotland

To
Z T G
A J B G
L M C G

The Spiritual Jurisdiction in Reformation Scotland
A Legal History

Thomas M. Green

EDINBURGH
University Press

Edinburgh University Press is one of the leading university presses in the UK. We publish academic books and journals in our selected subject areas across the humanities and social sciences, combining cutting-edge scholarship with high editorial and production values to produce academic works of lasting importance. For more information visit our website: edinburghuniversitypress.com

© Thomas M. Green, 2019, 2021

Edinburgh University Press Ltd
The Tun – Holyrood Road
12 (2f) Jackson's Entry
Edinburgh EH8 8PJ

First published in hardback by Edinburgh University Press 2019

Typeset in 10/12 Goudy Old Style by
IDSUK (DataConnection) Ltd

A CIP record for this book is available from the British Library

ISBN 978 0 7486 9998 8 (hardback)
ISBN 978 0 4744 8429 9 (paperback)
ISBN 978 0 7486 9999 5 (webready PDF)
ISBN 978 1 4744 5235 9 (epub)

The right of Thomas M. Green to be identified as author of this work has been asserted in accordance with the Copyright, Designs and Patents Act 1988 and the Copyright and Related Rights Regulations 2003 (SI No. 2498).

Contents

Acknowledgements	vii
Abbreviations	ix
Introduction	1
1. The Suppression of the Courts of the Catholic Church in Scotland	**7**
The courts of the Catholic Church in Scotland	7
Revolution and reform	9
The Wars of the Congregation	13
The deposition of Regent Guise	16
The Inquiry of La Brosse and Cleutin	17
The ordinance against the courts of the Catholic Church	21
Effectiveness of the suppression of the Catholic courts spiritual	25
2. Revolution and Law: The Reformation Parliament, the Proclamation of Leith and the Law of Oblivion	**33**
The 'First Legal Framework'	34
The Government of Scotland, August 1560 to August 1561	44
The 'Second Legal Framework'	47
The Reformation Parliament legislation and the spiritual jurisdiction	53
3. Papal and Episcopal Jurisdiction in Scotland following the Reformation Crisis	**57**
The validity of the legislation of the Reformation Parliament	57
Archbishop Hamilton's papal and episcopal jurisdictions	66
Eglinton v. Hamilton, Hamilton v. Eglinton	67
The restoration of spiritual jurisdiction to Archbishop Hamilton	69
Gordon v. Hepburn, Hepburn v. Gordon	73
Ordinary episcopal jurisdiction following the Reformation crisis	75
Conclusion	79
4. The Rise of the Courts of the Church of Scotland	**80**
Consistorial actions before kirk sessions prior to the Reformation Parliament	82
Consistorial actions before superintendents' courts and kirk sessions following the Reformation Parliament	87
The consistorial jurisdiction of the new church courts following the queen's return	94
Consistorial actions before superintendents' courts and kirk sessions following the queen's return	98
The General Assemblies of the kirks of Scotland	106
Conclusion	109

5.	**The Lords of Council and Session**	**110**
	The circumspection of the Lords of Council and Session during the Reformation crisis	112
	Litigants petitioning the Court of Session with spiritual causes	114
	Papal jurisdiction	118
	Litigants' understanding of what had befallen the old courts spiritual	121
	Court of Session commissions and the prefiguration of the Court of the Commissaries of Edinburgh	123
	Conclusion	126
6.	**The Court of the Commissaries of Edinburgh**	**128**
	The need for a more sustainable order	129
	The creation of the commissary system	132
	The Commissaries of Edinburgh	142
	The inferior commissaries	144
	The restoration of order	146
	The Commissaries of Edinburgh's consistorial jurisdiction and the courts of the Church of Scotland	148
	The pre-1564 consistorial judgements of the courts of the Church of Scotland	150
7.	**The Commissary Courts and the Jurisdiction of the Courts of the Church of Scotland**	**158**
	The interplay between disciplinary and consistorial jurisdictions	161
	Jurisdictional co-operation and divergence: the staying of banns	163
	The exception of St Andrews	166
	Forbes v. Sandilands	168
	The continued interplay of disciplinary and consistorial jurisdictions at St Andrews	170
	Kay v. Arnot	172
	Dalgleis & Wemyss; Boswell v. Wemyss	173
	Church Jurisdiction Act 1567	177
	St Andrews and the Commissaries of Edinburgh post-1567	180
	Johnston v. Morris; Morris v. Johnston & Winram	183
	Conclusion	184
Conclusion		**187**
Appendix		191
Outline Chronology, 1558–1567		195
Select Bibliography		201
Index		207

Acknowledgements

The research interests upon which this monograph are based were developed while the author was a postgraduate and doctoral candidate at the School of Divinity, University of Edinburgh, between 2004 and 2010. Between 2006 and 2009, the author was in receipt of a doctoral scholarship from the Stair Society, which has a distinguished history in publishing works concerning the ecclesiastical history of Scots law. During this period in particular the author was the beneficiary of a unique research context. On the one hand, the author's doctoral supervisors, Professor Jane E. A. Dawson at the School of Divinity, and Professor John W. Cairns at the School of Law, were in possession of a unique combined knowledge of sixteenth-century Scottish ecclesiastical and legal history. On the other hand, the membership of the Stair Society itself provided a rich context of unlooked-for expertise in respect of the legal history of the Scottish Reformation. This was especially true in respect of the author's encounters with the late Sheriff David B. Smith and the late Sheriff Peter G. B. McNeill. In these respects, the years 2006 to 2010 involved a unique confluence of opportunity, supervisory expertise and direct contact with a living tradition of specialised historical knowledge.

Between 2011 and 2014 further research funding was provided by the British Academy, through a postdoctoral fellowship at the School of Law, University of Edinburgh. Towards the end of that fellowship the proposal for this monograph was submitted to and accepted by the commissioning editor for law and history at Edinburgh University Press, John Watson, and the author is grateful both to him and to the two anonymous peer reviewers who read the proposal and a draft of the first chapter. The author is grateful to John Watson and to his successor at EUP, Laura Williamson, for their good will and patience in awaiting the submission of this work.

Encouragement to persist with this work has been variously received and the author is particularly grateful to Professors Mark Godfrey, John D. Ford and Hector L. MacQueen. The author also wishes to acknowledge the award of an honorary research fellowship by the School of Law, University of Glasgow, between 2015 and 2018, which afforded the author access to the resources of a university library during the period when work on this monograph was completed. Above all the author wishes to acknowledge the support received from his wife, without which this work could not have been completed.

Thomas M. Green,
at Crookston,
Easter Saturday, 2018

The author is also grateful to the anonymous reader who read the post-submission typescript of this work, and who provided full and generous feedback. Responsibility for such faults, omissions and errors as remain lies solely with the author.

Abbreviations

Balfour's Practicks	*The Practicks of Sir James Balfour of Pittendreich*, ed. Peter G. B. McNeill (Edinburgh: The Stair Society, 1962–3), 2 volumes.
CSP Foreign, Eliz.	*Calendar of State Papers, foreign series, of the reign of Elizabeth*, ed. Joseph Stephenson et al. (London: Longman, Roberts and Green, 1863–1950), 23 volumes.
CSP Scot.	*Calendar of the State Papers Relating to Scotland and Mary, Queen of Scots, 1547–1603*, ed. J. Bain et al. (Edinburgh: H. M. General Register House, 1898–1969), 13 volumes.
Diurnal	*A Diurnal of Remarkable Occurents that have passed within the country of Scotland since the death of King James the Fourth till the year 1575*, ed. T. Thomson (Edinburgh: Bannatyne Club, 1833).
Fasti	*Fasti Ecclesiae Scoticanae: the Succession of Ministers in the Church of Scotland from the Reformation*, ed. Hew Scott (Edinburgh: Oliver and Boyd, 1915–1928), 8 volumes.
First Book of Discipline	*The First Book of Discipline*, ed. James K. Cameron (Edinburgh: Saint Andrew Press, 1972).
Knox's History	*John Knox's History of the Reformation in Scotland*, ed. W. C. Dickinson (London: Thomas Nelson, 1949), 2 volumes.
NRS	The National Records of Scotland, formerly the National Archives of Scotland, formerly the Scottish Record Office.
ODNB	*Oxford Dictionary of National Biography*, ed. H. C. G. Matthew and B. Harrison (Oxford: Oxford University Press, 2004), 60 volumes; www.oxforddnb.com.
RMS	*The Register of the Great Seal of Scotland (Registrum Magni Sigilli Regum Scotorum)*, ed. J. M. Thomson et al. (Edinburgh, 1882–1914), 11 volumes.
RPC	*The Register of the Privy Council of Scotland*, ed. J. H. Burton et al. (Edinburgh, 1877–), 37 volumes.

RPS	*The Records of the Parliament of Scotland*, ed. Keith Brown et al. (St Andrews, 2007); www.rps.ac.uk.
RSS	*The Register of the Privy Seal in Scotland (Registrum Secreti Sigilli Regum Scotorum)*, ed. M. Livingstone et al. (Edinburgh, 1908–), 8 volumes.
Shaw, Acts and Proceedings	*The Acts and Proceedings of the General Assemblies of the Church of Scotland, 1560–1618*, ed. Duncan Shaw (Edinburgh: Scottish Record Society, 2004), 3 volumes.
St Andrews	*The Register of the Minister, Elders and Deacons of the Christian Congregation of St Andrews*, ed. D. H. Fleming (Edinburgh: Scottish History Society, 1889–90), 2 volumes.
Watt and Murray, Fasti	*Fasti Ecclesiae Scoticanae Medii Aevi ad annum 1638*, ed. D. E. R. Watt and A. L. Murray (Edinburgh: Scottish Record Society, 2003).

Introduction

At first flush the sources of evidence concerning the history of the spiritual jurisdiction in Reformation Scotland appear confused, disorderly and contradictory. Various problems as to chronology, constitutional theory, competent authority and lawful jurisdiction confront the historian on almost all sides. Engagement with the vexed problems of the validity of the rebellion by which Protestant ecclesiastical reform was initially achieved in Scotland, of the consequences and validity of the legislation of the Reformation Parliament, of the status and jurisdiction of the courts of the Church of Scotland, and of the concept of episcopacy following the overthrow of the Catholic ascendancy, cannot be avoided. Within the traditional confines of Scottish ecclesiastical history, these problems have tended to defy enduring resolution, primarily because there appears to be only two contemporaneous perspectives from which these problems can be viewed, the one Catholic, the other Protestant. The outcomes suggested, or even dictated, by these perspectives have, of course, tended to be contradictory. A third contemporaneous perspective from which to view these problems within Scottish ecclesiastical history is provided by a focus on a jurisdictional history of the Reformation.

A jurisdictional history brings into view a distinctive group who lived through those momentous times, and who appear to have viewed matters not primarily through the prism of Catholicism and Protestantism, but through the prism of moderatism and radicalism. This group were all in one way or another trained lawyers, be they jurists, judges, officers of state or all three at once. While divisions as to religion are of course found among this group, it does not appear to have dominated their frames of reference. Rather, when faced with a revolution of the most far-reaching potential consequences for the Scottish legal system, both as to jurisdiction and as to law, care, moderation and nuanced judgement appear to have been the order of the day. For the leading lawyers of the day the Scottish Reformation presented them with a constitutional and jurisdictional crisis of the first order. On an intellectual level this crisis cast into sharp relief almost every aspect of the Scottish polity and it is hard to resist the view that, notwithstanding the stakes involved, many of them must have found living through the Reformation a remarkable intellectual experience. Yet at the same time the crisis within the legal system occasioned by the Reformation was not one of intellectual interest only. Rather, this group of lawyers were intimately involved in restoring order to the legal system through a series of comprehensive interventions, at a time when straying too far towards the Catholic position, or too far towards the more radical Calvinist position, would have resulted in the failure of their interventions, and consequently a failure of their duty to restore order in a time of revolution.

Despite the identification of this third potential perspective from which a contemporaneous understanding of the Reformation might be obtained, none of these lawyers left written accounts of their actions during the years 1558 to 1572. Accordingly their various responses to the consequences of the revolution of March 1558/9 to September 1561, together with the thoughts and motivations underpinning their responses, have for the most part been neglected by historians. It seems certain that Gordon Donaldson perceived the value of a legal history of the Scottish Reformation during the late 1950s, and to that end influenced the research of two young advocates, Peter McNeill and David Smith, during the 1960s. In light of the research and publications of Donaldson, McNeill and Smith, there was one final area of research required to be undertaken prior to writing this monograph, and that concerned the history of the commissary courts. This system of courts was established during the personal reign of Mary, Queen of Scots, and proved to be the enduring successor system of courts to those of the Catholic Church in Scotland. To this end the author has published variously on the subject, as may be ascertained by consulting the appended bibliography. With this inter-generational groundwork in readiness, the remaining areas of research still outstanding could be published within the compass of a single work.

Gaining a detailed understanding of the intellectual responses of the leading lawyers of the day and their corresponding actions during the Reformation nevertheless remained an arduous task. As can again be ascertained from consulting the bibliography, evidence drawn from primary source materials dominates this monograph. The basic approach adopted in this work had been to establish the practical and legal contexts within which the leading lawyers of the day found themselves, and to interpret their determinable actions within that context. Knowledge of the practical realities attending the contexts within which they acted has been either recovered *de novo* from the extant sources, or elaborated and recapitulated from the works of Donaldson, McNeill and Smith, together with those of the author of the present work. Practical contextual factors such as the suppression of the courts of the Catholic Church in Scotland during the Reformation crisis, the creation of legal frameworks in response to the crisis, and the position of the spiritual jurisdiction in law following the Reformation Parliament are considered in the first two chapters of this monograph.

Having set the scene as to the legal problems and contexts generated by the Reformation crisis, attention is turned to those aspects of this history which may be viewed as exceptional, or yet more complicating, and which in time were obviated by the actions of the Lords of Council and Session and the Commissaries of Edinburgh. Chapter 3 accordingly deals with the survival and ongoing exercises of papal and episcopal jurisdiction in Scotland following the Reformation Parliament. Papal jurisdiction was supposed to have been abrogated in Scotland by statute in August 1560, and understanding why this proved not to be the case from the lawyerly perspective is rendered at least comprehensible within the contexts outlined in the first two chapters. Chapter 3 also concerns what may be considered to have been the more radical Catholic solution to the crisis within the legal system by the mid-1560s: simply restore things to how they had been before the crisis. In contrast, Chapter 4 concerns the more radical Protestant solution to the crisis: simply allow the courts of the Church of Scotland to succeed to part of the spiritual jurisdiction of the old church courts, and hive off the residual functions of the old church courts on to the remainder of the Scottish legal system. This proposed succession is exceptionally pronounced in respect of what Scots lawyers still on occasion refer to as the consistorial jurisdiction, which to the layperson needs to be understood as a jurisdiction in respect of matrimonial litigation. Succession, however, may be a misleading way of describing what the leading Scottish reformers thought they were doing in their capacity as judges within the new Reformed church courts. Rather, their actions appear to indicate a fundamental rejection of the Catholic constitutional understanding of spiritual jurisdiction, and the adoption of what is a recognisably Calvinist spiritual jurisdiction, albeit one apparently uniquely Scottish. This radical alteration within the Scottish legal system as to spiritual jurisdiction brought with it the potential for a wholesale rejection of medieval Canon law and the adoption of a new marriage law founded upon a Calvinist understanding of the 'law of God'.

From this point on the relative confusion encountered within this history begins to be resolved. Chapter 5 concerns the assumption of the spiritual jurisdiction of the old Catholic church courts by the Court of Session in December 1560. This assumption appears to have been undertaken by the judges of the Court of Session as a temporary expedient in the interest of order. It is also during the course of Chapter 5 that the leading Protestant nobles of the Reformation and the Scottish reformers begin to recede into the background, and the group of judges and officers of state by which order was restored to the legal system come into sharper focus. While the names of Henry and John Sinclair, John Spens of Condie, Sir John Bellenden of Auchnoul, James MacGill of Nether Rankeillour and James Balfour will already have been encountered in earlier chapters, it is from this point on that their combined actions and judgements in response to the crisis within the legal system come to the fore.

The intervention of the judges of the Court of Session in respect of the spiritual jurisdiction looks to have provided the basis upon which the creation of the Court of the Commissaries of Edinburgh, and the commissary system more generally, was effected from February 1563/4. Chapter 6 concerns the creation of this new system of courts, which was occasioned by a decisive and direct intervention of royal authority in respect of the crisis within the legal system, an intervention guided by and accomplished through the advice and actions of many of the leading lawyers of the day. This system of commissary courts succeeded directly to the old Catholic church courts, and was considered in constitutional and conceptual terms to be administering the spiritual jurisdiction of the bishops and other prelates of the Scottish Church. In this respect part of the pre-Reformation concept of spiritual jurisdiction survived the Reformation crisis, and the Canon law enforced by that jurisdiction continued for the most part to be enforced. In this the commissary system was itself a moderate response to the earlier suppression of the old church courts during the Reformation crisis, which response charted a careful course between Catholic restoration and radical Calvinism.

The restoration of order considered in Chapters 5 and 6 directly contradicted the more radical Protestant narrative of what was occurring within the legal system. Chapter 7 accordingly considers the interaction of the consequences of these two narratives, namely jurisdictional relations between the commissary courts and the courts of the Church of Scotland. Jurisdictional divergence, and at times conflict, is most pronounced in respect of the consistorial, or matrimonial, jurisdiction of the Commissaries of Edinburgh and the matrimonial jurisdiction of the new church courts at St Andrews during the period 1564 to 1572. On the one hand, the Commissaries of Edinburgh had been commissioned by royal authority to exercise jurisdiction in respect of all matrimonial litigation within the kingdom. On the other hand, the courts of the Church of Scotland had proceeded to hear all manner of matrimonial litigation, and to pronounce judgements as the result of such processes, from the winter of 1559/60. These two consistorial jurisdictions were in effect mutually contradictory, and the manner in which the Church of Scotland sought to disentangle its disciplinary jurisdiction from its involvement in matrimonial litigation, and the manner in which the Commissaries of Edinburgh sought in effect to suppress the competence of the new church courts at St Andrews in respect of matrimonial litigation, form the basis of the final chapter of this work.

The general structure of this monograph has been dictated by a focus on jurisdiction, without which the evidence provided by the extant source materials would have crowded in in so undifferentiated and chaotic a manner as to be quite bewildering. For example, during the course of 1566 matrimonial actions are known to have been heard by papal judges delegate appointed by virtue of the legatine authority of the Catholic Archbishop of St Andrews, by the Protestant superintendent of Fife, Fotherick and Strathearn holding court at St Andrews, and by the Commissaries of Edinburgh. This is indicative of the multifaceted confusion which a strict chronological approach would have encountered. A jurisdictional focus brings a welcome degree of differentiation and relative clarity, but requires that the same chronological periods be variously visited and re-visited during the course of this work. Accordingly, Chapter 1 concerns the spiritual jurisdiction of the Catholic Church, and covers the period c.1558 to August 1560. Chapter 2 concerns the two principal legal frameworks created in response to the Reformation crisis during the period 1560 to 1563, to which the perennial and thorny problem of the Reformation Parliament and its legislation is intimately bound. Chapter 3 deals with papal and episcopal jurisdiction during the period August 1560 down to c.1567. Chapter 4 concerns the development of the courts and jurisdiction of the early Church of Scotland from c.1559 to February 1563/4. Chapter 5 concerns the jurisdiction of the judges of the Court of Session in spiritual causes from December 1560 to *c*.February 1563/4. Chapter 6 concerns the jurisdiction of the Court of the Commissaries of Edinburgh, and the commissary system more generally, from February 1563/4, and the manner in which the Commissaries of Edinburgh dealt with matrimonial judgements pronounced by the courts of the Church of Scotland during the period prior to the Commissaries' appointment. Chapter 7 concerns the jurisdictions of the commissary courts and of the courts of the Church of Scotland from February 1563/4 to *c*.1572. While these various jurisdictions have been thus differentiated by the structure of this work, an outline chronology has been provided for the particularly confused period of 1558 to 1567, so as to give an overall impression of how some of the principal aspects of this history fell out at the time.

One final point ought to be noted here. The evidence upon which extensive parts of Chapters 3 to 7 are based has been drawn from the documentation generated by exercises of jurisdiction during the period under consideration. This tends to mean that the evidence upon which these chapters are based has been furnished by extant court records for the period. The nature of this evidence and its proper discussion has inevitably involved the use of procedural terminology found in those records. Legal historians who happen to read this work will be quite at home with such terminology, but those without prior knowledge of such terminology may wish to familiarise themselves with the same. To this end, the author has already provided in print two points of reference, which can usefully be consulted in conjunction.[1]

---

[1] Namely a glossary of procedural terminology in Green, *Consistorial Decisions*, 399–403, together with Green, 'Romano-canonical Procedure'.

Chapter 1

The Suppression of the Courts of the Catholic Church in Scotland

The courts of the Catholic Church in Scotland were suppressed during the Wars of the Congregation, principally following the deposition of Mary of Guise from the regency and the attempted assumption of government by the Lords of the Congregation. In order to understand why the suppression of the courts of the Catholic Church resulted in a considerable degree of uncertainty and even crisis for the Scottish legal system and the Scottish polity, it is necessary to consider the Wars of the Congregation and to understand that they were themselves uncertain and chaotic, from their theoretical justification to their vacillating and often violent progress.

THE COURTS OF THE CATHOLIC CHURCH IN SCOTLAND

On the eve of the Reformation, the courts of the Catholic Church in Scotland formed an integral part of the Scottish legal system, and were arguably the most developed system of courts in the kingdom. This system of courts was concentrated for the most part in lowland Scotland and they were to be found from Shetland to Whithorn, and from St Andrews to Argyll.[1] These courts sat relatively permanently throughout many of the cathedrals, collegiate churches and other ecclesiastical buildings of Scotland, and were staffed by beneficed churchmen, from local deans and Commissaries to the Officials and Officials Principal of the archiepiscopal sees, many of whom enjoyed a high level of education and legal expertise. The jurisdiction of these church courts was held to be spiritual, and formed one of the three jurisdictions of the Scottish legal system, alongside the criminal and civil jurisdictions emanating from the Scottish Crown, these more familiar jurisdictions being administered variously by the court of the Lord Justice General, Parliament, the Privy Council, the Court of Session, the sheriff courts, the burgh courts and the old feudal franchise courts. The spiritual jurisdiction emanated principally from the ordinary episcopal jurisdiction of the Scottish hierarchy, and as such most Scottish Commissaries and Officials were appointed by the Scottish episcopate, although some Commissaries were appointed by archdeacons and religious houses in respect of their peculiar spiritual jurisdictions.

---

[1] For maps providing the locations of pre-Reformation Officials' and Commissaries' courts throughout Scotland see *Atlas of Scottish History*, ed. McNeill and MacQueen, 379–380.

In this respect, the native Scottish spiritual jurisdiction may be best described as 'prelatical', since although dominated by episcopal authority, it also in part emanated from archdiaconal and abbatial authority.

Within these courts spiritual appeal lay from regional Commissaries and Officials to Officials Principal at Glasgow and St Andrews, which archepiscopal courts were in turn subject to the supreme appellate jurisdiction of the bishops of Rome. Appeals to Rome were often heard within Scotland through the device of appointing Scottish churchmen as papal judges delegate on an appeal-by-appeal basis. Nevertheless, papal jurisdiction within Scotland was not limited to final appeals, since Scottish litigants could either petition Rome directly or petition papal legates to hear their spiritual actions at first instance, thereby bypassing the older native Scottish courts spiritual. Where first instance spiritual causes were heard by virtue of papal jurisdiction, such causes were often heard in Scotland by papal judges delegate, such judges being usually Scottish churchmen, and on occasion Scottish spiritual judges, commissioned to hear such actions either directly by Rome, or by the Archbishop of St Andrews exercising a delegated papal legatine authority. Appeal lay from such papal judges delegate to Rome. In this respect Ollivant has noted that by the late medieval period 'the operation of the two systems was at times so closely intermingled that the distinction between the two must often have seemed obscure to laymen'.[2] This intermingling of episcopal and papal jurisdictions within the Scottish spiritual jurisdiction appears to have led to a conflation of papal and episcopal jurisdiction among some parts of the Protestant party during the first stage of the Scottish Reformation, while a distinction between the two appears to have been maintained by many Scottish jurists, lawyers and officers of state involved with the spiritual jurisdiction during the same period.

The spiritual jurisdiction encompassed all matters relating to the internal administration of the Catholic Church in Scotland, which, as the largest and wealthiest institution in Scotland, involved the courts spiritual in a range of areas concerning rights and titles to Scottish benefices and the collection of ecclesiastical revenues, although by the sixteenth century the majority of litigation concerning titles to Scottish benefices appears to have been heard at Rome,[3] to the detriment of the native Scottish courts. Beyond the considerable confines of the institutional Church, these courts also dealt with a number of areas of law which are now considered civil, but which prior to the Reformation fell within the purview of the spiritual jurisdiction. These areas included exclusive competences in all legal matters concerning: matrimony, including divorce and legitimacy; succession in movables; the appointment of tutors and curators for minors and pupils; all contracts of whatever kind when either fortified by an oath, or containing some clause submitting the contracting parties to the jurisdiction of the courts spiritual; together with a non-exclusive competence in actions concerning slander

---

[2] Ollivant, *Court of the Official*, 40.
[3] Ibid., 126.

and defamation.[4] Heresy trials appear to have proceeded by virtue of direct and collective exercises of episcopal, or more generally prelatical, authority through the convention of extra-ordinary courts spiritual.

When the courts spiritual were suppressed during the early stages of the Reformation, a series of wide-ranging constitutional, legal and practical problems were occasioned. On the constitutional level the legal position of the Catholic Church within the Scottish polity was thrown into confusion, and, while the ordinary jurisdiction of the Scottish episcopate may be said to have survived the Protestant revolution, papal authority and jurisdiction did not. The rejection of papal claims not only abolished the appellate jurisdiction of Rome over the spiritual jurisdiction in Scotland but threw into doubt the authority and validity of Canon law. Canon law was not only directly enforced throughout Scotland by the courts spiritual, but was a major constituent part, together with Roman law, of the common law of Europe, the *ius commune*, to which Scottish lawyers and the judges of Scotland's supreme civil court, the Court of Session, had habitual recourse. Many Scottish lawyers were well versed in the *ius commune* as a result of their continental educations, and, where Scots law could not be brought to bear on a case, *ius commune* decisions and principles were routinely incorporated into Scots law through the decisions of the judges of the Court of Session.[5] On a purely practical level, the overthrow of the legal system of the Catholic Church within Scotland caused considerable confusion for many Scots in search of a court by which their spiritual actions could subsequently be heard, and caused considerable difficulties for the Scottish civil courts as they sought to contain the fallout from so sudden and momentous an act of revolution.

REVOLUTION AND REFORM

The Wars of the Congregation broke out in the spring of 1559 and began a series of events which are variously referred to as the 'uproar for religion' and the 'Reformation crisis'. The wars were at least initially an attempt by the Protestant nobility of Scotland both to protect the early Protestant congregations of Scotland against the threat of persecution, and to implement a programme of reform in respect of the Catholic Church. The Protestant nobles who began the wars constituted the Lords of the Congregation, and their numbers grew steadily during the progress of their campaigns, until in the autumn of 1559 they moved to depose the Regent, Mary of Guise, and to assume the government of the realm for themselves.

That a programme of purportedly ecclesiastical reform was commenced in Scotland by a section of the nobility was from the beginning predicated upon a departure from the received theories of earlier magisterial Protestant Reformations.

---

[4] For the workings of these courts see generally Ollivant, *Court of the Official*, and for a breakdown of their jurisdiction see specifically chapter V.
[5] For the pre-Reformation context concerning the reception of Canon law into Scots civil law see Dolezalek, 'Court of Session as a Ius Commune Court'.

The classical Protestant Reformation, predicated upon a rejection of the sole right or capacity of the Catholic Church to reform itself, was to invoke the 'godly' prince or magistrate to press their traditionally secular powers into the service of Protestant programmes of reform. This tended to result in an orderly seizure of the institutional structures of the Catholic Church within a particular kingdom, electorate or city state, which assured a degree of centralised control over the implementation of reform, and resulted in a sense of at least partial continuity with the late medieval Church. In Scotland, continued fidelity to this classical Protestant conception of reform by the temporal power effectively meant that there would be no Protestant reformation. As is well known, the unchallengeable sovereign of the realm was Mary, Queen of Scots, the only legitimate child of James V, and heiress to one of the oldest royal houses in Europe. Mary was in turn married to Francis Valois, eldest son of Henry II of France, and had spent most of her life in Catholic France. Following the couple's marriage in April 1558, Mary's husband had been granted the crown matrimonial by the Scottish three estates the following November,[6] further embedding Scotland into a dynastic union with Catholic France and creating the potential, should Mary and Francis have issue, for a full union of the crowns. While Mary had long been absent from the Scottish realm, her mother, Mary of Guise, widow of James V, had successfully gained the regency of Scotland in 1554, at the expense of the governorship of James Hamilton, second Earl of Arran,[7] and, while she was willing to occasionally countenance the Protestant faction, she remained firmly of the old religion.

Within this context there was no real prospect of a programme of Protestant reform being implemented in Scotland by the lawful government of the realm, the supreme authority of which was vested in the person of Mary, Queen of Scots, and delegated to her regent in Scotland, Mary of Guise. Nevertheless, by the time of the Scottish Reformation crisis various continental Protestant reformers had begun to reconsider the earlier Protestant position of passive resistance to persecution, and had begun to advocate and recognise the role of 'lesser magistrates' in coercing tyrants.[8] The problem of prosecuting ecclesiastical reform within a kingdom ruled by a Catholic sovereign was addressed by John Knox in a series of tracts published in 1558.[9] In the *First Trumpet Blast Against the Monstrous Regiment of Women*, published in Geneva in 1558, Knox argued that the rule of women was unnatural, and that as such the authority of queens might be lawfully resisted. This radical approach had the potential to solve the Scottish impasse, although it was specifically intended as a solution for England, in that it offered a theoretical justification for English subjects to resist the rule of Mary Tudor, which had stifled the Edwardian Reformation. In the *First Trumpet*, however, Knox differentiated

---

[6] RPS, 1558/11/8.
[7] Keith, *History*, i, 141–142.
[8] Kirk, *Patterns of Reform*, xiv–xv.
[9] The following discussion of Knox is based on Mason, *Knox on Rebellion*, xv ff.; Dawson, 'The Two John Knoxes', 555–576; Kellar, *Scotland, England, and the Reformation*, 178–180.

Scotland from England by arguing that, while England has entered into a formal covenant with God during the reign of Edward VI, Scotland had not yet taken this step, and as such English Protestants were bound to uphold their covenant through radical political action, while the Scots were not. This distinction did not permanently preclude the Scots from deposing their queen, should the Scots enter such a covenant themselves, as Knox was to hold them to have done during the Reformation Parliament of August 1560. Nevertheless, within the context of 1558, this meant that for Knox English Protestants might overthrow a female sovereign, while the Scots were still enjoined to obey Mary, Queen of Scots. Knox had however made a serious error in supporting his theory for the English Protestant overthrow of Mary Tudor in universal terms of the un-natural rule of all female sovereigns. The death of Mary Tudor and the succession of Elizabeth I almost immediately highlighted this error, and his theory received condemnations from across Protestant Europe.

Yet mindful of his native Scotland, Knox set forward a second theory of political resistance in a series of works also published in 1558, which were addressed to a Scots audience, and which developed a justification for the implementation of a programme of Protestant reform in Scotland, without the direct aid of the authority of the Scottish sovereign. Within the context of the medieval Scottish polity, if recourse could be had neither to the Catholic Church nor to the Scottish Crown, the range of alternative sources of authority by which ecclesiastical reform might be implemented were few. The three estates by which Parliament was constituted were one alternative source of authority and legitimacy, but the basic impasse here was that they had to be summoned by the sovereign in order to enact legislation which would be countenanced by the Scottish legal system, which itself administered civil and criminal jurisdictions emanating from the Crown. Another alternative was the Privy Council, but this was appointed by the sovereign, and might not presume to issue ordinances in the names of Mary and her husband Francis, Queen and King of Scots, without their, or their regent's, direction and consent. This left the nobility, lairds and commons of Scotland, to whom Knox therefore had recourse.

The problem for Scottish Protestantism, then, was how this rump of the Scottish polity might be justified in enforcing a programme of church reform, contrary to the will of the sovereign. The main principle to elide was the Pauline injunction, accepted by Calvinists, to obey lawful government: 'Let euery soule submit him selfe vnto the auctoryte of the hyer powers. For there is no power but of God. The powers that be, are ordeyned of God. Whosoeuer therfore resysteth power, resysteth the ordinaunce of God. But they that resist, shall receaue to them selfe damnacion.'[10] Knox's solution to this seeming impasse was to emphasise that

---

[10] *The Byble in Englyshe* (London, 1539), Romans chapter 13, verses 1 and 2; being the first edition of the English *Great Bible*, which Knox 'developed a great affection for' during his time in England (Dawson, *John Knox*, 26). Knox's 1558 tracts were published prior to the printing of the *Geneva Bible* by Rouland Hall in 1560.

St Paul had referred to 'powers', rather than power, and that as such God had ordained a plurality of powers which ought to be obeyed. Within the Scottish context, this meant that while the sovereign enjoyed the right to be obeyed, and to reform the Church, so too did the other powers in Scotland, which Knox equated with the nobility. In this respect, Knox argued that while the nobility ought not to resist the sovereign, thereby causing conflict between two powers ordained by God, they were entitled to reform the Church, should the sovereign decline to do so. This suggestion of a plurality of powers allowed Knox to argue that, since Mary Stewart and her regent were unwilling to reform the Scottish Church in accordance with the word of God, the nobility themselves were bound by virtue of their station so to proceed, thereby resisting idolatry and superstition, and upholding the cause of those faithful to God and his true Church. Within this context, Knox was able to argue that Protestants had been martyred for the sake of true religion in Scotland because the nobility had passively permitted them to be so persecuted, contrary to their divinely appointed duty.

The problem with a programme of reform predicated upon such a justification was that its relative novelty rendered it unlikely to be acceptable to all. While James Kirk has noted that, within the context of continental Protestant political theory, 'there were clearly ample precedents for Calvinist revolutionaries in Scotland when they came to advocate what, in effect, was rebellion in 1559',[11] it would appear that this departure from a classical form of a magisterial reformation would occasion considerable difficulties in Scotland in terms of the constitutional and legal frameworks within which reform occurred. Neither the queen and king of Scots, nor more immediately their regent in Scotland, could be expected to passively permit a section of the nobility to take up arms and engage in a wide-ranging assault upon the religious, material and legal fabric of the Catholic Church in Scotland, while simultaneously protecting the congregations and ministers of a new religion forbidden by law. The Scottish Reformation therefore began with rebellion, war and revolution from the perspective of Scotland's sovereigns and regent. While the Protestant party variously sought to legitimate their revolution through deposing the regent, exercising the authority of the Privy Council, and summoning the three estates to Parliament in 1560, serious problems as to the legitimacy of this phase of the Reformation were at times pronounced, and various aspects of reform lacked the legitimate backing of sovereign authority and attendant ordered control. Thus while reform by the 'lesser' magistrate proved effective as to suppression of public Catholic worship, ritual and practice and its replacement with Reformed Protestantism, matters more clearly dependent upon the regulation of law, such as ecclesiastical finance and the administration of legal jurisdictions, were thrown into a pronounced degree of disorder. The absence of classical magisterial reform in Scotland during the first phase of the Reformation is brought sharply into focus by the complex and at times disordered history of the

---

[11] Kirk, *Pattern of Reform*, xv.

spiritual jurisdiction, the first part of which concerns the suppression of the courts of the Catholic Church in Scotland during the Wars of the Congregation.

THE WARS OF THE CONGREGATION

The Wars of the Congregation began in earnest in May 1559, but the antecedents of the wars may of course be traced back further still, usually to the 'first band' of Protestant nobles entered into in December 1557 for the establishment of the true Church in Scotland, and whose signatories included three of the nobles and lairds who would go on to be leading Lords of the Congregation, namely Alexander Cunningham, fourth Earl of Glencairn, John Erskine of Dun and Archibald Campbell, fifth Earl of Argyll.[12] By November 1558 it appears to have been well understood by the Protestant faction that reform would either be orderly or tumultuous, in that it would either be achieved through lawful government or carried through by revolution. This is apparent from a protestation made openly before the three estates in Parliament in that month, following the regent's rejection of various Protestant articles which had been given in for consideration. The third point of that protestation stated that 'if any tumult or uproar shall arise among the members of the realm for the diversity of religion, and if it shall chance that abuses be violently reformed, the crime be not imputed to us, who now do most humbly seek that all things may be reformed by order'.[13] It is one of the curiosities of the Scottish Reformation that perceived abuses within the Church were in the event 'violently reformed' by the Lords of the Congregation, and that the 'crime' was not imputed to them, since they were granted indemnity by the Act of Oblivion of 1563.

According to the Act of Oblivion of 1563, the rebellion of the Protestant Lords of the Congregation against the regency of Mary of Guise and the authority of the Scottish Crown began, in statutory terms, on 6 March 1558/9. The precise significance of this date is unclear, but following the resumption of lawful government in Scotland following Mary Stewart's return to Scotland in August 1561, an Act of Oblivion was passed by the three estates in the first Parliament of Mary Stewart's personal reign, whereby those who had participated in what had proved to be the successful Protestant rebellion and the early stages of the Reformation were indemnified against prosecution.[14]

Whatever the true significance of 6 March 1558/9 as the 'appointed day' of the Scottish Reformation, the initial outbreak of the actual Protestant rebellion with which the Wars of the Congregation began occurred in and around Perth during May 1559. These events are well known, and arose out of a combination of the regent's determination to suppress the activities of unlicenced Protestant preachers, by formally summoning them to appear at Stirling on 10 May 1559,

---

[12] *Knox's History*, i, 136–137, xxix.
[13] Spottiswoode, *History*, i, 267–270; *Knox's History*, i, 157.
[14] The Act of Oblivion of 1563, its relation to the Act of Oblivion enacted by the Reformation Parliament, together with the significance of 6 March 1558/9, are discussed at length in Chapter 2.

and of the reformation of Perth. In advance of 10 May, a multitude of Protestants, including John Erskine of Dun and Sir John Wishart of Pittarrow, made their way to Perth from Angus and the Mearns in support of their preachers, but in the event did not proceed to Stirling.[15] Rather, on 11 May, John Knox, having but recently returned to Scotland, preached his now famous sermon against idolatry at St John's church, Perth, which sparked an iconoclastic riot within that burgh. During the course of the riot, St John's was cleansed of the 'trappings' of Catholicism, the Dominican and Franciscan monasteries were sacked, and the charterhouse, or Carthusian Priory, which contained the tomb of James I, was razed to the ground.[16]

In response to this perceived outrage, the regent and her predominantly French forces marched upon Perth from Stirling, where they had been awaiting the appearance of the summoned Protestant preachers. In response to this perceived act of aggression, various Protestants set out in support of Perth from Angus, the Mearns, Fife and the Lothians. The Earl of Glencairn marched day and night from Ayrshire to Perth for the defence of the Protestants there, and among his company of some two-and-a-half thousand men marched two other sometime Lords of the Congregation, Robert Boyd, fifth Lord Boyd, and Andrew Stewart, second Lord Ochiltree.[17] The Protestant reformer John Willock also marched with Glencairn's forces,[18] and so at Perth were to be found three notable reformers of the early Church of Scotland, Knox, Willock and Erskine of Dun, two of whom would be among the first superintendents of the Kirk, and all three of whom who go on to sit in judgement in a variety of actions formerly competent before the courts of the Catholic Church.[19]

The regent and her forces retook Perth without a fight, having negotiated terms with the Protestant faction, but her subsequent actions in Perth, namely garrisoning some of her forces on the town and restoring the Mass, violated the same, and caused the open defection of Archibald Campbell, fifth Earl of Argyll, and Lord James Stewart, Prior of St Andrews, to the cause of the Congregation. With the defection of Argyll, three of the signatories of the first Band of 1557 were now to be found among the Lords of the Congregation.[20] These three, along with Lord James Stewart, the Lords Ochiltree and Boyd,[21] and the lairds Erskine of Dun and Wishart of Pittarrow, were all to form part of the 'Protestant Council' which attempted to assume the government of Scotland following the deposition

---

[15] *Knox's History*, i, 159–161.
[16] McRoberts, 'Material Destruction', 429–430; *Knox's History*, i, 162–164; Spottiswoode, *History*, i, 272.
[17] Spottiswoode, *History*, i, 272–273.
[18] *Knox's History*, i, 177.
[19] As is discussed at length in Chapter 4.
[20] The fourth Earl of Argyll had died in 1558, while the Earl of Morton held off openly joining the Congregation until after English support had been obtained for the Wars (G. R. Hewitt, 'Douglas, James, fourth Earl of Morton (c.1516–1581)' in *ODNB*, accessed October 2017).
[21] A 'second band' was subscribed at Perth on 31 May 1559 by Argyll, Lord James, Glencairn, Boyd and Ochiltree (*Knox's History*, i, 178–179).

of Mary of Guise from the regency, and which first attempted to suppress the courts spiritual throughout the kingdom.

It is not necessary to narrate here in further detail the vacillating fortunes of the Lords of the Congregation prior to October 1559,[22] other than to say that the wars developed into open conflict between the Congregation and the regent's forces during the summer of 1559. The more salient features and events of the wars in respect of the spiritual jurisdiction are discussed below in respect of the deposition of Mary of Guise from the regency, the ordinances subsequently issued against the courts of the Catholic Church and the effectiveness of the Lords of the Congregations' suppression of the same. As a general reflection upon the Congregation's reforming activities, however, it is difficult to consider their actions in respect of the Catholic Church to have been a programme of reform relative to earlier European Reformations. The avowed intent of the Protestant nobility engaged in the campaign was on the one hand to protect congregations of the Protestant faithful, which had been meeting in 'privy' kirks in many Scottish burghs throughout the 1550s,[23] and on the other to overthrow the Catholic establishment which had been actively engaged in the prosecution of Scottish heretics since the days of James Beaton, Archbishop of St Andrews.[24] In this respect there was not one Catholic Church in Scotland which would be reformed so as to conform to the religious tenets of Scottish Protestantism, but rather there were two Churches in Scotland, one a small, persecuted, predominantly underground Protestant Church, made up of various congregations which had arisen spontaneously among many of Scotland's principal burghs, the other the Catholic Church, the largest institution in Scotland, variously recognised and privileged in law. The programme of ecclesiastical reform thus pursued by the Lords of the Congregation prior to July 1560 was one of disorderly open assault upon the old establishment and the protection of the Protestants of Scotland by force of arms. This phenomenon of the 'two Kirks' was the cause of several of the early Church of Scotland's considerable difficulties, in that it necessitated the transfer of property rights and legal jurisdictions from the Catholic Church to the Church of Scotland, a process which was often disorderly, and which involved a range of third parties who competed with the Church of Scotland for the same.

The hallmarks of this early programme of reform were the purging of parish churches of their Catholic furnishings and embellishments so that they might be given over to Protestant worship, the sacking of religious houses,[25] the suppression of the Mass and, as is argued below, the suppression of Catholic church courts.

---

[22] For a full and readable account of the actions and development of the Lords of the Congregation see Jane E. A. Dawson, 'Lords of the congregation (act. 1557–1560)' in *ODNB*, accessed February 2016. Perhaps the best narrative account of the Wars remains Spottiswoode's *History*, i, 265–325.
[23] Kirk, *Patterns of Reform*, chapter 1.
[24] For the earliest statement of the Congregation's intent see the 'first band' of 1557, printed in *Knox's History*, i, 136–137.
[25] For which see McRoberts, 'Material Destruction', 429 ff.

There was, however, no centralised will behind the implementation of reform, nor a comprehensive raft of legislation by which it might be regulated in law. Rather, the progress of the Reformation was sporadic, and bound to the military fortunes of the Lords of the Congregation, which seemed at best precarious prior to the full-scale military intervention of England in late March 1560. These general patterns of revolutionary reform may be discerned in the suppression of the courts of the Catholic Church in Scotland.

THE DEPOSITION OF REGENT GUISE

The Congregation was at the height of its unaided success in October 1559, having taken Edinburgh for the second time on 18 October as a prelude to an assault upon the principal position of the regent's forces at Leith. On 21 October the Lords of the Congregation, whose number by then included the Duke of Chatelherault and his son, the third Earl of Arran,[26] having assembled in the Tolbooth of Edinburgh, moved to suspend Mary of Guise from the regency and to assume her authority for themselves. In the Act of Suspension issued by the Lords of the Congregation on that day, they styled themselves the 'borne councillers of the realm' and moved to suspend the regent on the grounds that she had 'overpassed our Sovereign Lord and Lady's commission given and granted unto her' and had acted 'plane contrary unto our Sovereign Lord and Lady's mind'.[27] The offences committed by the regent were itemised, by virtue of which she was suspended 'in the name and authority of our Sovereign Lord and Lady'.[28] This was something of an enormity against the authority of the Scottish Crown, in that a group of Scottish nobles had presumed to suspend a lawfully appointed regent in the name and authority of the undoubted queen and king of Scots, without any mandate whatsoever from them, and that in stark contrast to the circumstances which had attended Mary of Guise's appointment as regent on 10 April 1554.[29] Rather than having received a mandate from Francis and Mary thus to proceed, the Protestant Lords contented themselves with ascertaining the will of their sovereigns by inference.[30] In this the Lords were perhaps able to persuade themselves that they were not engaged in an act of usurpation, although their protest of obedience to the higher power was at best a tenuous avoidance of occasioning an open conflict between the 'powers ordained by God'.

The Act of Suspension was signed simply 'by us, the nobility and commons of the Protestants of the Church of Scotland', but further particulars are provided

---

[26] Chatelherault joined the Congregation only after his eldest son's return to Scotland on 10 September 1559 from France, where he had been held as surety for his father's loyalty to the regency of Mary of Guise (*Knox's History*, i, 207–208, 228–229; Spottiswoode, *History*, i, 290–291).

[27] It is noteworthy that Mary of Guise was not suspended on the cited ground of her religion.

[28] A transcription of the Act of Suspension is contained in *Knox's History*, i, 251–255.

[29] For which see Keith, *History*, i, 141–142.

[30] The manifest illegality of this Act is well summarised by Keith, *History*, i, 236–237; cf. Donaldson, *James V–VII*, 97.

by the letter sent by the Protestant Lords to Mary of Guise on 23 October. This letter informed her that she had been suspended from, or deprived of, the office of regent of Scotland, and requested that she quit Leith within twenty-four hours, lest the Protestant Lords be compelled to achieve the same by force of arms. This letter was signed by 'The Council having the authority unto the next Parliament', the members of which had been appointed by the leading nobles and barons of the Congregation. This 'Protestant Council', held by Donaldson, Kirk and Cameron to have adopted the appellation 'Great Council of the Realm' at around this time,[31] consisted of the Duke of Chatelherault, his eldest son the Earl of Arran, the Earls of Argyll and Glencairn, Lord James Stewart, Lord Ruthven, Sir William Murray of Tullibardine, John Erskine of Dun, Sir John Wishart of Pittarrow and the provost of Aberdeen.[32] This list is based upon a manuscript consulted by Robert Keith in the Advocates Library, and is by and large verified by a similar list calendared by Joseph Bain, which was dated 22 October 1559, but which included in addition John, Master of Maxwell,[33] and which replaced the provost of Aberdeen with the provost of Dundee.[34]

THE INQUIRY OF LA BROSSE AND CLEUTIN

What is certain is that these Protestant 'Lords of Council' pretended to the government of Scotland, and accordingly desired to begin issuing ordinances in the names of their lawful sovereigns, Mary and Francis, as though various members of the rebel government constituted the lawful Privy Council:[35] one such ordinance was the instrument by which a full-scale suppression of the courts spiritual was first attempted. Considerable evidence concerning this period of the rebellion has been furnished by the proceedings of an Inquiry commissioned by Mary and Francis on 10 November 1559, and held in Holyrood Palace from February 1559/60. The aim of this Inquiry, headed by two French officers stationed in Scotland, Jacques de la Brosse and Henri Cleutin, was to gather together documentary evidence and depositions which could be used to try the Duke of Chatelherault and his eldest son, the Earl of Arran,[36] for treason.

La Brosse and Cleutin, having received their commission from France, secured the assistance of John Spens of Condie, Queen's Advocate, in drawing up the

---

[31] Donaldson, *James V–VII*, 97; Kirk, *Patterns of Reform*, xiv; *First Book of Discipline*, 85, n.1.
[32] Keith, *History*, i, 235. Thomas Menzies was provost of Aberdeen at this time.
[33] John Maxwell, second son of Robert, Lord Maxwell.
[34] *CSP Scot.*, i, no. 551. James Halyburton was provost of Dundee at this time.
[35] Although that is not to say that various of the Lords of the Congregation had not been Privy Councillors during the regency of Mary of Guise, although obtaining precise details on this head is difficult due to the fact that the Register of the Privy Council is no longer extant for the period of her regency (*RPC*, i, 153–157).
[36] In the commission Chatelherault was referred to as the Earl of Arran, since the French held him to have been stripped of his French dukedom because of his rebellion, while his eldest son was called just that, rather than the Earl of Arran.

interrogatories which would be used in examining witnesses during the Inquiry.[37] In addition, since French translations of the documentary evidence produced, and the depositions taken, during the Inquiry were required, the services of James MacGill of Nether Rankeillour, Lord Clerk Register, and Sir John Bellenden of Auchnoul, Lord Justice Clerk, were also secured.[38]

The interrogatories – being written questions put to witnesses – were drawn up as twelve articles, which listed the principal acts of treason committed by Chatelherault and Arran from the time they had joined the Lords of the Congregation in September 1559 until November 1559. Nevertheless, since depositions were taken at Holyrood from 5 February 1559/60, some documentary evidence of a date later than November was also included in the Inquiry's final report, known as the *Information*. The first article concerned the Convocation at Hamilton and the subsequent letter sent by the Lords of the Congregation to the regent, desiring her to suspend immediately the fortification of Leith and to remove all French forces in Scotland furth of the realm. The second article concerned the muster of the Lords at Stirling and their subsequent armed invasion of Edinburgh on 18 October 1559. The third article concerned the attempted suspension of Mary of Guise from the regency, while article five concerned a public proclamation made at the market cross in Edinburgh, whereby the rebels 'usurpans le nom des roy et royne noz souerains, destituerent ladite dame [Mary of Guise] de son auctorite et administration . . .'[39]

Articles seven and eight provide valuable further details concerning the issuing of ordinances by the Lords of the Congregation in the names of Francis and Mary. It was alleged that around the time that the rebels were shelling Leith from Calton Hill, which had commenced on 1 November 1559, an Edinburgh goldsmith, James Cockie, had been pressed into the service of the Lords for the engraving of a counterfeit signet and also 'cunzie irons' for the minting of coin. Cockie was summoned before the Inquiry and examined on 10 February 1559/60, when he deponed that two of Chatelherault's servants had come to his dwelling in Edinburgh early one morning before he arose, and commanded him to come to Hamilton's lodgings in the town. When he arrived at the lodging he found 'the Earl of Arran [i.e. the Duke of Chatelherault], the Earl of Glencairn, Lord Ruthven and Lord James Stewart', together with various other Lords of the Congregation, who took Cockie to the Tolbooth and there commanded him to engrave a signet and coining irons. The signet, which was finished, was engraved with the arms of the king and queen. The coining irons, which were never finished, were intended for the minting of coins which would have borne on one side a crown of thorns and a cross, and on the other the legend 'Verbum Dei'. The signet was

---

[37] Dickinson, 'Report by de la Brosse', 89.
[38] Ibid., 98. Only the French translations of the documents generated by the Inquiry are still extant.
[39] Ibid., 90–92: 'usurping the names of the king and queen our sovereigns, deprived the said lady of her authority and administration'.

received by Chatelherault at some point prior to 6 November 'out of Cockie's own hands', 'et en sa presence en feit signer deux lettres, ne scay ou il les envoya depuys'.[40] The need for a counterfeit signet implies that the Lords at Edinburgh were not then in possession of a genuine signet. While the Secretary, William Maitland, had defected to the Lords by this time,[41] it would appear that he was not in possession of a genuine signet at that time.[42] While the history of the Scottish signet is not known in sufficient detail for the period of the Reformation,[43] in the reign of James V there has been three 'little signets' together with a 'great signet', two of the little signets being used by 'the sessioun and justice airis', with the third being used to issue 'the kingis grace directiouns'.[44] It seems probable that, at the time of the granting of the crown matrimonial to Francis Valois in 1558, new signets bearing the arms of Mary and Francis would have been made,[45] but details both as to the number of genuine signets in use at the time of the Reformation crisis and as to the names of their keepers are not presently known.[46]

Article eight of the interrogatories concerned the issuing of ordinances under this counterfeit signet.[47] During the Inquiry, William Chisholm, Bishop of Dunblane, deponed that Patrick Lindsay had had 'ung signet countrefaict', which Lindsay had said was to be used for the issuing of letters and commandments in the name of the king and queen, at the behest of Chatelherault 'et de son conseil'.[48] Given that article seven of the interrogatories alleged that the rebels had used the signet to authorise their 'pretended laws and ordinances', which had been published in Edinburgh, St Andrews, Glasgow, Dundee, Linlithgow, Perth, Cupar-Fife 'et aultres lieulx par les provinces et villes de ce royaulme',[49] it is remarkable how few of these ordinances were procured by the Inquiry. James Beaton, Archbishop of Glasgow, produced a letter issued by various Protestant Lords at Glasgow on 23 January 1559/60, and deponed that he had seen various other letters issued by the rebels,[50] but there is no specific mention of the ordinance which intended the suppression the courts of the Catholic Church in Scotland. Nevertheless, given the gravity of the allegations being brought against the Hamiltons, it is likely that the

---

[40] Ibid., 123–125: 'and in his presence caused two letters to be sealed, but knows not where he sent them since'.
[41] Maitland defected around 29 October 1559 (*Knox's History*, i, 263–264).
[42] The earliest Secretary of the reign of Queen Mary, David Paniter, had been entrusted with the queen's signets (*RSS*, iii, no. 42).
[43] See Hannay, 'History of the Scottish Signet', 273–323.
[44] *Acts of the Lords of Council*, ed. Hannay, 485.
[45] Inference drawn from *RPS*, 1558/11/9.
[46] It is therefore a possibility that the Lords of the Congregation, having obtained Cockie's counterfeit signet, subsequently came into the possession of a genuine signet.
[47] Dickinson, 'Report by de la Brosse', 93–94.
[48] Ibid., 103.
[49] Ibid., 93: 'and other places throughout the provinces and towns of this kingdom'.
[50] Ibid., 101.

Protestant faction made every effort to keep such evidence of treason discreetly concealed during the Inquiry.

Complementary to the gathering of evidence by the Inquiry was the commissioning of James MacGill and John Bellenden by Mary of Guise to compile what became known as the *Discours Particulier d'Ecosse*. This was commissioned between the issuing of the commission to La Brosse and Cleutin and the examination of witnesses in conformity with the same. The *Discours* was a statement of the laws of Scotland on various heads, and was meant to allow French lawyers to determine how the evidence of the Inquiry would relate to any subsequent prosecutions for treason in Scotland according to Scots law. In particular, the *Discours* dealt 'with the patrimony of the crown, the courts and the law of treason', and, as Peter McNeill has noted, there is 'some congruence' between the aspects of treason dealt with and 'the various items which the rebels were committing and with the sundry articles of charge against the Duke which are set forth in the *Information* [that is, the report issued by the Inquiry]'. The points of congruence were the most serious faults committed by the rebels prior to the Treaty of Berwick, namely 'illegal convocation and assembly, treasonable actings against a regent, rebelling against royal authority, the purported suspension of the regent, and coining without royal authority'.[51] It is nevertheless no surprise that the contents of the *Information* and the *Discours* did not coincide exactly: this could have happened only if the depositions of the witnesses had been obtained prior to the compilation of the *Discours*, which was not the case. In addition, the *Discours* was written by MacGill and Bellenden, while the interrogatories were prepared by John Spens, following which MacGill and Bellenden undertook the translation into French of the depositions taken by the Inquiry.[52] As such, while MacGill, Bellenden and Spens worked closely together at various points, they were nevertheless working on separate commissions, the outcomes of which were therefore congruous, but not perfectly accorded. In the event, the proposed prosecutions for treason were never carried through, not because there was no sound basis in law and fact for such proceedings, but because the rebel Lords won the Wars of the Congregation with the military aid of England.

From the evidence of the Inquiry it is clear that the Lords of the Congregation, having deposed Mary of Guise, procured a counterfeit signet and began issuing ordinances as though they constituted the Scottish Privy Council. Copies of two such ordinances not procured before the Inquiry remained in the possession of one of these Protestant 'Lords of Council', John Erskine of Dun, some of whose papers came into the possession of Alexander Petrie, first minister of the Scots congregation at Rotterdam, during the seventeenth-century. Petrie included

---

[51] McNeill, 'Discours', 86, 97.
[52] Dickinson, 'Report by de la Brosse', 98.

transcriptions of both ordinances in his *Compendious History of the Catholick Church*.[53] The originals seem to be no longer extant, but Petrie's transcriptions were included by Robert Keith in his *History of the Affairs of the Church and State in Scotland*, first published in 1735,[54] and the second of these ordinances, which concerned the suppression of the consistorial courts of the Catholic Church in Scotland, was calendared by Joseph Stevenson in 1865.[55] There seems little reason to doubt the authenticity of these no-longer-extant documents: Petrie provided a vivid detail suggestive of authenticity in his *History*, when he stated that 'I have them by mee, as yet with the Signet whole and entire; which I received (as I have hinted before) among the papers of John Erskin of Dun'.[56]

The first of these ordinances transcribed by Petrie was issued at Glasgow on 29 November 1559, the second at Dundee on 14 December 1559. This second, 'Dundee' ordinance concerned the courts spiritual, and itself referred to an earlier ordinance of the Protestant 'Lords of Council', by which the courts of the Catholic Church were first suppressed in Scotland. The tenor of this earlier ordinance against the courts spiritual is now known only from the contents of the later 'Dundee' ordinance, and the date of this earlier ordinance is also unknown. In order to speculate as to the date of this earlier ordinance it is helpful to reconstruct the movements of the Protestant 'Lords of Council' prior to discussing the contents of the ordinances which they are known to have issued.

THE ORDINANCE AGAINST THE COURTS OF THE CATHOLIC CHURCH

The Protestant 'Lords of Council' convened for the first time at Edinburgh at around the same time as the Act of Suspension was issued against the regent on 21 October 1559. According to James Cockie's deposition before the Inquiry, he was commissioned to produce the counterfeit signet for the Protestant Lords around 1 November. Cockie deponed that he delivered the signet to James Hamilton and had seen Hamilton use it to issue ordinances. Yet Cockie also deponed that he had been commissioned to fabricate irons for the minting of coin by the Lords of the Congregation, but that they had left Edinburgh before he had the irons in readiness.[57] The Lords retreated from Edinburgh on 6 November, following their unsuccessful attempt upon Leith, retreating via Linlithgow to Stirling, which they reached on 8 November, and there immediately convened

---

[53] Petrie, *Compendious History*, second sequence of pagination 215–216.
[54] Keith, *History*, i, 247–248.
[55] *CSP Foreign, Eliz.*, ii, no. 421.
[56] Petrie, *Compendious History*, second sequence of pagination 216.
[57] Cockie's deposition has already been discussed and cited above.

in Council.⁵⁸ From Stirling the Lords of the Congregation dispersed, and, of those chosen as members of 'the Council', Chatelherault, Argyll and Glencairn passed to Glasgow, while Arran, Rothes, Lord James Stewart, Lord Ruthven, John Erskine of Dun and Sir John Wishart of Pittarrow passed to St Andrews, where each group was thought to be keeping council, 'each council advertising the other, for unity'.⁵⁹ From here there seems to have been further movements of these 'Lords of Council', Chatelherault reportedly passing to Hamilton, possibly with Argyll and John, Master of Maxwell, while Arran, Lord James Stewart and Ruthven were reportedly at Perth.⁶⁰

The Protestant Lords of Council that had passed to the west, as already noted, issued an ordinance in the names of Francis and Mary at Glasgow on 29 November 1559. This ordinance summoned to St Andrews all those members of the clergy who had not yet renounced Catholicism and joined the Protestant Congregation, under the pain of deprivation of their benefices. The ordinance also provides a further valuable insight into the Protestant Lords' understanding of what had happened to the authority of the regent. The ordinance narrated that 'it is understood by the Lords of our Privy Councell that be reformed, of the suspension of the Queen Dowrier's autority, the samine is by the consent of the Nobility and Barons of our realm, now by Gods [sic] providence devolved unto them'.⁶¹ This assertion that the authority of the regent had devolved upon the Protestant 'Lords of Council' is found again in an intelligence report sent into England from Scotland, which offers a narrative of events up to 7 November 1559. It recounts that, at the time of the deposing of the regent, Chatelherault, Arran, Argyll, Glencairn, Ruthven, Lord James Stewart and John, Master of Maxwell, together with the Earl of Huntly⁶² and William Maitland of Lethington,⁶³ were 'made regents by the congregation, to govern the realm till they have a righteous prince'.⁶⁴

Of the Protestant 'Lords of Council' who had passed initially from Stirling to St Andrews, it may be presumed that some were assembled at Dundee on 14 December 1559, where they issued an ordinance in the names of Francis and Mary against the court of the Commissary of Brechin. The ordinance began by narrating that the members of the court of the Commissary of Brechin had recently convened their court and in so doing had disobeyed an earlier ordinance issued by the

---

⁵⁸ *Knox's History*, i, 262–265, and 271.
⁵⁹ *CSP Scot.*, i, no. 584; cf. *Knox's History*, i, 298 and 276.
⁶⁰ *CSP Scot.*, i, no. 585, 21 November 1559.
⁶¹ Petrie, *Compendious History*, second sequence of pagination 215; cf Keith, *History*, i, 246–247.
⁶² George Gordon, the Catholic fourth Earl of Huntly, was thought by Bishop Spottiswoode to have joined the Congregation only when he heard that English forces were directly to back the military campaigns of the Protestant Lords (Spottiswoode, *History*, i, 315).
⁶³ Actually 'lord Levingeton' in the source, but presumably this was a reference to William Maitland of Lethington.
⁶⁴ *CSP Scot.*, i, no. 566, 10 November 1559.

'Lords of Council' by which the courts spiritual had purportedly been suppressed. The ordinance, as transcribed by Petrie, ran:

> Francis and Marie, by the Grace of God King and Queen of Scots, Dauphin and Daulphiness of Viennois, To our lovets . . . our shirefs in that part conjunctly and severally specially constitute, greeting. For so much as the Lords of our Council, understanding the great hurt and iniquity that in times past hath proceeded to the members of Christ's Church, by maintaining and upholding of the Antichrist's lawes and his consistory, boasting and fearing the simple and ignorant people by their cursings, gravatures and such like other their threatnings, whereby they sate on the consciences of men of long time by gone, Ordained that no consistory should be afterward holden, hanted, nor used, having respect that there be enough of Civil ordinary Judges to which our Leiges may have recourse in all their actions & causes; And not the less, the said Lords are informed that certain wicked persons within the City of Brechin, malevolent members of the said Antichrist, contemptuously disobey the said ordinance, and cease not still to hold consistory and execute his pestilent lawes within the said City, in contempt of Vs and our authority; Our will is therefore, and we charge you straitly, and command, that incontinent these our letters seen, yee pass and in our name and authority command and charge the Commissary and Scribe of Brechin, and all other members of the said Consistory, and other our Leiges whatsoever having interess, That non of them tak in hand to hold any consistory for administration of the said wicked lawes, or assist there to in any way from thenceforth, Vnder the pain of death, As yee will answer to us thereupon. The which to do we commit to you conjunctly and severally our full power . . . Given under our signet at Dundy, the 14 day of December, and of our reignes the second and 18 years.[65]

It is therefore most likely that the initial ordinance issued against the courts spiritual by the Protestant Lords of Council was issued after the first week of November, after the counterfeit signet had been delivered by Cockie, and sufficiently prior to 14 December for the Commissary of Brechin to have contravened the same. Specifically, therefore, the ordinance against the courts spiritual may have been given at Edinburgh during the first week of November, at Stirling on 8 November 1559 following the retreat of the Lords from Edinburgh but prior to their dispersal to Glasgow and St Andrews, or it may have been issued by a group of the 'Lords of Council' following their dispersal from Stirling, just as had the ordinance of 29 November 1559. In terms of chronology, the earlier dates seem more likely: it would presumably have been unreasonable to expect the court of the Commissary of Brechin to have conformed to an ordinance issued in mid-to-late November at Glasgow, although this is not out of the question. The original ordinance seems more likely to have been issued either at Edinburgh during the first flush of power

---

[65] Petrie, *Compendious History*, second sequence of pagination 215–216; cf. Keith, *History*, i, 247–248; cf, *CSP Foreign, Eliz.*, ii, no. 421.

following the deposing of the regent in early November 1559, or at Stirling on 8 November as a way of continuing the attacks of the Congregation upon the Catholic Church following their demoralising retreat from Edinburgh. The principal point, however, is that the ordinance was issued, and that it was contravened by the court of the Commissary of Brechin.

The rationale which seems to have underpinned the suppression of the courts spiritual by the Protestant 'Lords of Council' is of interest. From the perspective of constitutional theory, the ordinance suggests an underlying conception of Canon law and the Scottish courts spiritual as being manifestations of the authority of Antichrist, and in this it is possible that the framers of the ordinance held papal jurisdiction to be the sole basis of the spiritual jurisdiction of the Scottish Church. If the document is considered from the perspective of authorship, there appears to be something of an odd admixture of radical Protestant polemic, standard legal formulae and possibly a more statesmanlike moderation. In this it is tempting to imagine the ordinance being framed in the Protestant Council at Stirling, where the voices of Knox and his fellow preachers were modified by the more measured voices of the likes of William Maitland of Lethington.[66]

The more radical voice is redolent of Knox's *Appellation from the cruel and most injust sentence pronounced against him by the false bishops and clergy of Scotland etc* of 1558. The *Appellation* had been published in response to Knox's condemnation for heresy in 1556, in conformity with which he had been burnt in effigy, he being then in Geneva following his exile from Marian England and expulsion from Frankfurt. In the *Appellation* Knox petitioned the nobility of Scotland to grant

> that just defences be admitted to us that sustain the battle against this pestilent generation of Antichrist, and that they be removed from judgment in our cause, seeing that our accusation is not intended against any one particular person, but against the whole kingdom, which we doubt not to prove to be a power usurped against God . . . Yea, we doubt not to prove the kingdom of the pope to be the kingdom of the Antichrist.

In the *Appellation* the bishops of Scotland were described as 'cruel beasts', whom the nobility were obliged to compel, by virtue of their noble office, to desist 'from their cruel murdering of such as do study to promote God's glory',[67] since 'the tyranny of those raging beasts should have no force if by your strength they were not maintained'.[68] It may also be noted that Canon law, being the law administered by the courts spiritual, had been dismissed by Knox in this work as being 'accursed by God'.[69]

---

[66] Both Knox and Lethington were present in the Council at Stirling (*Knox's History*, i, 271).
[67] Mason, *Knox on Rebellion*, 74–75.
[68] Ibid., 112.
[69] Ibid., 75.

This potent blend of apocalyptic rhetoric about the kingdom of the Antichrist and the emotive language about the burning of Scottish Protestants for heresy was well calculated to stimulate direct action, both during the Wars of the Congregation and in 1566.[70] Similar language may well have been used when the suppression of the courts spiritual was discussed by the Protestant 'Lords of Council', and the stinging remark, that members of the Scottish Protestant faithful would not have been burnt as heretics had not the nobility maintained the Catholic hierarchy, may have found expression in the clause of the ordinance of suppression concerning 'the great hurt and iniquity that in times past hath proceeded to the members of Christ's Church, by maintaining and upholding of the Antichrist's lawes and his consistory . . .' Within this context it seems reasonable that the 'Lords of Council' at Dundee on 14 December 1559 gave no quarter to the Commissary of Brechin and his principal clerk, who 'cease not still to hold consistory and execute [the Antichrist's] lawes', branding them 'malevolent members of the Antichrist', and warning solemnly that 'non of them tak in hand to hold any consistory for administration of the said wicked lawes . . . under the pain of death'.

The ordinance is also of interest in terms of what it did not mention. On the one hand, no mention was made of the fact that the Commissary of Brechin was exercising the ordinary jurisdiction of the bishop of Brechin, and it would appear that the pronounced emphasis on the Antichrist's laws and courts eclipsed any distinction between papal and ordinary Scottish episcopal, or more generally prelatical, jurisdiction. The omission of this distinction may be compared with its presence among the reasoning of the Lords of Council and Session and the commissioners who proposed the creation of the commissary system, as is discussed at more length in Chapters 5 and 6. On the other hand, the framers of this ordinance clearly envisaged a transfer of litigation and legal functions from the suppressed church courts to 'civil ordinary judges', with no mention being made of the courts of the early Church of Scotland. Yet as is discussed at length in Chapter 4, there is wide-ranging evidence that the new church courts did proceed to hear various types of actions and causes previously heard by the suppressed courts spiritual, and that such activity began between the suppression of the courts spiritual during the autumn of 1559 and the convening of the Reformation Parliament in July 1560.

EFFECTIVENESS OF THE SUPPRESSION OF THE CATHOLIC COURTS SPIRITUAL

To what extent this attempted suppression of the courts spiritual was achieved by the Lords of the Congregation is a nice point, since the registers of the courts spiritual for this period are no longer extant. Generally speaking, if the suppression

---

[70] As was demonstrated during Mary's restoration of Archbishop Hamilton's spiritual jurisdiction, which is discussed below in Chapter 3.

was not entirely effective from the autumn of 1559, and reflected merely the operational effectiveness of the Lords of the Congregation during the period between November 1559 and July 1560, it must have become increasingly effective with the ascendancy of the Lords and their increasingly firm hold upon the government of the realm, particularly from the time of the Reformation Parliament in August 1560 until Mary Stewart's return a year later. Despite the lack of the most obvious sources of direct evidence as to how each Catholic court fared, various helpful fragments of evidence are noted in Watt and Murray's invaluable *Fasti Ecclesiae Scoticanae Medii Aevi* in respect of Commissaries and Officials for the period after October 1559.

In respect of the *Fasti* evidence, the distinction needs to be made that spiritual judges had been prohibited by the Protestant Lords from convening their courts only, and do not appear to have been formally stripped of their offices and titles. This parallels the Lords' suppression of the celebration of Mass and other sacraments according to Catholic rites, without a corresponding, or at least an effective, suppression of ecclesiastical titles and their corresponding livings held by the churchmen of the medieval Church. In this, post-October 1559 *Fasti* references to spiritual judges must be distinguished between those references which relate to titles and those references which relate to the actual exercise of jurisdiction pertaining to those titles.

For many pre-Reformation courts of the Commissaries and Officials the last known references in the *Fasti* to the judges who presided over them fall within the period December 1557 to July 1559, which suggests nothing more that a lack of extant evidence to allow a full reconstruction of these judges' periods of office. The judges who fall into this category are George Strang, Official of Orkney, Malcolm Reid, Commissary of Caithness, Nichol Hay, Commissary of Aberdeen, William Cranston, Official of St Andrews, James Rolland, Commissary of St Andrews, John Abercromby, Commissary of the Chapel Royal at Stirling, James Balfour, Official of Lothian, John Hamilton, Commissary of Hamilton, John Hamilton, Commissary of Kilbride, and Andrew Hamilton, Commissary of Bute and Arran.[71]

Of those references to judges after October 1559, the one which accords best with the present line of reasoning concerns the interruption of the court of Malcolm Chisholm, Commissary of Dunblane, shortly after October 1559, which is directly suggested by a reference to Chisholm on 12 March 1561/2. The date of this reference actually refers to a diet before the Lords of Council and Session, but the details recorded for that diet refer back two-and-a-half years to an action of executry pending before Chisholm, prior to the attempted suppression of the courts spiritual. The pursuer in that cause had petitioned the Court of Session in March 1561/2 because, although process had been led before Chisholm up

---

[71] Watt and Murray, *Fasti*, 344, 98, 33, 421, 426, 443, 423, 252, 253, 277. It has not here been determined whether the two John Hamiltons mentioned were one and the same person.

to the pronouncing of decreet, the diet for the pronouncement of the definitive sentence had been assigned *litteratorie*,[72] but in the event the same had never been pronounced. The reason for this interruption of process was specifically related to the Lords of Council and Session thus: 'And sen the said conclusioun of the said caus, quhilk wes in the moneth of October the zeir of God jaj vc lix zeris [i.e. 1559], the consitoriall lawis hes cessit'.[73] So here is good evidence of process being led before the Commissary of Dunblane in October 1559, but the final diet in the process having never occurred because of the suppression of the courts spiritual at about that time.

While the consistorial court of Dunblane thus appears to have been directly and effectively suppressed by the Lords of the Congregation around November 1559, there is evidence of continued activity northward at Aberdeen, in so far as William Gordon, Bishop of Aberdeen, together with his Official, John Leslie, are known to have appointed three tutors to William Gordon, pupil, on 12 April 1560.[74] The most unexpected evidence of similar continuing activity concerns William Broun, Commissary of Brechin, against whom the ordinance of 14 December 1559 had been directed. Two-and-a-half months after this date, on 26 February 1559/60, Broun issued a transumpt of an instrument of sasine, which transumpt is still extant. The transumpt was given under the seal of the Commissary of Brechin (still attached) at 'the cathedral church of Brechin, in the consistorial place of the same'.[75] On the one hand it may be that the 'sheriffs in that part' to whom the Lords' ordinance of 14 December 1559 had been directed had never proclaimed the same to Broun, while on the other, and supposing the ordinance to have been proclaimed, Broun may have engaged in a limited act of defiance. The original instrument of sasine in question, dated 11 August 1542, had presumably been recorded in one of the registers of the Commissaries of Brechin, whence a copy was required for some purpose in February 1559/60. In this, Broun was not hearing a first instance spiritual action, but was rather providing a useful legal service which could probably be provided only through recourse to the registers in his keeping. Nevertheless, it is clear that the consistorial court in Brechin cathedral was

---

[72] This was normal procedure, since future diets were either assigned a specific date while the litigants were in court, or the litigants where informed that they would be notified by letter of the date of the next diet.

[73] NRS, CS7/23, fo. 252v, cited in Watt and Murray, *Fasti*, 122, and discussed in Smith, 'Spiritual Jurisdiction', 13–14.

[74] *RMS*, iv, no. 1725, cited in Watt and Murray, *Fasti*, 32: it is not clear whether Gordon and Leslie had actually convened a consistorial court for the purpose of appointing tutors. Concerted efforts by the Congregation to 'reform' Aberdeen began with an attack on the spire of St Nicolas on 4 January 1559/60, but there was notable, if not entirely effective, resistance to the purging of the religious buildings of old and new Aberdeen (McRoberts, 'Material Destruction', 438–439).

[75] NRS, GD16/10/9, cited in Watt and Murray, *Fasti*, 77.

still intact by this date, and that Broun was still in possession of his court's records, despite the fact that the choir of the cathedral had been 'reduced to ruin' around January 1559/60.[76]

The survival of consistorial court records and their continued use is also suggested in a fragment of evidence for the Commissary of Wigtown. In a marriage contract dated 6 August 1562, it was stated that the same be registered in the 'commisseris buykis off Wigtoun' with a further statement that the contracting parties were 'content that this present contract be registrat and insert in the buykis of counsale and sessioun, and in the commisseris buykis of Vigtoun'.[77] While the reference to the books of the Court of Session may have been added as an afterthought, since it was perhaps anticipated there might be some problem in respect of the court of the Commissary of Wigtown, the double reference to the same does suggest that it was still a reasonable clause to insert in a marriage contract in 1562.

One final reference from the *Fasti* suggests on-going activity after November 1559 for Glasgow, while all other references refer to the office of spiritual judge, rather than an exercise of jurisdiction.[78] The Glasgow reference concerns Archibald Betoun, Official of Glasgow, and Robert Herbisoune, Commissary of Glasgow,[79] who were sitting in judgement in an action of divorce on 19 March 1562. This, however, was the action of Hugh Montgomerie, Earl of Eglinton, against his first countess, and was commissioned by John Hamilton, Archbishop of St Andrews. This action is evidence not of a continuity of the holding of consistorial courts at Glasgow, but rather of the continued exercise of the Archbishop of St Andrews's legatine authority during Mary's personal reign, and is discussed in its proper context in Chapter 3.

This fragmentary evidence may be further considered within the context of the effectiveness of the government of the rebel Lords during the Wars of the Congregation. The first point to note is that the ordinances issued against the courts spiritual were probably an extension of a policy already being pursued by the Lords of the Congregation, in much the same way as they suppressed the Mass in areas under their control long before this policy was expressed in the legislation of the Reformation Parliament. And by the same measure, just as the suppression of the Mass was not nationally effective even by December 1560,[80] minor acts of defiance on the part of spiritual judges against the will and authority of the Protestant

---

[76] McRoberts, 'Material Destruction', 439.
[77] *Correspondence of Sir Patrick Waus*, ed. Agnew, i, 25–27 (reference provided by David B. Smith).
[78] The references to offices only are for Michael Hawthorn, Commissary of Wigtown, 23 March 1559/60, Archibald Menzies, Official of Nith, 10 April and 31 August 1560, John Gibson, seemingly Commissary of Moray (Elgin), 18 March 1562/3, and George Strang, Commissary of Shetland, 12 June 1560 (Watt and Murray, *Fasti*, 186, 247, 320, 345).
[79] Watt and Murray, *Fasti*, 246 and 250, citing Fraser, *Memorials*, ii, 172.
[80] See Shaw, *Acts and Proceedings*, i, 6–7.

faction ought also to be expected. If the Lords suppressed church courts as they suppressed the Mass, the progress of the Lords from Perth to Stirling to Linlithgow to Edinburgh in the summer of 1559 may well have witnessed initial temporary suppressions of the consistorial courts at Stirling and Edinburgh,[81] but there is no direct evidence for this.

Evidence of an early policy of suppressing church courts is more forthcoming for St Andrews prior to October 1559, for which location there is an extant early Protestant kirk session and superintendent's court register. It is known that the Reformation was effectively implemented in St Andrews on Sunday 11 June 1559, instigated by John Knox and executed by the forces of the Lords of the Congregation under the command of the Earl of Argyll and Lord James Stewart, with strong support from the burgh's council, members of the city's university colleges and the citizens of the burgh. The places of worship within the burgh were stripped of their Catholic ornamentation, the houses of the Dominicans and Observant Franciscans were razed to the ground and the church of the Holy Trinity given over to Protestant worship.[82] Unlike Edinburgh and Stirling, St Andrews was never retaken by pro-Catholic forces.

At precisely what point the courts of the Official Principal of St Andrews and of the Commissary of St Andrews were suppressed cannot be established with certainty. A most tantalising sentence of adherence was pronounced by the superintendent of Fife, Fotherick and Strathearn[83] on 10 December 1561, which rejected a defence of non-adherence on the ground of lawful annulment, because the sentence of annulment in question was Catholic, and had been

> pronuncit into ane privat and prophane hows (as called in Papistre) wythin the reformit citie of Sanctandrois, and that lang efter the said citie was reformed be sinceir preaching and hearing of Goddis trew Word, all public idolotrie, Papistrie, and Papisticall jurisdiccione abolesched furth of the same, the consistorie hows dischergit and stekyt up, the multitud of the inhabitantis of the said citie be professione and protestacione adjonit into ane Cristiane congregacione.

Regrettably, the date of the Catholic sentence of annulment is not given, since the process for the action was not copied into the extant register, but rather 'wrttyn into ane buk be the self remanand wyth regester etc',[84] which appears to be no longer extant. Limited inferences may nevertheless be drawn. The defender had deserted her husband 'be the space of twa yearis or tharby' prior to 10 December 1561, dating the moment of desertion to around December

---

[81] There were no courts spiritual at Perth or Linlithgow.
[82] Dawson, 'Face of Ane Perfyt Reformed Kyrk', 416–419.
[83] For whose consistorial jurisdiction see Chapters 4 and 7.
[84] *St Andrews*, i, 133–134.

1559. If the defender had 'deserted' her husband by virtue of a sentence of annulment pronounced in her favour, it would follow that the old church courts at St Andrews had already been suppressed by this date. Unfortunately these inferences shed no further light on what may already been reasonably presumed, since at the very latest the old church courts at St Andrews ought to have been suppressed in conformity to the ordinance of the Protestant Lords of Council issued during the autumn of 1559.

Nevertheless, the reason for the reduction of the Catholic sentence of annulment given above does contain a suggestion that the consistorial courts of St Andrews were suppressed from the outset of the Reformation in St Andrews. It is noteworthy that the rationale for the reduction makes no mention of the ordinance of the Protestant Lords, nor any Act of Parliament, but rather suggests that 'Papistical jurisdiction' was abolished in St Andrews at the same time as 'idolatry', and that suppressing consistorial courts was a direct corollary of abolishing papal jurisdiction. If this is correct, it suggests that when the Reformation was first achieved most completely in part of Scotland, at St Andrews in June 1559, this model of Reformation included the suppression of the courts spiritual along with all other aspects of medieval Catholicism.[85] From this perspective, the Protestant Lords of Council's ordinance against the courts spiritual would appear to have been an attempt, having for the first time obtained a claim to exercise the authority of the Scottish Crown, to have imposed upon all Scotland the pattern of reform established in St Andrews in respect of the old church courts.

As to post-October 1559 suppressions per the Lords' ordinances, the quality of evidence is such that only the most general observations can be offered. If the original ordinance against the consistories was issued at Edinburgh during the first week of November it may be reasonably assumed that the court of the Official of Lothian, which sat in St Giles' collegiate church on the High Street of that burgh, would have been suppressed, only to be restored after the reoccupation of Edinburgh by the regent's forces following 6 November 1559. This court was presided over during this period by James Balfour, who went on to be the one of the first Commissaries of Edinburgh, and later Lord President of the Court of Session. The court of the Commissary of Brechin was self-evidently within the compass of the Congregation's activities,[86] although William Broun's on-going, if tentative, activities at Brechin have already been noted. If Brechin fell within the effective control of the rebel Lords from time to time, it is reasonable to suppose that similar circumstances also applied to the courts spiritual at Dunkeld[87] and Dunblane.

---

[85] This also coincides with the last known reference to James Rolland, Commissary of St Andrews, on 27 April 1559 (Watt and Murray, *Fasti*, 426).
[86] There was in fact a public Protestant congregation at Brechin by 1559 (Kirk, *Patterns of Reform*, 13).
[87] Dunkeld cathedral was not 'reformed' until after 12 August 1560 (McRoberts, 'Material Destruction', 442), although there is no evidence either way as to the activities of the Commissary of Dunkeld during the period in question.

It has already been noted that one piece of evidence cited in the *Fasti* for Dunblane strongly suggests the suppression of that court shortly after October 1559.

In the west, it would appear that Glasgow fell briefly to the Congregation in November 1559, only to be retaken by pro-Catholic forces,[88] and fell to the Congregation again shortly after 27 February 1559/60.[89] Around 15 March 1559/60 the regent's forces 'past to Glasgow, and thair chacit the congregatioun furth of the same', but left the city after only two nights.[90] It may therefore have been that the consistorial courts at Glasgow were briefly suppressed in November 1559 and late February to early March 1559/60, but, not unlike the court at Edinburgh, were probably only finally and permanently suppressed during the course of 1560. It is unclear, too, how things fell out among the 'peculiar jurisdictions of Glasgow cathedral's prebends', which included commissary courts at Hamilton, Kilbride, Campsie, Carnwath, Monkland and Cadder, Manor, Cardross, Douglas, Renfrew and Stobo, but the location of many of these minor courts in or near Hamilton territory, together with the proximity of many to Protestant Ayrshire, likely saw them suppressed during late 1559 and throughout 1560.[91]

From this evidence it seems that the Lords of the Congregation's suppression of the courts spiritual was certainly effective at St Andrews and Dunblane, and that the courts at Brechin, Stirling, Edinburgh and Glasgow were likely suppressed at least from time to time during the Wars of the Congregation. This picture accords generally with the evidence gathered together by the Inquiry held at Holyrood during the winter of 1559/60, which stated that the rebel Lords' ordinances were proclaimed, among other places, at St Andrews, Perth, Linlithgow, Edinburgh and Glasgow, and also accords with the relative strength of Protestantism in Angus, the Mearns, Fife, Strathearn, the Lothians and Ayrshire.[92] The fortunes of the courts spiritual within the dioceses of the 'reforming' bishops of Galloway, Caithness and Orkney are unclear, and there is an absence of evidence for Argyll and the Isles during the period in question. Nevertheless, it is clear that, following the victory of the Lords of the Congregation and the conclusion of the wars during the summer of 1560, the suppression of the courts spiritual became effective enough by 18 August 1560 for the Archbishop of St Andrews to write to the Archbishop of Glasgow, who had removed to France, that 'the elderis callit of every town takis all the causis of our ecclesiasticall jurisdiction, and intromettis with all our office'.[93] The assumption of the ecclesiastical jurisdiction

---

[88] Spottiswoode, *History*, i, 307–308.
[89] McRoberts, 'Material Destruction', 436.
[90] *Diurnal*, 273.
[91] Watt and Murray, *Fasti*, 252–256: there are no references here to the judges of these courts sitting between 1559 and 1563 inclusive.
[92] McRoberts, 'Material Destruction', 440; Spottiswoode, *History*, i, 271, 277; Kirk, *Patterns of Reform*, 13; Sanderson, *Ayrshire and the Reformation*, chapters 6 and 7.
[93] Letter dated 18 August 1560, transcribed in Keith, *History*, iii, 5, cited in Donaldson, 'Church Courts', 367.

by the courts of the Protestant Kirk, rather than by the civil courts as directed in the ordinances against the consistories, is discussed in detail in Chapter 4, but for now this evidence may be taken to suggest that the Lords' suppression of the courts spiritual gained in effectiveness as the legitimacy of their government increased during the course of 1560. This legitimacy reached its apotheosis prior to Mary's return with the Lords' 'reappointment' by the Reformation Parliament as a provisional government from August 1560, to which events attention is now turned.

Chapter 2

Revolution and Law: The Reformation Parliament, the Proclamation of Leith and the Law of Oblivion

The apparent problem for many of the lawyers who lived through the Reformation crisis, and who in the event were left with the task of containing the practical fallout from the suppression of a major constituent part of the Scottish legal system, was that the early stages of the Scottish Reformation were not part of an obviously magisterial reformation but rather a revolution. Had the queen and king of Scots, or even their regent, used their authority to press various aspects of the Scottish polity into the service of a Protestant programme of reform, it might have been irregular in strict constitutional terms, but lawyers would have been able to work within a coherent and authorised framework of change. As it was, while Protestants no doubt rejoiced that the work of reform was at last begun, and while Catholics may have looked on aghast at the wholesale overthrow of the Catholic ascendancy in Scotland, many Scottish lawyers, Catholic or Protestant, appear to have been disquieted by the apparent violence done to the legitimacy of almost all aspects of the Scottish polity. The rude shocks sustained by the institutional structures of the Catholic Church had been wide-ranging. The office of regent had been roughly handled. The authority of the Scottish Privy Council had apparently been usurped and pressed into the service of Protestant reform. Scotland's sovereigns and regent had clearly taken steps to show their opposition to such actions in authorising a compilation of the laws of Scotland relative to treason, and in commissioning an Inquiry into some of the more treasonable aspects of the early stages of the rebellion. To this situation, yet more uncertainty for the lawyerly mind was to be added, first by the summoning of the three estates of Parliament without royal authorisation, then by the summoned Parliament's disregard for the 'Concessions to the Nobility and People of Scotland' granted by Scotland's sovereigns, which had sought to legitimate the proceedings of the three estates, and finally by the appointment of a kind of Council of the Realm by the same Parliament, again without royal sanction.

At the time, this complex sequence of constitutional events and their consequences for the legal system were not mere theoretical abstractions. The 'uproar for religion' had very real and pressing consequences for the Scottish constitution, the authority of law and the functioning of the legal system. In response to the crisis various Scottish jurists, judges and lawyers, including some exercising offices of state, were obliged either to attempt to adhere to temporary legal frameworks within which they could continue to make coherent and consistent decisions or to make decisions without any clear guidance from an authoritative legal framework.

During the course of this chapter, two attempts to create legal frameworks in response to the revolution are considered. The first framework concerns the negotiations and concessions which surrounded the conclusion of the Wars of the Congregation, and which created a basis in law for a simultaneous acceptance of the fact that the wars had been won by the Congregation, while renewing the victors' obedience, at least as to form, to the queen and king of Scots. This framework broke down almost immediately through the actions of the Reformation Parliament, and lawyers found themselves once more working outwith the confines of an overarching authoritative legal and constitutional framework. The second framework concerns the policies adopted and legal frameworks created in the wake of Mary Stewart's return to Scotland. The return of the queen to her native realm was a constitutional event of the first order, and one which had been but a distant possibility at the time of the breakdown of the first legal framework. Yet return she did, from which point the old pretence on the part of the revolutionaries, of purportedly acting in the sovereign's inferred interests while undermining the constitution, became untenable. The commencement of Mary's personal reign created a second legal framework in response to the Reformation crisis, founded primarily upon the Proclamation of Leith, and it endured until undermined by the queen herself from late 1566. This second framework was substantially strengthened in 1563 by the enactment of a Law of Oblivion by the first Parliament of Mary's personal reign. This Act granted indemnity to all those involved in illegalities between the outbreak of the Wars of the Congregation and the return of the queen. The failure of the queen's personal reign during the course of 1567 and her subsequent abdication by and large obviated the need for this second framework. Following the overthrow of Mary's personal reign a Protestant regent was appointed, the three estates in Parliament regularly convened and lawful statutory provision made for abolition of the Catholic ascendancy and the establishment of Protestantism in Scotland. This third and final legal framework, parts of which still endure in law to this day, bore the traditional hallmarks of magisterial Protestant reformation, and was accordingly far simpler than the earlier responses to the Reformation crisis, in that it fully accepted and legitimated many of its consequences.

THE 'FIRST LEGAL FRAMEWORK'

As to the Wars of the Congregation, the Lords of the Congregation carried through their rebellion against the authority of Mary of Guise, with the aid of English military intervention, and thus brought the wars to a successful conclusion. An English fleet arrived in the Firth of Forth on 24 January 1559/60,[1] and, the Protestant

---

[1] *Diurnal*, 55.

faction having negotiated a military alliance with England, concluded at Berwick upon Tweed on 27 February 1559/60,[2] an English army arrived in Scotland on 30 March 1560.[3] This English intervention effectively confined the predominantly French forces loyal to Mary of Guise within Leith, which had been so heavily fortified that it could not be taken. The Lords of the Congregation felt sufficiently confident by 29 April 1560 to commission what became the *First Book of Discipline* as a full-scale programme of Protestant reform,[4] and by 25 May 1560 to summon the three estates in Parliament. The siege of Leith was broken by the death of Mary of Guise shortly after midnight on 11 June 1560, which paved the way for a series of negotiations between the commissioners of Mary and Francis on the one hand, and of Elizabeth I on the other, for the ending of Franco-English hostilities in Scotland. The English commissioners were Sir William Cecil and Nicholas Wotton, the French John de Monluc, Bishop of Valence, and Charles de la Rochefoucauld, Comte de Randan.[5] While there was no need for the appointment of Scottish representatives as parties to the negotiations, it may be presumed that various Scottish lawyers would have been conversant with the resultant agreements. For example, a year previously Henry Sinclair, Lord President of the Court of Session, and James MacGill of Nether Rankeillour had been commissioned by Mary and Francis 'to treat with the English commissioners on certain matters not settled by the treaty of Cambray', and in this there were at least two Scots lawyers of note for the purposes of this study who were well versed in such international negotiations.[6] In any event, the adjunct 'Concessions' were to be discussed at length during the Reformation Parliament of August 1560.

A resultant Treaty of Leith was entered upon 5 July 1560 for the ending of open hostilities, whereby French forces in Scotland would demolish the fortifications they had erected at Leith and effectively quit Scotland altogether, and whereby English forces would withdraw to Berwick, there to be disbanded. While the Treaty of Leith dealt with the immediate problem of ending what had developed out of the initial Protestant revolution into a complex international war on Scottish soil, relations required to be normalised between Elizabeth on the one hand and Mary and Francis on the other, through a further treaty, the Treaty of Edinburgh. At the same time, Mary and Francis had to treat with their own subjects in an attempt to obtain their renewed obedience in the wake of a successful rebellion, at a time when coercing obedience through military force had

---

[2] Keith, *History*, i, 258–262. The Scots who treated with the English at Berwick had done so 'in the name and behalf of the noble and mighty prince, James duke of Chatelherault' (Spottiswoode, *History*, i, 310–311).
[3] *Diurnal*, 56.
[4] *First Book of Discipline*, 85.
[5] Keith, *History*, i, 286–288. These were the English and French commissioners who actually negotiated in Scotland.
[6] *CSP Scot.*, i, no. 456. It may also be noted that William Maitland of Lethington had been involved in negotiating this treaty (Donaldson, *James V–VII*, 92).

manifestly failed. This attempt was made through the ostensible granting of formal 'Concessions' by Mary and Francis's commissioners to their Scottish subjects in return for renewed obedience. The legal aspects of the Treaty of Edinburgh and the 'Concessions', together with the failure of Mary and Francis to ratify the same and the resultant consequences for the proceedings of the Reformation Parliament, have been analysed in a seminal article by Peter McNeill,[7] to whose analysis the following comments are much indebted.

The device of the 'Concessions' was adopted since Scotland's sovereigns could not enter into a treaty with their own subjects, and as such the French commissioners held a separate group of negotiations with the Scottish nobility, while also negotiating a formal treaty with England for the resumption of peaceful accord between the two powers. In this respect the Treaty of Edinburgh of 6 July 1560 was a bilateral treaty between Elizabeth on the one side and Mary and Francis on the other, which, having been negotiated by each party's respective commissioners or deputies, was to be ratified by those sovereigns within sixty days.[8] The Treaty was not an agreement between the king and queen of Scots and of France on the one hand and the Scottish nobility on the other. Nevertheless, clause VIII of the Treaty of Edinburgh narrated that Mary and Francis had been moved to manifest clemency towards their Scottish subjects through the good offices of Queen Elizabeth, and had therefore 'granted their assent to certain supplicatory petitions presented by the saids Nobility and people' to them and that they would 'fulfil all those things which by their saids Commissioners they have granted to the saids Nobility and people of Scotland, at Edinburgh' 6 July 1560, upon condition that the Scots would return to the due obedience owed to their sovereigns.[9]

In this, Scotland's sovereigns were considered not to have entered into a treaty with their subjects, but to have benevolently granted concessions, the actual tenor of which was not to form part of the Treaty of Edinburgh.

The 'Concessions' therefore formed a document which was supplementary to the Treaty of Edinburgh, but which nevertheless enjoyed a direct legal relationship with the Treaty. The 'Concessions' were subject to ratification by the three estates of the Scots Parliament on the one hand and by Francis and Mary on the other, following which Francis and Mary would ratify the Treaty of Edinburgh entered into with Elizabeth. The French, however, would not, and in the event refused to, allow Francis and Mary to ratify the Treaty of Edinburgh with Elizabeth before the 'Concessions' had been duly ratified, since it was held that in that scenario Francis and Mary would have bound themselves to uphold the 'Concessions' granted to the Scots by virtue of clause VIII of the Treaty of Edinburgh, while the Scots would

---

[7] McNeill, 'Our Religion', 68–89.
[8] Keith, *History*, i, 295, article X.
[9] Ibid., i, 294, article VIII.

remain free to disregard the terms of the 'Concessions'. As is discussed at more length presently, in the event the Scots Parliament did not ratify the 'Concessions' in good faith, and accordingly neither the 'Concessions' nor the Treaty of Edinburgh were ever ratified by Francis and Mary, whereby all that followed upon the 'Concessions' was null and void in law.

The 'Concessions' were calculated to reduce the Scots to renewed obedience to their lawful sovereigns, without recourse to force of arms. Force of arms could not now be attempted by Mary and Francis without both entering Scotland into civil or religious war and risking open war with England. As such, the French were reduced on the one hand to testing the loyalty of the Scots to Mary Stewart, and on the other to offering attractive concessions such as indemnity against prosecution for rebellion through the enactment by the three estates of an Act of Oblivion. The ability of the French to carry through such prosecutions was perhaps never a realistic prospect, but, for those Scottish nobles who had recently engaged in armed rebellion and had entered into a treasonable alliance with a foreign power (the Treaty of Berwick), the promise of total indemnity against forfeiture, execution and attainder of blood was not without its attractions. It will also be noted that when Mary Stewart returned to Scotland in August 1561 she likewise had no realistic means by which she might coerce the Protestant party to obey her rule, but rather was obliged to trust to the principle of her own direct sovereignty and the granting of concessions. Such an approach was to prove insufficient both in 1560 and during Mary's personal reign.

The 'Concessions' had been framed in direct response to a series of articles, or supplicatory petitions, presented by the Scottish nobility to the French commissioners at Edinburgh. Article IV of the supplicatory petitions desired that 'Parliament shall assemble on 10th July, and its acts shall be valid'.[10] As already mentioned, the three estates had been summoned to assemble in Parliament shortly before 25 May 1560,[11] almost certainly by the Protestant 'Lords of Council',[12] but article IV indicates that doubts were entertained by the Lords themselves as to the validity of the Acts which would be passed by the forthcoming Parliament. The French commissioners therefore consented, in article IV of the 'Concessions', that Parliament should assemble on 10 July as summoned, and then adjourn until 1 August 1560, during which interval the consent of Francis and Mary would be obtained to this concession so that 'this Assembly [i.e. the forthcoming Parliament] shall be as valid in all respects as if it had been called and appointed by the express commandment of the King and Queen'.[13]

---

[10] *CSP Foreign, Eliz.*, iii, no. 280.
[11] Goodare, 'Scottish Parliamentary Records', 248, citing *CSP Scot.*, i, no.799.
[12] Spottiswoode maintained that the Lords of the Congregation had asserted their right to summon Parliament at the time Mary of Guise was deposed from the regency (Spottiswoode, *History*, i, 303).
[13] Keith, *History*, i, 300.

Articles VIII, X and XI submitted by the Protestant Lords aimed at securing indemnification against prosecution for any illegal acts committed since 6 March 1558/9,[14] and were directly reflected in articles VIII, X and XI of the 'Concessions'.[15] The centrepiece of these articles was that an Act of Oblivion was to be passed by the three estates in Parliament,[16] the legislation of which forthcoming Parliament, as already noted, would be rendered valid by the ratification of article IV of the 'Concessions' by Francis and Mary.

Article VI submitted by the Scottish Lords desired that 'a council of twelve shall be appointed to manage affairs', by which ought to be understood that the Protestant Lords wished to be formally appointed as members of a valid Council of State.[17] This request was partially granted in article VI of the 'Concessions', wherein it was conceded that the three estates would nominate twenty-four persons 'out of which number the Queen [i.e. Mary Stewart] shall select seven, and the States [i.e. the three estates in Parliament] five, for to serve as an ordinary Council of State during her Majesty's absence, for administration of the government'.[18]

The final article of the 'Concessions' (XVII) responded to 'certain articles concerning religion' presented by the Scottish nobility, but 'in which the Lords Deputies [i.e. the French commissioners] would by no means meddle, as being of such importance that they judged them proper to be remitted to the King and Queen'. It was therefore agreed between the Scottish nobles and the French commissioners that at the forthcoming Parliament 'some persons of quality shall be chosen for to repair to their Majesties, and to remonstrate to them the state of their affairs, particularly those last mentioned [i.e. those touching matters of religion]'. It was also agreed that those persons so chosen 'shall carry along with them to the King and Queen the confirmation and ratification made by the Estates of the several Articles which are presently granted by the Lords Deputies,[19] at which time they shall get delivered to them the confirmation and ratification done by their Majesties'.[20]

A general theme running through the 'Concessions' was that they would be observed by Francis and Mary provided that the Scottish nobility 'render to their Majesties all that obedience which the true, faithful, and natural subjects of this Crown owe to their Sovereigns'.[21] This was no empty caveat, for the rendering of the due obedience promised by the Scottish nobility was to be manifested by their

---

[14] *CSP Foreign, Eliz.*, iii, no. 280.
[15] Keith, *History*, i, 302–304.
[16] Ibid., i, 302–303, article VIII.
[17] *CSP Foreign, Eliz.*, iii, no. 280.
[18] Keith, *History*, i, 301.
[19] By which it may be supposed that article XIV of the 'Concessions' would also be fulfilled, whereby the nobility would 'bind and oblige themselves to observe, and to cause [to] be observed' all the points contained in the 'Concessions' (ibid., i, 305).
[20] Ibid., i, 306.
[21] Ibid., i, 297, cf. 304, article XI.

co-operation with the terms of the 'Concessions', without which the 'Concessions' would not be ratified by Francis and Mary.

The manifestation of due obedience required from the Scottish nobility was this: that, having assembled in Parliament on 10 July 1560, the three estates of the Scottish kingdom would ratify the 'Concessions' and convey them to France for ratification by Francis and Mary, and would moreover appoint representatives to be sent into France to discuss those articles concerning religion which had been submitted by the Scottish nobility to the French commissioners, but remitted by the same for discussion in France. In return for this due obedience Francis and Mary would ratify the 'Concessions' and further bind themselves thereto by ratifying the Treaty of Edinburgh. These ratifications would bestow validity upon the proceedings and subsequent legislation of the Parliament when it was reconvened on 1 August 1560 or thereafter, which would allow the three estates, among other items of business, to pass an Act of Oblivion and to select twenty-four of their number out of which a Council of State would be validly appointed. In this respect, valid legislation would be permitted only if those matters contained in the supplicatory petitions concerning religion were discussed in the first instance in France between representatives of the Scottish estates on the one hand and Francis and Mary on the other.

Quite why the Scottish nobles, who had given in their articles concerning religion, were prepared during the negotiations with the French commissioners to delay discussion of the matters thus raised until some future date is not at once apparent. John Leslie maintained that the English desired the 'Congregatione of Scotland' to received the discipline and ceremonies recently established under Elizabeth, so that both kingdoms might have a uniform religion. The 'ministers and congregatione of Scotland', however, held their Genevan discipline and ceremonies to be more pure than those of England, containing only those things expressly sanctioned by scripture.[22] In this it would seem that the Scots were content to let matters of religion pass until the English had departed, while the French expected that the Scots would be constrained to continue such discussions at the French court.

The 'Concessions' may be considered to have created a legal framework whereby the recent revolution might be reduced to some sort of order. In this respect the most relevant aspects of the 'Concessions' were the agreement of a procedure whereby the Parliament summoned by the Protestant 'Lords of Council' shortly before 25 May 1560 might be rendered lawful; provision for that Parliament to pass an Act of Oblivion; provision for the appointment of a Scottish Council of State; and the reservation to Francis and Mary of the discussion of those matters of religion contained in the supplicatory petitions proffered by the Scottish nobility, as a token of the renewed obedience pledged by the Scottish nobility to their lawful sovereigns. Had the terms of the 'Concessions'

---

[22] Leslie, *History of Scotland*, 292.

been observed by the three estates in Parliament, Mary and Francis would have augmented their subsequent ratification of the 'Concessions' by making any violation of the same on their part an indirect breach of the Treaty of Edinburgh, following that Treaty's ratification.

In the event, the process by which what became the Reformation Parliament might be rendered lawful was not observed, primarily because the Scots Parliament not only discussed those 'matters of religion' which were most likely contained in the supplicatory petitions and enacted legislation purporting to abolish papal jurisdiction and the celebration of the Mass in Scotland, but also attempted to ratify the Treaty of Berwick. The consequences in respect of the legal framework which might have been created by the 'Concessions' were fatal. The 'Concessions' were never ratified by Mary and Francis, and, because the 'Concessions' were referred to in the Treaty of Edinburgh, that too was never ratified.

Nevertheless, when Parliament did assemble, James Sandilands, Lord St John of Jerusalem, does appear to have been commissioned by the three estates to convey the estates' ratification of the 'Concessions' to Francis and Mary and to procure their ratification of the same. Sandilands's commission was printed by Alexandre Teulet in 1862, but in his notes Teulet somewhat unhelpfully referred to the 'traité conclu à Edinbourg, le 6 juillet' and also 'le traité d'Edimbourg'. This misled Gordon Donaldson into thinking that the Reformation Parliament ratified the Treaty of Edinburgh,[23] but it is clear from the commission that the 'treaty' or agreement referred to was that entered between the deputies of Mary and Francis on the one hand, and certain noblemen acting in the name of the nobility and people of Scotland on the other, as Teulet did in fact point out. That this 'treaty concluded at Edinburgh' was in fact the 'Concessions' and not the Treaty of Edinburgh is confirmed by the further particulars of Sandilands's commission, namely the selection by the three estates of the twenty-four nominees out of which a Council of the Realm would be selected (as per article VI of the 'Concessions'). In addition Sandilands's commission authorised him to deliver Parliament's confirmation of the 'Concessions' to Mary and Francis and to humbly request his sovereigns' ratification of the same.[24]

There is an appearance that the 'Concessions' were ratified by Parliament on 9 August, since the English agent in Edinburgh, Thomas Randolph, wrote to William Cecil that day relaying that the three estates had thought it good 'that the articles of peace be confirmed by common consent, that they might be

---

[23] Donaldson, *James V–VII*, 103. *CSP Scot.*, i, no. 883, is also misleading on this head. In both instances *tractatus* would have been more helpfully rendered 'agreement' rather than 'treaty' when referring to the 'Concessions'. The point is that, when encountering a phrase indicating a treaty or agreement made at Edinburgh on 6 July 1560, it is necessary to differentiate the actual Treaty of Edinburgh from the 'Concessions' by examining the parties by which the agreement was entered into, together with the contents of the agreement.

[24] Teulet, *Relations Politiques*, ii, 147–150; cf. *CSP Scot.*, i, no. 884.

sent with speed to France to be ratified. Being read, they were agreed to . . .',[25] although William Maitland thought them to have been ratified on 8 August.[26] That the 'articles of peace' was a contemporaneous name for the 'Concessions' is suggested by the summary of the legislation passed by the Reformation which was probably written by Archbishop Hamilton. Article XIII of the 'Concessions' concerned the giving in of complaints to Parliament by prelates, so that any harm they had suffered in person and goods during the wars might be redressed. On this head Hamilton's summary of statutes reported that 'the Lordis and Nobilitie had don thair duetie conform to the Articles of Peax, quhilk sayis, "Gif ony Kirkman war hurt, let him gif in his bill to the Parliament, and he suld be answerit as resson wald"'.[27]

Nevertheless, the renewed obedience of the Scots to their lawful sovereigns envisaged by the French commissioners was not to be forthcoming. The three estates had technically ratified the 'Concessions' as a legal document, but disregarded some of the provisions contained therein. This must have been brought home to the French court with considerable force when James Sandilands eventually arrived from Scotland bearing the 'ratified Concessions' and somehow thought it an appropriate moment to desire his sovereigns to confirm him in his lands of Torphichen, which he held as Lord St John of Jerusalem by virtue of a papal provision, which provision he thought to be no longer valid title in Scotland by virtue of the Papal Jurisdiction Act enacted on 24 August 1560.

Yet notwithstanding the legislation enacted by the Reformation Parliament in respect of religion, the fundamental impasse encountered by Mary, Francis and their French councillors, and which caused them to decline to ratify both the 'Concessions' and the Treaty of Edinburgh, thereby rendering void the Acts of the Reformation Parliament, was that the three estates had presumed to ratify the Treaty of Berwick. The significance of this ratification seems to have been often overlooked, but a consideration of the contents of the Treaty of Berwick reveal just how remarkable an act of contempt against the authority of Mary and Francis this was.

It will be recalled that the Protestant 'Lords of Council', having purportedly deposed the regent and assumed her authority, had entered a military alliance with a foreign power, England, at Berwick on 27 February 1559/60, some time after the close of the 1559/60 Inquiry.[28] That this Treaty would be ratified by the three estates in Parliament in August 1560 had been keenly anticipated by Randolph. On the evening of 8 August 1560 Randolph had written to Cecil that the estates had 'devised to have the contract with England confirmed by

---

[25] *CSP Scot.*, i, no. 879 per McNeill, 'Our Religion', 79.
[26] *CSP Scot.*, i, no. 880.
[27] Keith, *History*, i, 304–305 and 325.
[28] The 1559/60 Inquiry appears to have examined witnesses for the last time on 10 February 1559/60 (Dickinson, 'Report by de la Brosse', 121 ff.).

Parliament' adding that 'for more assurance, I would, besides the ratification by Parliament, that every nobleman in Scotland had put his hand and seal to it, which may always remain as a notable monument, though the act of parliament be hereafter "dysannulled"'.[29] The final phrase suggests that the English, having been party to the negotiations leading to the Treaty of Edinburgh, were alive to the fact that Francis and Mary could decline to legitimate the Acts passed by Parliament by declining to ratify the 'Concessions'.

The Treaty of Berwick was one of the principal illegalities of the Wars of the Congregation, for which dealings indemnity had been offered by Mary and Francis in the form of the proposed Act of Oblivion. That Parliament could both pass the act of indemnification and ratify one of the principal illegalities of the rebellion is remarkable. It had been agreed in the Treaty of Berwick that English forces would enter Scotland for the expulsion of the French, and that in return, should France invade England, the Scots would furnish at least two thousand each of horsemen and footmen for the defence of England. This Treaty was to remain in force so long as the marriage of Francis and Mary endured, and for one year thereafter.[30] Given that Francis and Mary had been crowned king and queen of France following the death of Henry II on 10 July 1559, and given that they were lawfully queen and king of Scots, the ratification of the Treaty of Berwick by Parliament was another apparent mockery of Parliament's ratification of the 'Concessions', over and above that communicated by James Sandilands's remarkable request. It simply could not follow that a Scots Parliament which agreed 'that the saids Nobles and the rest of the subjects [of the realm of Scotland shall] render unto their Majesties such an entire obedience as is due from faithful and natural subjects to their proper Sovereigns',[31] could also ratify a military alliance with England for the defence of that kingdom against the forces of the king and queen of Scotland and France.

The manifest inconsistency of passing an Act of Oblivion and ratifying the Treaty of Berwick was well understood at the time by at least some parties. There seems to have been an attempt to get each Scottish nobleman to subscribe the Treaty of Berwick prior to its ratification by Parliament, as per Randolph's preference. When asked for a second time to subscribe, the Earl of Crawfurd objected that 'since the law of oblivion was granted, he saw not how any man could, reserving his duty to his sovereign, give consent to any such contract', an idea attributed by Randolph to James MacGill of Nether Rankeillour.[32]

---

[29] CSP Scot., i, no. 879. The 'Lords of Scotland' may previously have attempted to ratify the Treaty of Berwick 'by their subscriptions at the camp before Leith' on 10 May 1560 (Spottiswoode, History, i, 314).

[30] Keith, History, i, 258–262.

[31] Ibid., i, 304, 'Concessions', article XI.

[32] CSP Scot., i, no. 881. Randolph also reported that 'the Earl Marischal is too well "scholed" by Mr James Magill, to do his country any good' (CSP Scot., i, no. 891).

On 27 August William Maitland wrote to Cecil that 'the treaty of Berwick is by act of parliament confirmed, which I doubt not shall highly "irrite" the French'.[33] Other aspects of Parliament's proceedings were also to exasperate the French. The general tenor of Randolph's and Maitland's reports to Cecil about the proceedings of the three estates during the third week of August is of pro-English sentiment, the centrepiece of which was the ratification of the Treaty of Berwick. Hopes for Anglo-Scottish amity and union, together with dynastic union between the houses of Hamilton and Tudor, seem to have run high, and there was also a general sense of excitement at the prospect of an embassy to Elizabeth, with many leading Scottish Protestant nobles desirous of seeing that queen.[34] This pro-English sentiment was in pronounced contrast with the dispatch of the lone James Sandilands, Lord St John, to the queen and king of Scots, a point fully appreciated by Mary Stewart when Sandilands finally attempted to discharged his commission at the French court in November 1560.

Queen Elizabeth ratified the Treaty of Edinburgh on 2 September 1560 at Windsor,[35] but by 15 September the English ambassador to the French court, Sir Nicholas Throckmorton, was still seeking French ratification of the same. Since the French had not yet received the 'Concessions' ratified by the three estates of the Scots Parliament – James Sandilands left Scotland only on 12 September 1560 'on his leisurely way to France'[36] – they were unwilling to let the Treaty of Edinburgh be ratified by Francis and Mary. It was explained to Throckmorton that since clause VIII of the Treaty of Edinburgh obliged Francis and Mary to uphold the 'Concessions' granted to the nobility and people of Scotland on 6 July 1560, the Treaty could not be ratified, since not only had the estates' ratification of the 'Concessions' yet to be received, but also the Scots had 'committed sundry disorders, contrary to their duty'. Throckmorton tried to argue that the Treaty of Edinburgh and the 'Concessions' were not interdependent, to which it was answered that either clause VIII of the Treaty of Edinburgh must be 'left forth' of the same or Elizabeth must find some means of compelling the Scots to 'perform that which they are bound to'. If neither of these approaches were adopted, the Treaty of Edinburgh could not be ratified, for, were it so, Francis II would be 'bound to his [Scottish] subjects' while 'they remain at large to continue in their follies and disobedience'.[37]

On 14 November Lord St John gained audience at the French court, but there was to be no ratification of the 'Concessions'. On 16 November Throckmorton gained an audience with Francis II, who informed him that 'as his subjects had

---

[33] Ibid., i, no. 892.
[34] Ibid., i, nos 885, 886.
[35] McNeill, 'Our Religion', 79.
[36] Ibid., 81. The author of the *Diurnal* thought Lord St John 'depairtit to France throw the realme of Ingland' on 23 September (*Diurnal*, 62), but see *CSP Scot.*, i, no. 902.
[37] *CSP Foreign, Eliz.*, iii, no. 534; cf McNeill, 'Our Religion', 79–80.

in no point observed their duty to him, he could not ratify the treaty'.[38] During this audience Mary had entered the room and declared her own reasons to Throckmorton for withholding the ratifications: 'My subjects in Scotland do their duty in nothing, nor have they performed their part in one thing that belongeth to them ... I will have them assemble by my authority, and proceed in their doings by the law of the realm, which they so much boast of, and keep none ...' Touching the mission of Lord St John, Mary declared that the Scots 'have sent hither a poor gentleman to me, who I disdain to have come in the name of them all, to the king and me, in such a legation. They have sent great personages to your mistress [Elizabeth]. I am their Sovereign, but they take me not so ...' That same day Francis wrote to the Scottish three estates informing them that 'we have decided to send to you, two good and notable personages, our deputies, to come and have the parliament summoned lawfully'.[39]

Neither the 'Concessions' nor the Treaty of Edinburgh were ever ratified by Francis or Mary. The consequent situation has been summarised thus by McNeill: 'Since there was no ratification of the treaty [of Edinburgh] ... there was no valid treaty, and no valid concessions ... Since there were no valid concessions, there could not be a valid parliament. And since there was no valid parliament, there could be no valid legislation, [which] invalidity applied not just to the ... measures dealing with religion, but to all of the purported acts of that assembly.'[40]

This perspective, or something very much like it, appears to have enjoyed considerable currency in Scotland among judges, lawyers and officers of state, including those involved in the creation of the commissary courts by which the old courts spiritual were in large part replaced, in so far as the legislation of the Reformation Parliament was neither enforced in Scotland during Mary's personal reign nor widely countenanced among legal practitioners. These points are considered at more length in Chapter 3, yet for now the problem of the government of Scotland between the Reformation Parliament and Mary's return falls to be considered.

THE GOVERNMENT OF SCOTLAND, AUGUST 1560 TO AUGUST 1561

It is sometimes held that lawful government was restored in Scotland following the Wars of the Congregation by the Treaty of Edinburgh, the 'Concessions' and the Reformation Parliament. Although this was the intention, it was in fact not the case. As already noted, provision had been made in clause VI of the 'Concessions' for the appointment of a Council of the Realm. The three estates in Parliament

---

[38] McNeill, 'Our Religion', 83.
[39] Ibid., 84.
[40] Ibid., 87.

were to nominate twenty-four persons, from among whom twelve persons would variously be selected by the queen and the three estates as members of the proposed Council of the Realm.[41]

Twenty-four persons were nominated by the three estates on 24 August 1560,[42] and their names conveyed to France by James Sandilands.[43] Yet the total failure of Sandilands's mission meant that Mary never made her selection of those she wished to form part of the proposed Council of the Realm. Since the 'Concessions' were not ratified, and since the actual selection of the twenty-four was bound up with the general invalidity of the proceedings of the Reformation Parliament, no lawful provision was made for the government of Scotland during Mary's continued absence in France. This is why, when a valid Act of Oblivion was passed by the three estates during the first Parliament of Mary's personal reign in 1563, the Act encompassed all illegalities committed 'during the time of the late troubles in her majesty's absence' up to and including 1 September 1561.

It may therefore be wondered by what authority Scotland was governed during the period between August 1560 and August 1561. This is an important point in respect of the history of the spiritual jurisdiction in Reformation Scotland. On the one hand, and as is discussed at more length in Chapter 4, it was during this period that the Privy Council both nominated the superintendents of the Church of Scotland and commissioned various kirk sessions and superintendents' court to hear matrimonial actions. On the other hand, and as is discussed at more length in Chapter 6, it is also important for the early history of the commissary system, and of the Court of the Commissaries of Edinburgh in particular, since the Commissaries of Edinburgh were obliged to reduce to order the chaotic legacy of the years 1559 to 1563 in respect of actions and litigation formerly competent before the courts of the Catholic Church. In particular, many of the complicating jurisdictional factors with which the Commissaries were faced, particularly the involvement of the courts of the Protestant Kirk in matrimonial actions, were to become imbedded into practice during the period from the Reformation Parliament until Mary's return.

It has already been seen how the process for the nomination of twenty-four persons by the three estates out of which a Council of the Realm was to be chosen proved abortive, but the common bruit and fame of the these proceedings within Scotland at the time seems to have been that the twenty-four nominees were themselves the new Council. This is suggested by a report of these proceedings by the author of the *Diurnal*: 'And vpoun xxiij day of August [1560], the saidis nobilitie and lordis past to the tolbuit, and ther chesit xxiiij regentis'.[44] This idea that Parliament had appointed a Council to exercise the authority of a regent is

---

[41] Keith, *History*, i, 301.
[42] *CSP Scot.*, i, no. 893; cf. *Diurnal*, 62.
[43] Teulet, *Relations Politiques*, ii, 147–150; *CSP Scot.*, i, no. 884; Keith, *History*, iii, 209–210.
[44] *Diurnal*, 62.

redolent of the earlier assumption of such an authority by the Protestant 'Lords of Council' from 21 October 1559 at the time of the attempted deposition of Regent Guise; and indeed, compared to that earlier attempt at forming such a government, the proceedings of the Reformation Parliament, although still highly irregular, were a marked improvement.

It is no surprise to find among the names of the twenty-four 'regentis' appointed by way of a provisional government the familiar names of the earlier Protestant 'Lords of Council', including the Duke of Chatelherault, the Earls of Arran, of Argyll, and of Glencairn; Lord James Stewart, Lord Ruthven; John, Master of Maxwell, Sir John Wishart of Pittarrow and John Erskine of Dun; together with other early Lords of the Congregation such as the Earls of Menteith,[45] of Morton,[46] and of Rothes,[47] the Lords Boyd[48] and Ochiltree,[49] and William Maitland of Lethington.[50] At the time of the formation of this second 'at best . . . provisional government in a dubious legal position',[51] the leaders of the Protestant faction had no reason to anticipate Mary Stewart's return to Scotland, since her husband Francis II did not die until 5 December 1560. In this respect there was, in late August 1560, a reasonable expectation that the victorious Lords of the Congregation would be left to govern Scotland relatively indefinitely, and to enforce the legislation of the Reformation Parliament.[52] Even if the predominantly Protestant government of Scotland entertained doubts as to the legality of the Reformation Parliament, this made little difference to the political reality that the *de facto* government appointed by the Reformation Parliament was going to implement the legislation enacted by the same Parliament: such legislation would be law by virtue of the fact that it would be countenanced and enforced, rather than by virtue of the fact that it had been lawfully enacted.

This provisional government was in effect the victorious Lords of the Congregation continuing to govern the realm, principally through the Privy Council.

---

[45] Menteith has been described as 'one of the most zealous protestants of this country' (Kirk, *Patterns of Reform*, 329).

[46] Morton signed the 'first band' of 3 December 1557 (*Knox's History*, i, 136–137).

[47] Andrew Leslie, fifth Earl of Rothes.

[48] Robert Boyd, fifth Lord Boyd.

[49] Andrew Stewart, second Lord Ochiltree. Boyd and Ochiltree were among the signatories of the 'Perth band' of 31 May 1559 (*Knox's History*, i, 178–179).

[50] *Diurnal*, 62.

[51] Donaldson, *Scottish Reformation*, 55; cf. Kirk, *Patterns of Reform*, 326, where mention is made of the 'protestant provisional government' in August 1560.

[52] That they moved to enforce the legislation of the Reformation Parliament is illustrated by a mandate issued by the Privy Council to superintendent Spottiswoode on 10 March 1560/1, wherein he was charged 'to take inquisitioun quhat persones sen the last parliament aganis the tenour of the actis and statutis maid thairin hes said mess or hard mess . . .' (Donaldson, *Scottish Reformation*, 226, appendix item Ia). The General Assembly also urged the Privy Council to enforce the Mass Act 1560 (Shaw, *Acts and Proceedings*, i, 6, 27 December 1560, and 9–10, 27 May 1561).

This has been observed by James Cameron, in that following the Reformation Parliament 'the government of the country was in the hands of the Duke of Chatelherault and a small number of prominent Protestant lords, who acted as the Privy Council. The names of Arran, Lord James, Morton, Glencairn, Ruthven, Menteith, Rothes, Boyd, and Ochiltree, together with that of the Secretary, Maitland, appear most frequently on official documents which the Council issued.'[53] The General Assembly certainly countenanced the legitimacy of the Privy Council during this period, stating in a supplication to the Privy Council dated 27 May 1561 that 'your honours shall find us not only obedient to you in all things lawful, but also ready at all times to bring under order and obedience such as would rebel against your just authority, which, in the absence of our sovereign, we acknowledge to be in you hands'.[54] Under this provisional government, the courts of the early Church of Scotland developed a wide-ranging and officially countenanced competence in respect of various actions previously heard by the suppressed courts spiritual, and that often with the direct support of the Privy Council, as is discussed at more length in Chapter 4.

This revolutionary government might well have been established and legitimated in time had it been left to its own devices, but the return of Mary Stewart in August 1561 meant that this second provisional government and all its programmes of reform were subsumed into and captured by the overarching structures of legitimate government and polity reaffirmed and at least partially reimposed upon Scotland by the return of the Catholic Queen of Scots.

THE 'SECOND LEGAL FRAMEWORK'

There were two clear policies open to the widowed Queen of Scots when she returned to Scotland in 1561. The first option was to land at Aberdeen where it was proposed that twenty thousand men-at-arms would be assembled for the crushing of the Protestant faction and the reaffirmation of the Catholic establishment.[55] In the event, Mary declined this proposition, communicated to her by John Leslie, while still in France.[56] There are various reasons why she may have declined to plunge Scotland into a full-scale war of religion. On the one hand, there were the clear lessons of the Wars of the Congregation, and a real prospect of renewed English military intervention in Scottish affairs should the Protestant cause be threatened; and, of course, French support could no longer be expected. On the other hand, such an approach would have been at variance with attempts then being made in France to avoid its own wars of religion.

---

[53] *First Book of Discipline*, 10.
[54] Shaw, *Acts and Proceedings*, i, 10.
[55] Dawson, *Scotland Re-formed*, 244.
[56] Rosalind Marshall, 'Lesley, John (1527–1596)' in *ODNB*, accessed March 2018.

The second option upon Mary's return was one of diplomacy, conciliation and compromise, which can reasonably be described as an insistence upon the collective observation of the 'rule of law' or of lawful government. This policy was advocated by William Maitland and Lord James Stewart, who 'promised Mary that they would win for her recognition of her claim to succeed Elizabeth on the English throne, in return for the maintenance of the religious *status quo* in Scotland'.[57] This policy was adopted by Mary's arrival at Leith on 19 August 1561 without occupying forces and her subsequent Proclamation of Leith of 25 August, in effect an edict of toleration and a moratorium upon the tumultuous affairs of the realm. The Proclamation acknowledged the divisions in the realm 'for the differens in materis of religioun' and warned that no one should 'tak upoun hand, privatlie or oppinlie, to mak ony alteratioun or innovatioun in the state of religioun, or attempt ony thing aganis the forme quhilk hir Majestie fand publict and universalie standing at hir Majesteis arrival in this hir realme, under the pane of deid'.[58] Mary's proclamation gave the *de facto* religious situation which she found upon her return some form of legal validity,[59] an effect clearly understood by both the General Assembly[60] and the kirk session of St Andrews.[61] The position of both the Protestant and the Catholic Churches as they stood on her return was given legal protection by the Proclamation. Protestants gains to date were not to be reversed, yet nor was the disestablishment of the Catholic Church in Scotland to proceed yet further. The policy was aimed at avoiding religious and civil war, buying time for Mary and her government, but could only really be considered temporary, depending in great measure upon Mary and the principle of her personal sovereignty for its success.

The legal framework created by the Proclamation of Leith was a deft but clear one. While the legislation of the Reformation Parliament was not to be formally enforced during Mary's personal reign, the fact remained that it had been enforced by the provisional government appointed by the Reformation Parliament. So, the Proclamation of Leith gave legality to the religious situation which had been created by the Wars of the Congregation, the legislation of the Reformation Parliament and the actions of the provisional government, without actually directly and explicitly legitimating the processes by which the religious situation had been created. Thus, while the Proclamation of Leith did not lend binding force to the legislation of the Reformation Parliament, much of the order expressed in that legislation was maintained by virtue of the terms of the Proclamation.

---

[57] Mark Loughlin, 'Maitland, William, of Lethington (1525x30–1573)' in *ODNB*, accessed January 2017.
[58] *RPC*, i, 266–267.
[59] Goodare, 'First Parliament', 62–63; McNeill, 'Our Religion', 74–75; cf. Smith, 'Reformers and Divorce', 25.
[60] Shaw, *Acts and Proceedings*, i, 66, 28 June 1564.
[61] *St Andrews*, i, 270, 17 April 1566.

There is a particularly noteworthy example of this framework being applied. The Mass had clearly been suppressed throughout Scotland by August 1561, in part because of the initial successes of the Lords of the Congregation, and more fully because of the continuation and expansion of their policy through the enforcement of the Mass Act 1560 by the post-August 1560 provisional government. Had Mary not returned to Scotland, it would have been normal for those who celebrated or heard Mass to be tried by virtue of the Mass Act 1560. Yet following her return such prosecutions proceeded by virtue of the Proclamation of Leith, an alteration as to the legal basis of such prosecutions at least countenanced by the General Assembly.[62] Thus when a co-ordinated attempt was made by the Archbishop of St Andrews and some of his co-religionists to restore the Mass in parts of the west of Scotland on Easter Sunday 1563, they were subsequently tried by assize before the Lord Justice General, the fifth Earl of Argyll. Prior to the trial, 'the Queen asked counsel of the Bishop of Ross [Henry Sinclair] and the old Laird of Lethington [Sir Richard Maitland] . . . who affirmed "That she must see her laws kept, or else she would get no obedience"'.[63] The trial proceeded on the ground that, in making innovations and alterations to the state of religion as found publicly and universally standing at Her Majesty's arrival within Scotland, those who had celebrated or heard Mass had contravened the Proclamation of Leith. No mention was made of the Mass Act 1560.[64]

This second legal framework was augmented on 4 June 1563, when the first Parliament of Mary's personal reign passed an Act of Oblivion. The legal reasoning surrounding the Act, as well as its effect in law, reveal a number of aspects of lawyerly opinion surrounding the Reformation crisis. Something very similar in tenor to the 1563 Act of Oblivion had been anticipated by the articles given in to the French commissioners by the Protestant Lords, during the negotiations between the French and English at Leith and Edinburgh at the conclusion of the Wars of the Congregation in July 1560. At that time, the Protestant Lords had requested of the French commissioners an 'amnesty for all things done since 6th March 1558[/9]', so that 'neither the party of the Congregation, nor their adversaries shall reproach one another with anything done since the 6th March 1558[/9]', and so that 'the King and Queen shall not take vengeance for anything done since the 6th March 1558[/9]'.[65] These articles were duly reflected in the 'Concessions' provisionally granted by the French commissioners on behalf of Mary and Francis, principally in clause VIII. Here it was narrated that the commissioners had agreed that an Act of Oblivion should be passed by the three

---

[62] See Shaw, *Acts and Proceedings*, 6 and 29.
[63] *Knox's History*, ii, 76.
[64] Pitcairn, *Ancient Criminal Trials*, i, 427–430. Those who attacked Reformed practices and doctrines could also be tried in the justiciary court for violating the Proclamation of Leith (e.g. NRS, JC1/11, 31 December 1561, and JC1/12, 1 October 1563; thanks are due to John G. Harrison for providing these references).
[65] *CSP Foreign, Eliz.*, iii, no. 280.

estates in Parliament, with the intention of 'burying the memory of all bearing of arms, and such things of that nature as have happened since the 6th day of March 1558[/9]' so that 'all those who have any manner of way contravened the laws of the kingdom, shall be exempted from the pains and penalties contained therein, as if they had never offended'.[66] This 'first' Act of Oblivion was subsequently passed in the Reformation Parliament of August 1560,[67] and, although its detailed contents are no longer extant, it may be presumed to have conformed to the articles of the Protestant nobility and the 'Concessions' granted thereupon, and consigned to oblivion all illegal acts committed since 6 March 1558/9. The same start date of the period of indemnity was adopted in the Act of Oblivion 1563.

It therefore appears that, notwithstanding the Act of Oblivion enacted by the Reformation Parliament, a new Act of Oblivion was deemed necessary by the Parliament of 1563. This cannot be explained simply by the fact that the 1563 Act must have extended the period of indemnity considerably beyond that of the 1560 Act. Rather it is apparent that the 1563 Parliament provided a forum within which the view that the legislation of 1560 had been invalid was actually aired, a view directly reflected in the 1563 Act of Oblivion, as is discussed at more length in Chapter 3.

The period encompassed by the indemnity granted by the Act of Oblivion 1563 ran from 6 March 1558/9 to 1 September 1561, and an attempt to establish the significance of these dates provides some further insight into the lawyerly view of the first stages of the Reformation. The precise significance of 6 March 1558/9 still proves elusive, although, as already noted, it was clearly a date fixed upon during negotiations by which the Wars of the Congregation were concluded, and was reflected in the proceedings of the Reformation Parliament.[68] Donaldson[69] and McNeill[70] both considered the significance of this 'appointed day' of the Scottish Reformation, albeit inconclusively, with Donaldson going as far to state that it was 'a date on which nothing of significance is known to have happened in Scotland'. John Leslie, Bishop of Ross in succession to Henry Sinclair, provided a suggestion for the selection of 6 March 1559 in his near contemporaneous *History*. Leslie narrated that, responding to the on-going religious ferment within the realm, the regent caused the Catholic prelates of the realm to convene what was to prove their last reforming Provincial Council.[71] The Council met from

---

[66] Keith, *History*, i, 302–303, translated from the French original.
[67] Goodare, 'Scottish Parliamentary Records', 252.
[68] This date also appears to have been used in a no longer extant Act of the Reformation Parliament concerning feus and tacks of teinds (*RPS*, A1560/8/8); cf. *RPC*, i, 234–235.
[69] Donaldson, *James V–VII*, 92.
[70] McNeill, 'Legal Aspects of the Scottish Reformation', 84.
[71] For the history of Catholic attempts at reform of the Scottish Church prior to the Reformation see Winning, 'Church Councils', 332–358.

1 March 1558/9 to 10 April 1559.[72] Leslie notes that the Council finally resolved to compel the prelates and beneficed clergy of the Church 'to mak thame selffis able, and use thair awin offices according to thair fondationis and callingis, within the space of sax monethes, onder the pane of deprivation'. The Council appeared actually to be in earnest, and as such many churchmen decided to throw in their lot with the Protestant cause, hoping thereby to avoid any serious alteration in respect of their possession of ecclesiastical wealth.[73] Although Donaldson dismissed this idea out of hand,[74] the Provincial Council of March 1558/9 was the only obvious ecclesiastical event in progress on 6 March, and Leslie's idea is the only one which suggests a causal link between the Provincial Council and the statutory date assigned to the outbreak of the rebellion.

By 1567 the memory of this 'appointed day' of the Scottish Reformation was still remembered by the Scottish legislature, albeit imperfectly. The Marriage Act of that year reformed the forbidden degrees of consanguinity and affinity, and declared that marriages contracted since 8 March 1558/9 in conformity with the Act would be valid.[75] The alteration of the day of March from the sixth to the eighth may be attributed to faulty recollection. Yet by 1573 this 'appointed day' seems nevertheless to have been forgotten, or possibly overlaid by a new narrative of the Reformation. In the Divorce Act of that year, it was declared that malicious desertion had been a ground for Scottish Protestant divorce since 'the trew and Christiane religioun' had been publicly established in August 1560.[76] While it may now be demonstrated that this act was in no historically accurate sense declaratory and was, rather, prescriptive,[77] it is nevertheless noteworthy that the month during which the Reformation Parliament sat was chosen as the 'appointed month' for this piece of marriage legislation, whereas an Act also legislating on marriage six years earlier had chosen the more widely accepted 'appointed day' of the Scottish Reformation.

The end date of the period of indemnity defined by the 1563 Act of Oblivion, namely 1 September 1561, is also instructive. That this Act did encompass the years of revolution up to 1 September 1561, rather than 1 September 1560, requires a brief affirmation. Some confusion has been occasioned on this head because of what appears to be a clerical error in the original Acts of the 1563 Parliament passed in relation to the law of oblivion. The actual Act of Oblivion gives 1 September 1561 as the end date, but the Act by which the Lords Interpreters of the Law of Oblivion

---

[72] *Statutes of the Scottish Church*, ed. Patrick, 149–191.
[73] Leslie, *History of Scotland*, 271.
[74] While Donaldson dismissed Leslie's suggestion as 'merely comic' (*James V–VII*, 90), it was acknowledged by David Hay Fleming, although he doubted, in very general terms, whether this could really have been the case (*St Andrews*, i, xiii).
[75] RPS, A1567/12/15.
[76] RPS, A1573/4/2.
[77] Green, *Consistorial Decisions*, lxii–lxiv.

were appointed initially gives the end date as 1 September 1560.[78] While this earlier date has sometimes found its way into the historiography for the period, it is nevertheless incorrect, as may be demonstrated through recourse to the Acts of the Lords Interpreters of the Law of Oblivion.[79]

The choice of 1 September 1561, like the choice of 6 March 1558/9 for the beginning of the period encompassed by the Act, is problematic in terms of attributing it to a specific event, but it very nearly coincided with the resumption of lawful government in Scotland following Mary's return. Unfortunately, the register of the Privy Council is not extant between 1554 and 4 September 1561, but on that latter date Mary was at Holyrood Palace, seemingly in Council, appointing wardens for the Marches of Scotland. On 6 September 'for gude reule to be observit within hir realme' Mary elected fourteen noblemen together with the great officers of state 'to be hir Greit Counsale'.[80] In this the lawful government of Scotland, at least partially interrupted since the deposition of Regent Guise, was resumed in full.

What appears to be certain is that the three estates in Parliament in 1563 deemed it necessary to specify a period of indemnity which encompassed not only the Wars of the Congregation and the Reformation Parliament but also the period of rule by the provisional government appointed in August 1560: or, put another way, the entire period of the Scottish Reformation prior to Mary Stewart's personal reign. The effect of this legislation meant that it was no longer competent to discuss in courts of law any illegalities committed during the first two-and-a-half years of the Scottish Reformation. If this principle is taken together with the legitimating effect of the Proclamation of Leith, then it may be said that by June 1563 it was lawful neither to reverse the gains of the Reformation during its first phase nor to inquire into the causes of those gains. In respect of the spiritual jurisdiction, this would have meant that circumstances surrounding the issuing of the ordinance by which the Catholic courts spiritual were suppressed during the autumn of 1559 could not be formally discussed in such a way as to be the subject of legal judgement. Yet at the same time, the fact that the courts spiritual were suppressed at the time of Mary's return meant that to seek to restore such courts would have been a violation of the Proclamation of Leith. Such considerations, along with several others, appear to have been present in the minds of those who erected the commissary system, as is discussed in Chapter 6.

---

[78] RPS, A1563/6/1-2; cf. *Acts of the Parliaments of Scotland*, ed. Thomson and Innes, ii, 535–536, c.1 and 2. The near contemporaneous *Black Acts* of 1566 give the year as 1561 in both Acts (*Acts and Constitutions of the Realm of Scotland* (1971), fos clxx–clxxii).

[79] As may be determined from an examination of NRS, CC8/2/2, fos 257v–258r, 9 January 1567/8, *Newbattle v. Dundas* and NRS, PA9/1, fos 14v–15r, 10 January 1567/8, *Newbattle v. Dundas*. For further evidence on this head see NRS, PA9/1, fos 11v-12r, 13 July 1566, *Colesoun v. Robesoun* and NRS, PA9/1, fo. 17r, 3 April 1568, *Cunningham v. Knox*.

[80] RPC, i, 157–158.

THE REFORMATION PARLIAMENT LEGISLATION AND THE SPIRITUAL JURISDICTION

When the three estates assembled in Edinburgh in August 1560 it must have been fairly common knowledge that the courts spiritual had already been suppressed by the government of the Protestant 'Lords of Council'. Unless this is taken for granted, the legislation of the Reformation Parliament makes less sense, for although the abrogation of papal jurisdiction and its consequences were dealt with directly, the problem of the suppressed courts spiritual was considered only in such respects as to infer that the three estates already both held the courts spiritual to have been abolished, and held that provision had already made in respect of which courts ought now to hear those actions previously heard in the Scottish consistories. If it is presumed that the three estates held the courts spritual to have been abolished by royal ordinance during the autumn of 1559, with prospective litigants being redirected to 'civil ordinary judges', this would explain the absence of legislation which both directly and expressly abolished the courts of the Catholic Church in Scotland and made provision for the consequences of that abolition.

There are three Acts concerning the spiritual jurisdiction thought to have been enacted by the Reformation Parliament: a no-longer-extant Act which concerned the suppressed courts spiritual known only from a brief summary of the Act made by Archbishop Hamilton; the Papal Jurisdiction Act; and the 'Jurisdiction of Rome' Act, known only from its ratification in 1581. The Papal Jurisdiction Act is of course well known. The other, less well-known Acts are mentioned in a summary of the legislation of the Reformation Parliament received by Archbishop Beaton, who had passed to France with the French forces following the Treaty of Leith. This summary was bequeathed by Beaton among his papers to the Scots College in Paris, from whence a transcription was made of it by Thomas Innes during the early eighteenth century and sent to Robert Keith, who included the same in his *History*.[81] Goodare has argued that the original summary was probably written by Archbishop Hamilton, shortly after the close of the Reformation Parliament.[82] One of the entries in this summary reads: 'Item, Thair is certan statutis and ordinancis maid, in quhat manner appellationis and supplicationis, *per modum querelae*, should be pursuit befoir the temporal Judge, and na mair befoir the spiritual Judge; and siclyke, how letteris sall be gevin upon acts without cursing, upon liquidat dett, and four formes for fulfilling of an deid'. Goodare has treated this as a summary of two acts, the first being the 'Jurisdiction of Rome' Act, the other being no longer extant, but which concerned the enforcement of sentences pronounced by, and deeds registered with, spiritual judges.[83]

---

[81] Keith, *History*, i, 323–326, including footnotes.
[82] Goodare, 'Scottish Parliamentary Records', 254.
[83] Ibid., 251.

The problem of the suppression of the Scottish courts spiritual therefore appears to have been dealt with to a limited extent by the no-longer-extant Act concerning 'how letteris sall be gevin upon acts without cursing, upon liquidat dett, and four formes for fulfilling a deid'. The two specific issues thereby intimated concerned how parties were to get sentences enforced which had already been pronounced in their favour by courts spiritual, and also how parties were to get deeds and obligations enforced which had been registered with courts spiritual. This Act therefore appears to have presupposed that the courts spiritual no longer functioned, and that some procedural provision needed to be made whereby business already dealt with by those courts prior to their suppression could be enforced. No provision appears to have been made either in respect of hearing new first instance business which would previously have been heard by the Catholic church courts, or in respect of transferring actions which had been pending before those courts at the time of their suppression.

The Papal Jurisdiction Act and the 'Jurisdiction of Rome' Act dealt almost exclusively with papal jurisdiction, the first abolishing papal jurisdiction, the second making provision for the consequences of that abolition, although it may by extension have made provision for appeals pending before Officials Principal at Glasgow and St Andrews. Most of the Papal Jurisdiction Act actually concerned the prohibition of 'barratry', that is to say of the trade in titles to Scottish benefices at Rome. Statutory provisions in respect of 'barratry' had long been a feature of this aspect of Scottish relations with the see of Rome.[84] The final sentence of this Act, however, ordained 'that no bishop or other prelate of this realm use any jurisdiction in time to come by the said Bishop of Rome's authority'.[85]

From the wording of the Act it is at once apparent that the Reformation Parliament did not abolish episcopacy, but rather prohibited bishops and other prelates of the Scottish Church from exercising papal jurisdictions within the kingdom. It is more than fifty years since Donaldson pointed out that such an Act 'did not make a very serious change in the *de facto* position, it went no further than the anti-papal clauses of an English act of supremacy, if, indeed, it went so far, and while it ought to have been fatal to the archbishop's legatine authority it did not – so at least it might have been argued – affect the normal episcopal powers'.[86] The distinction between ordinary episcopal jurisdiction and papal jurisdiction is fundamental to clearly differentiating the different authorities at play within the spiritual jurisdiction of the medieval Church. Grants of legatine jurisdiction from Rome to the Archbishops of St Andrews could not be held valid by the terms of the Papal Jurisdiction Act; nor too could the appointment of papal judges delegate for the hearing of first instance business, nor appeals to

---

[84] For example *RPS*, 1424/16; 1428/3/10; 1488/10/49–50; A1493/5/4; A1496/6/3; cf. Cameron, *Apostolic Camera*, xxviii–xxix, n.1.
[85] *RPS*, A1560/8/4.
[86] Donaldson, *Scottish Reformation*, 60.

Rome from the Officials Principal of Glasgow and St Andrews in spiritual causes, nor the appointment of papal judges delegate by which such appeals could be heard. Yet there is nothing in the Act to suggest that the ordinary jurisdiction of the Scottish episcopate had been abolished. From this it follows that the Papal Jurisdiction Act had no direct bearing upon the exercise of ordinary episcopal jurisdiction in spiritual causes by the Commissaries, Officials, and Officials Principal of the Scottish courts spiritual.

Provision for the practical consequences of abolishing papal jurisdiction within the Scottish Church were made by the 'Jurisdiction of Rome' Act. The contents of this Act are known only from its ratification in 1581, and there are as yet no known instances of the Act being cited in litigation before Scottish courts during the era of the Reformation.[87] The lack of references to the Act among the extant court records for the period does not, however, necessarily preclude the passage of the Act in 1560: none of the legislation of 1560 appears to have been countenanced by the Court of Session, or by the Commissaries of Edinburgh, or by the wider legal system during the personal reign of Mary Stewart because of problems surrounding its validity: only from December 1567 did those Acts of 1560 ratified in 1567 gain the force of statute within the legal system, and clearly the 'Jurisdiction of Rome' Act was not ratified in 1567, which could explain its lack of citation in litigation.

In terms of the contents of that Act,[88] provision was made in respect of actions then pending in Rome or before papal judges delegate, with litigants with such 'pleas in dependence' redirected to the Lords of Council and Session or other 'temporal ordinary judges within this realm'. In addition, provision was made in respect of appeals which would have been made to Rome from papal judges delegate or from 'consistories', which may be understood as reference to appeals from Scottish Officials Principal, redirecting such appeals to the Lords of Council and Session. Thus, while this Act made reference to the courts of the Scottish episcopate, it did so only indirectly within the context of papal appellate jurisdiction, with no direct provision being made in respect the problem of the suppression of the Scottish courts spiritual.

The relevant legislation of the Reformation Parliament concerning the spiritual jurisdiction, in concerning itself primarily with papal jurisdiction in Scotland, may be considered to have had three direct effects in law, setting aside for the moment the question of the validity of such statutes. In respect of the native Scottish courts spiritual, the supreme appellate jurisdiction of Rome was abolished, with the consequences that appeals pending either in Rome, or before Scottish churchmen appointed papal judges delegate in such causes, were transferred to the Court of

---

[87] Smith notes that the Act 'does not appear to have been known to the lieges or the lords' ('Spiritual Jurisdiction', 16); and the author of the present work has yet to find a reference to the Act among the extant court records of the period.

[88] For the text of which see *RPS*, 1581/10/39.

Session. In respect of the direct petitioning of Rome by Scots who wished to bring first instance business directly within the purview of papal jurisdiction to the detriment of native Scottish episcopal courts, the hearing of such first instance business in Rome, or in Scotland by papal judges delegate with subsequent right of appeal to Rome, were no longer competent. In respect of the legatine authority by which aspects of papal jurisdiction in Scotland were delegated from time to time to the Archbishops of St Andrews, so that dispensations from impediments to marriage could be obtained without direct recourse to Rome, or by which papal judges delegate, and by extension sub-delegate, could be appointed to take cognisance of first instance business outwith the context of the native Scottish courts spiritual, such authority was abolished. In these respects, it would appear that the conflation of the spiritual jurisdiction of the Scottish episcopate and native courts spiritual with the spiritual jurisdiction of the bishops of Rome, howsoever exercised over, or in, Scotland, was not an error to be found within the legislation of the Reformation Parliament itself. Rather, it seems likely that, during the era of the Reformation, such a view was the product in part of what Ollivant has referred to as the conflation of the two in popular reckoning, and in part of an overly simplistic polemic against Canon law, episcopal jurisdiction and papal jurisdiction as aspects of the Antichrist.

If the 'Privy Council' ordinance against the Catholic courts spiritual of the autumn of 1559 and the legislation of the Reformation Parliament are taken together as part of a complementary programme of reform pursued by the predominantly Protestant Lords of the Congregation, then it is clear that the civil courts were intended to be the heirs of the spiritual jurisdiction in Scotland. This is particularly striking because of a pronounced silence among all these provisions, namely the total absence of any mention of the courts of the early Church of Scotland: as is described at length in Chapter 4, it was these new church courts which succeeded for a time to the pre-Reformation Commissaries and Officials in respect of matrimonial litigation.

One final point must also be made in respect of the legislation of the Reformation Parliament. From the foregoing chapters it is clear that the suppression of the native courts spiritual was not a consequence of the legislation of the Reformation Parliament, being already at least a *de facto* reality, and from the Protestant perspective arguably a legal reality, prior to August 1560. The misconceived theory that has long attributed the suppression of the courts of the Catholic Church in Scotland, both as to timing and as to law, to the legislation of the Reformation Parliament in Scottish legal historiography must therefore be treated with circumspection by those who would read earlier accounts of this history.[89]

---

[89] For a full discussion of previous Scottish legal historiography on this subject see Green, 'Court of the Commissaries of Edinburgh', 7 ff.

Chapter 3

Papal and Episcopal Jurisdiction in Scotland following the Reformation Crisis

The suppression of the native Scottish courts spiritual during the Wars of the Congregation and the abrogation of papal jurisdiction in Scotland by enactment of the Reformation Parliament formed the two principal features of the Reformation crisis concerning the spiritual jurisdiction of the Catholic Church. In order to understand the subsequent history of that jurisdiction following the Reformation Parliament, it is necessary to consider several aspects of those two principal features. On the one hand, and in so far as the native Scottish courts spiritual were presided over by Commissaries, Officials and Officials Principal appointed by the Catholic episcopate, the suppression of those courts ought to be understood in constitutional terms as a repudiation of ordinary episcopal jurisdiction. Since some commissaries within that system were actually appointed by the abbots and chapters of religious houses, the suppression may be understood more broadly as a repudiation of the spiritual jurisdiction of the higher churchmen, known collectively as prelates, of the Scottish Church. On the other hand, the legislation of the Reformation Parliament clearly sought to abrogate papal authority and to outlaw the exercise of papal jurisdiction in Scotland by any bishop or other prelate of the realm in times coming. This clear differentiation of episcopal, or more generally prelatical, authority and jurisdiction on the one part, and papal authority and jurisdiction on the other, was not only one dictated by the sequence of events by which the Protestant party sought to overthrow the spiritual jurisdiction of the Catholic Church in Scotland but also one maintained by those judges and officers of state who proposed the creation of the commissary courts during the winter of 1563–4, as is discussed at more length in Chapter 6. In these respects, this chapter is concerned with the various issues and events surrounding papal and episcopal jurisdiction in Scotland following the Reformation crisis.

THE VALIDITY OF THE LEGISLATION OF THE REFORMATION PARLIAMENT

Before entering into a discussion of papal and episcopal jurisdiction after the Reformation Parliament, it is necessary to consider the vexed problem of the extent to which the 1560 legislation was held to be valid during Mary's personal reign. While the Protestant party in Scotland for the most part held the legislation to be valid, and while the Privy Council active in the wake of the Reformation Parliament, together with the General Assembly, desired that it be enforced, there is no evidence that it was enforced in Scotland during Mary's personal reign.

As to general considerations, there were clearly contemporaneous objections to be found in Scotland as to the Reformation Parliament before and during its progress, in addition to the known view of the Queen of Scots and her then husband, Francis II, as to those proceedings. Archbishop Spottiswoode, son of the Scottish reformer and superintendent of Lothian, John Spottiswoode, records in his history that at the time of the Parliament there was at first

> great altercation – divers holding that 'no Parliament could be kept, seeing their sovereigns had sent no commission, nor authorised any to represent their persons.' Others (alleging that article of the peace whereby it was agreed, '. . . that the same should be as lawful in all respects, as if it were ordained by the express commands of their majesties') maintained that 'the said article was a warrant sufficient for their present meeting;' and this opinion by voices prevailed. So after some eight days spent in these contentions, they began to treat of affairs; but as they had no commission, so the solemnities accustomed of crown, sceptre, and sword, which are in use to be carried at these times, were neglected.[1]

On the one hand, further 'altercations' appear to have developed during the course of the Reformation Parliament, with the opinion of James MacGill of Nether Rankeillour in respect of the *non sequitur* of enacting the Act of Oblivion and ratifying the Treaty of Berwick having already been noted in Chapter 2. On the other, the absence of the regalia was a sufficiently memorable part of the solemnities surrounding the Reformation Parliament as to be recorded by the author of the *Diurnal*, an omission which he contrasted with the processing of the regalia in respect of the Parliaments of 1563 and 1564.[2]

The failure of the Reformation Parliament, both to observe the procedures prescribed in the 'Concessions' of July 1560 for the regularisation and legitimation of its own proceedings and to ratify the 'Concessions' in good faith, resulted in the queen and king of Scots declining to ratify the 'Concessions' for their own part. From this basis the queen and her then husband are known to have maintained the logical outcome of this sequence of events, namely that the three estates had not been summoned in Parliament by royal authority in May 1560 and that as such the legislation of that Parliament was invalid. Given that this position was well established in Mary Stewart's mind prior to her husband's untimely death and her subsequent return to Scotland, it is difficult to see on what ground Scotland's sovereign might have been persuaded that the legislation was valid, and that it ought to be enforced by organs of royal government which derived their authority from her sovereign person.

As to specific considerations, there is fairly wide-ranging evidence that various Lords of Council and Session and officers of state, together with various lawyers who went on to be Commissaries of Edinburgh from February 1563/4, held the

---

[1] Spottiswoode, *History*, i, 325–326.
[2] *Diurnal*, 61, 76, 78.

1560 legislation to be invalid in law. In respect of the Lords of Council and Session, the actions and opinions of two Scottish brothers, Henry and John Sinclair, who remained Catholics notwithstanding the Reformation, are to the fore. Both were judges of considerable reputation, with the author of the *Diurnal* remarking that 'sik twa honest and cunning letterit men as thir wes, will be seindill [i.e. seldom] or rather neuer sene to come of ane hous and familie of this realme; the ane for his singular eruditioun had in the lawis ... the vther for his singulare intelligence had in theologie, and in lykwise the lawis'.[3] Even John Knox acknowledged that 'they were both learned of the laws' albeit 'given to maintain the Popish religion, and therefore great enemies of the Protestants'.[4] Both brothers were consecutively Lord Presidents of the Court of Session, Henry holding that highest judicial office in the kingdom from 1558 until his death at Paris on 2 January 1565 and being succeeded by his brother in November of that year. Notwithstanding the Papal Jurisdiction Act of 1560, Henry Sinclair received papal provision to the Scottish bishopric of Ross on 2 June 1561, having been elected to the see around 1560.[5] On 7 September 1565 John Sinclair received papal provision to the Scottish bishopric of Brechin, following Crown nomination.[6] Henry Sinclair's provision is particularly noteworthy, because it was issued at a time when the provisional government appointed by the Reformation Parliament was enforcing the legislation of 1560: indeed, six days prior to the issuing of the papal provision, the General Assembly had resolved to petition the 'Privy Council' 'for order to be taken for the punishment of such as purchase, bring home or execute, within this realm, the pope's bulls'.[7] John Sinclair's provision is also noteworthy, because it was issued within the context of the second legal framework created in response to the revolution: from the perspective of the General Assembly of July 1562, the giving of institution in respect of papal bulls of provision was an example of 'breaking of the queen's acts', to which end the Assembly petitioned Mary's Privy Council desiring that those who 'have entered into benefices by the pope's bulls, and such other transgressors of the law made at your grace's arrival within this realm, may be severely punished; or else men will think that there is no truth meant in the making of such laws'.[8] The General Assembly was clearly referring to the Proclamation of Leith. Naturally, Henry Sinclair's papal provision had been issued on June 1561, thus prior to the return of the queen and the issuing of the Proclamation, although clearly the later provision of his brother to Brechin would have been a case in point. Given that Henry Sinclair went on to be a figure of central importance in respect of the assumption of the spiritual jurisdiction by the Court of Session in December 1560 and the subsequent proposal of the new commissary

---

[3] Ibid., 98.
[4] *Knox's History*, ii, 185.
[5] Watt and Murray, *Fasti*, 351.
[6] Ibid., 56.
[7] Shaw, *Act and Proceedings*, i, 10.
[8] Ibid., i, 24 and 29.

courts from February 1563/4, it ought to be noted in passing that Sinclair was clearly aware of the consequences of the Proclamation of Leith in law, and that there is considerable evidence that he sought to uphold the policy of toleration established by the Proclamation. Mark Dilworth has noted that Sinclair's 'commitment to Catholicism, however, was combined with his upholding of the rule of law and his outstanding integrity as a senior judge, exemplified by his personal conduct'.[9] Among the various examples of this personal conduct are to be found: his furnishing of 'breid and wyne to the halie communion continewalie sen the Reformation of religion within this realm' to the parishioners of Glasgow at Easter in his capacity as parson of Glasgow;[10] his declining to be commissioned by the Archbishop of St Andrews to take cognisance of *Eglinton v. Hamilton* in 1562;[11] and his dismissal of a charge of treason made against John Knox before Mary's Privy Council in 1563, which judgement Sinclair maintained proceeded from 'neither affection to the man, nor yet love of his profession . . . but the simple truth, which plainly appears in his defence'.[12] In these respects it would appear that Henry Sinclair's acceptance of a papal provision to the bishopric of Ross in June 1561 proceeded upon a considered view of the legal position created by the Reformation crisis prior to the return of the queen, and that in so doing he adopted a moderate position in respect of the Reformation, a position subsequently maintained following the Proclamation of Leith.

The point in hand, however, is the fact that two Scottish judges received and accepted papal provisions to Scottish bishoprics while either holding the office of Lord President of the Court of Session or being nominated for the same, subsequent to the passage of the Papal Jurisdiction Act. This suggests that the force of lawyerly opinion against the validity of the legislation of the Reformation Parliament was held at the highest levels of the Scottish judiciary. This suggestion is expressly confirmed by the proceedings of the first Parliament of Mary's personal reign in June 1563, during the course of which matters concerning the legality of the 1560 legislation appear to have come to a head. Prior to the dissolution of that Parliament, John Knox preached a sermon to the 'most part of the nobility', which included the following passage:

> Yea, I hear that some say that we have nothing of our Religion established, neither by Law nor Parliament . . . the speaker for his treason against God committed, and against this poor Commonwealth, deserves the gallows. For our Religion being commanded, and so established by God, is accepted within this Realm in public Parliament; and if they will say that was no Parliament, we must and will say, and also prove, that that Parliament was as lawful as ever any that passed before it within this Realm. Yea, if the King then living was King, and the Queen now in this Realm be lawful Queen, that Parliament cannot be denied.

---

[9] Mark Dilworth, 'Sinclair, Henry (1507/8–1565)' in *ODNB*, accessed January 2017.
[10] *RPC*, i, 492; Donaldson, *Scottish Reformation*, 66.
[11] Smith, 'Spiritual Jurisdiction', 9; *Eglinton v. Hamilton* is discussed below.
[12] For which he was directly reprimanded by the Queen (*Knox's History*, ii, 93–100).

Knox recorded this sermon in his *History*, and noted in the margin that the speaker in question was the dean of Restalrig, John Sinclair.[13] It seems reasonable to suppose that the view taken by John was taken by Henry, a supposition confirmed at least in part by their acceptance of papal provisions to their respective bishoprics.

Despite Knox's invective against John Sinclair's position, Sinclair's view appears to have been reflected by various features of the Act of Oblivion enacted by the 1563 Parliament. As noted in Chapter 2, the 1563 Act made no reference to the Act of Oblivion of 1560, which lack of reference suggests that the earlier Act was held to be invalid. Neither did the 1563 Act refer to, or proceed upon, the provision made for the enactment of such a piece of legislation by the 'Concessions' of July 1560. On this head, Spottiswoode records that the queen expressly prohibited the 1563 Act of Oblivion to proceed upon the 'Concessions', which she 'would never acknowledge. Wherefore it was advised that the lords in the house of parliament should, upon their knees, entreat the passing of such an act, which accordingly was done.'[14] In terms of the actual contents of the 1563 Act, the period for which indemnity was granted brought within its purview the proceedings of the Reformation Parliament, a point taken by Keith to betoken the 'tacite or rather open acknoweldgement in the States, that they had no right to frame Acts in that meeting'.[15] Keith's position appears to be confirmed in so far as the actual wording of the 1563 Act discharged all judges whatsoever from hearing actions encompassed by the Act included all 'legates, archbishops, abbots, commendators, priors and all uther judges'.[16] If the three estates in Parliament in 1563 had accepted the Papal Jurisdiction Act 1560 as statutory law, there could have been no cause to refer to legates in the 1563 Act, since legatine authority and jurisdiction could be derived only from the bishops of Rome.

During the course of 1566 a yet more formal and authoritative refutation of the legislation of the Reformation Parliament came to pass. On 1 May 1566 Mary, with the advice of her Privy Council, issued a commission for the correction of the laws of the kingdom. The commission narrated that since 'the misknowledge and ignorance of the laws' resulted in 'misorder, inobedience, tumult and troubling of the common weel', various nobles, bishops, judges and officers of state were being commissioned to 'visie, sycht and correct the Lawis of this our Realme maid be vs, and our maist Nobill progenitouris, be the avise of the thre Estatis in Parliament' down to the date of the granting of the commission. No other statutes except those seen and corrected by the commissioners and subsequently printed were to have either 'place, faith or authority' or 'to be alleged or rehearsed before any our judges and justices whatsoever in judgement and outwith'. Among the list of those so commissioned were to be found two of the 'reforming' bishops of

---

[13] Ibid., ii, 80–81.
[14] Spottiswoode, *History*, ii, 24; although note *RPC*, i, 203.
[15] As commented upon by Keith in his *History*, ii, 201.
[16] *RPS*, A1563/6/1.

the early Church of Scotland, namely the bishops of Galloway and Orkney; John Leslie, Catholic Bishop of Ross in succession to Henry Sinclair; William Ballie, Lord President of the Court of Session in succession to John Sinclair; Sir Richard Maitland of Lethington, Lord of Council and Session; John Bellenden of Auchnoul and John Spens of Condie; and James Balfour and Edward Henryson, two of the first Commissaries of Edinburgh.[17] By 1566 the Court of the Commissaries of Edinburgh had been erected as the principal court by which the jurisdictions of the courts of the Officials and Commissaries continued to be administered in Scotland. Balfour had been the first 'chief' Commissary of Edinburgh from February 1563/4, although he had demitted office by 1566, while Henryson still remained a Commissary of Edinburgh.[18] The work of this commission resulted on 12 October 1566 in the publication by royal licence of the statutes of the realm from the reign of James I down to 1564. Between the legislation of the Parliament held during the regency of Mary of Guise in 1555 and that of the June 1563 Parliament,[19] the legislation of the Reformation Parliament was conspicuous by its absence. A second impression was printed on 28 November 1566, with various corrections and additions, including the insertion of additional legislation for the Parliaments of 1548, 1555, 1557 and 1564; yet still the 1560 legislation was omitted from the volume.[20] Both editions contained a preface by Edward Henryson, in which Balfour was singled out for praise in respect of his labours and it is clear that much of the material printed was based on authentic copies prepared and signed by him. In addition to the presence of Bellenden and Spens on the commission, it may also be noted that the third officer of state involved in the 1559/60 Inquiry held at Holyrood, James MacGill of Nether Rankeillour, had also provided the commission with some of the authentic copies of statutes.[21] The omission of the legislation of the Reformation Parliament, given the open disputations held as to its validity during the 1563 Parliament, was clearly intentional, and brought with it a judgement backed by learned opinion and authorised by royal commission as to the validity of the 1560 legislation.

This weight of learned opinion may also be seen to have left its mark among the judgements both of the Lords of Council and Session and of the Commissaries of Edinburgh. As is discussed at length in Chapter 5, the Lords of Council and Session began hearing spiritual actions from December 1560, as a direct response to the earlier suppression of the courts spiritual. Among the judgements of the Court of Session during the period 1562/3 to 1563/4 are to be found two instances of the Lords of Council and Session suspending their own letters of poinding until the

---

[17] See *Acts and Constitutions of the Realm of Scotland* (1971), which begins with the licence to print the statutes followed by the commission.
[18] The first Commissaries of Edinburgh are discussed in Chapter 6.
[19] *Acts and Constitutions of the Realm of Scotland* (1971), fos clix ff.; fos clxx ff.
[20] Ibid., for which see the 'Anhang', or 'Attachment', at end of the volume, for which various of the folios are not numbered.
[21] Ibid., fo. clxxx verso.

outcomes of two appeals in spiritual causes then currently pending before papal judges delegate appointed by Rome were known. Following the appointment of the Commissaries of Edinburgh in February 1563/4, the Commissaries appear to have accepted as valid, albeit indirectly and tacitly, a sentence pronounced by a papal judge delegate in the diocese of Ross in 1565.[22] The judgements of the Lords of Council of Session are particularly noteworthy, since they presuppose that the judges of the Court of Session declined to consider either the Papal Jurisdiction Act 1560 or the 'Jurisdiction of Rome' Act 1560, the latter having explicitly directed litigants with appeals pending before papal judges delegate to bring them before the Lords of Council and Session or any other temporal judges.[23]

Beyond the opinions and judgements of these judges and officers of state, it falls to consider the opinions found among the acts and proceedings of the General Assembly of the Church of Scotland. Donaldson has noted that the 'precarious situation of the reformed church between 1560 and 1567' was a matter not 'only of constitutional theory, thought it must have been especially plain to lawyers like John Sinclair, who remarked, as Knox complained, that "we have nothing of our religion established, neither by law nor parliament"; for the general assembly itself implied the truth of Sinclair's assertion' in 1565.[24] Donaldson referred to an article framed in the General Assembly on 26 June 1565, but it appears appropriate for the present purpose to set that article within the chronological context of various positions and opinions advanced by the General Assembly. It has already been noted above that in July 1562 the General Assembly petitioned the queen to the effect that 'the law made at your grace's arrival within this realm' might be enforced in respect of those who received papal bulls of provision to Scottish benefices, no mention being made of the Papal Jurisdiction Act 1560. By June 1564 the General Assembly resolved to present Mary's Privy Council with various articles, the first of which, although its tenor is not entirely clear, appears to contain a desire that the statutes of 1560 be ratified so that 'Christ's religion be *de novo* established'.[25]

On 26 June 1565 the General Assembly, as noted by Donaldson, gave in further articles to Mary's Privy Council, desiring: 'Firstly, that the papisticall and blasphemous mass, with all papistry and idolatry, and pope's jurisdictions, be universally suppressed and abolished throughout the realm . . . and these heads to be provided by act of parliament with the consent of the estates, and the ratification of the queen's majesty'.[26] From this it may be seen that the General Assembly was clearly aware that papal jurisdiction had not been universally suppressed within the kingdom, which may suggest that the Archbishops of St Andrews's

---

[22] As discussed at more length in Chapter 6.
[23] RPS, 1581/10/39.
[24] Donaldson, *Scottish Reformation*, 68.
[25] Shaw, *Acts and Proceedings*, i, 65.
[26] Ibid., i, 80.

continued exercise of legatine powers during this period – discussed below – was common knowledge. Moreover, the problems surrounding the legality of the 1560 legislation as a whole were clearly of sufficient strength for the General Assembly to call for new legislation of similar tenor to be enacted by the three estates in Parliament and ratified by the sovereign. In a reply made to this article on 25 December 1565 the queen appears to have offered to ratify anything on that head which the three estates would agree in the next Parliament held, and in the meantime offered renewed assurance that no man would be troubled for practising religion according to his conscience, nor that men's heritages should be in hazard for religion's sake.[27]

In these respects it would appear that, within the context of the legal framework created by the Proclamation of Leith and the Law of Oblivion, the General Assembly was prepared to grant either that the legislation of the Reformation Parliament required ratification or that provision for the establishment of the Protestant religion in Scotland required new legislation. Yet by late 1566 the queen's policy of toleration was beginning to break down, a process possibly set in motion, as discussed below, by the restoration of spiritual jurisdiction to Archbishop Hamilton in December 1566. In any event, by 25 July 1567 the position within the General Assembly had clearly departed from its earlier conciliatory opinions, in that certain articles were formed, to be signed by all the Protestant faithful of Scotland, apparently on pain of excommunication. The first article ran that

> for as much as there was a parliament held in this realm before the queen's majesty's arrival in the same, by the estates convened for the time, authorised with her highness's own power and commission, in which parliament, [August 1560] it was concluded that the religion of Jesus Christ, then universally received within this realm, should be universally established and approved within the same, and all papistry, with the pope's usurped jurisdiction, all idolatry, and especially the blasphemous mass, to be abolished and put away *simpliciter*, as the acts made thereupon purport; which acts, together with the queen's majesty's power to hold the same parliament, the noblemen, barons and others undersubscribing, desire to be extracted and put into full execution as a public law, and the transgressors thereof to be punished according to the same, throughout the whole realm without exception. Which parliament, in all things concerning the religion [of Christ], they shall defend and maintain to their uttermost in the first parliament which shall be held, and in all other times and occasions convened.[28]

By July 1567 it would therefore appear that the General Assembly was no longer willing to entertain doubts about the validity of the 1560 legislation, and was rather insisting that the Protestants of Scotland maintain the validity of the statutes of the Reformation Parliament, including in the next Parliament to be held.

---

[27] Ibid., i, 90.
[28] Ibid., i, 136. This article may also have been framed in response to the publication of the *Black Acts* in 1566.

The overthrow of the personal rule of Mary followed shortly thereafter, and by the end of the year the 'second' Reformation Parliament of December 1567 was in session. That Parliament, summoned by Regent Moray on the authority of the infant King James VI, ratified the four principal Acts of the Reformation Parliament as to religion, and added a raft of further statutes whereby the Protestant religion and Kirk were established in law. Whether or not the ratification of the 1560 Acts proceeded upon an acceptance of the lawyerly view as to their invalidity is perhaps beside the point; in any event, the process of ratification by a Parliament lawfully summoned laid that aspect of the Reformation crisis to rest.

In view of the ratification of the Papal Jurisdiction Act in 1567, it is noteworthy that the Act was still considered by lawyers to have left untouched the ordinary jurisdiction of the Scottish episcopate as to the laws and constitution of Scotland. This appears from the evidence contained in *Balfour's Practicks*, as has been noted by McNeill. James Balfour is thought to have compiled his *Practicks* intermittently between 1574 and 1583,[29] and McNeill has drawn attention to the fact that Balfour retained all the 'pre-Reformation legislation relating to the church – subject to the abolition of the mass and the papal jurisdiction – and apparently applie[d] it to the reformed church'. In particular, McNeill notes how Balfour retained 'the decisions (all of which are pre-Reformation) which relate to the spiritual judges and the jurisdiction of bishops. This retained law might have referred (until 1564) to the jurisdiction of the bishops which had been dispensed by the officials; but Balfour notes these had been assumed in 1564 by the new commissaries; and this was not restored to the ersatz bishops until 1609.'[30] McNeill also offers some thoughts as to the range of possibilities as to where this episcopal jurisdiction might have been actually vested within the context of the Reformation, and notes that an absence of explanation of the law and its principles is a feature of the *Practicks*. While it is unclear where episcopal jurisdiction was actually vested, the constitutional principle remained part of the Scottish constitution. From this perspective the creators of the commissary courts sought principally to continue to acknowledge the survival of the constitutional concept of episcopal, or prelatical, spiritual jurisdiction in Scotland, and to entrust the administration of jurisdictions emanating from the same to the commissary courts, with the latent possibility of those jurisdictions being restored to the Scottish episcopate, Catholic or Reformed, as and when Scotland's constitutional and ecclesiastical future became clearer. The theme of the survival of this constitutional concept in law and practice is discussed at more length in Chapters 5 and 6, and is likewise relevant to a proper understanding of the constitutional basis upon which the restoration of spiritual jurisdiction to Archbishop Hamilton proceeded in December 1566, as is discussed at more length below.

---

[29] *Balfour's Practicks*, i, xxxii–xxxiv.
[30] Ibid., i, xliv.

ARCHBISHOP HAMILTON'S PAPAL AND EPISCOPAL JURISDICTIONS

Outwith the confines of royal government and the extant Scottish legal system, John Hamilton, Archbishop of St Andrews, continued to exercise his papal legatine authority throughout Mary's personal reign in respect of granting commissions for the confirmation of abbatial charters, granting dispensations from impediments to marriage and in commissioning papal judges delegate to take cognisance of matrimonial litigation. Hamilton's exercise of papal jurisdiction in Scotland between 1561 and 1567 was augmented in December 1566, when the queen restored him to 'all and sundry' his jurisdictions within the diocese of St Andrews.

Within a late medieval Scottish context, delegated legatine powers were particularly useful for granting dispensations from the impediments to marriage of the forbidden degrees of consanguinity and affinity,[31] an aspect of Canon law not lawfully reformed in Scotland until the Marriage Act 1567.[32] The Archbishop of St Andrews is known to have issued dispensations from Canon law impediments to marriage in November 1561,[33] August 1562,[34] 17 February 1565/6,[35] 28 February 1565/6[36] and November 1566.[37] The dispensation of August 1562 was granted in favour of Hugh Montgomerie, Earl of Eglinton, and his second wife, Agnes Drummond, the archbishop being styled 'Legatus natus ac cum potestate Legati a latere sedis apostolice legatus'; and the same style was used in the dispensation of 17 February 1565/6, granted in favour of James Hepburn, fourth Earl of Bothwell, and his first wife, Jane Gordon. Beyond matrimonial matters, Hamilton also appears to have issued commissions by virtue of legatine authority in July 1561 for the confirmation of charters granted by the abbots of Glenluce and Crossraguel to the Earl of Cassilis.[38]

Such exercises of legatine authority following the Reformation crisis demonstrate that the Archbishop of St Andrews and those in whose interests he acted still adhered to the old religion, and as such continued to set store by papal jurisdiction. Nevertheless, such dispensations were the result of the personal exercise of a papal authority vested in the person of the archbishop, and it would appear that the granting of dispensations proceeded quietly. In apparent contrast, when the archbishop issued commissions to churchmen in respect of actions for annulment, such papal judges delegate appear to have convened courts. No such exercises of legatine authority are known to have occurred after the ratification of the Papal Jurisdiction Act in December 1567.

---

[31] Herkless and Hannay, *Archbishops*, v, 81–82.
[32] I.e. Green, 'Authority of the Sources', 128–134.
[33] Donaldson, 'Church Courts', 367.
[34] Fraser, *Memorials*, ii, 189–190.
[35] Stuart, *Lost Chapter*, 93–94.
[36] *Lag Charters*, ed. Murray, 6 and 55, appendix item 23.
[37] *St Andrews*, i, 268, n.2.
[38] Robertson, *Concilia Scotiae*, clxxiv, n.1.

Two specific series of events from the history of Hamilton's on-going exercise of papal jurisdiction are worthy of closer scrutiny, highlighting as they do the intermingling of the matrimonial jurisdiction of Archbishop Hamilton, of the courts of the early Church of Scotland, and of the Court of the Commissaries of Edinburgh during Mary's personal reign. While details concerning the rise of the courts of the Church of Scotland are dealt with in Chapter 4, and the appointment of the Commissaries of Edinburgh in Chapter 6, it is sufficient for the present purpose to note that both the courts of the Church of Scotland and the Commissaries of Edinburgh exercised consistorial, that is to say matrimonial, jurisdictions, with the new church courts active from at least February 1559/60, and the Commissaries from February 1563/4, notwithstanding differences as to the constitutional basis and authority by which they exercised such jurisdictions. The first specific series of events concern the attempts of Hugh, third Earl of Eglinton, and his first wife, Jane Hamilton, daughter of the Duke of Chatelherault, to procure both a Catholic annulment on the ground of consanguinity and a Protestant divorce on the ground of adultery from one another during the course of 1562, through recourse to litigation both before judges appointed by the archbishop and before the Protestant kirk session of Edinburgh by virtue of a Privy Council commission. The second concern the attempts of James Hepburn, fourth Earl of Bothwell, and his first wife, Jane Gordon, daughter of the Earl of Huntly, to procure both a Catholic annulment on the ground of consanguinity and a Protestant divorce on the ground of adultery from one another during the course of 1567, through recourse to litigation both before judges appointed by the archbishop and before the Commissaries of Edinburgh. These two sequences of litigation were punctuated by Mary Stewart's ill fated and abortive restoration of spiritual jurisdiction to Archbishop Hamilton within the diocese of St Andrews during the winter of 1566–7.

EGLINTON V. HAMILTON, HAMILTON V. EGLINTON

The earliest extant example of a marital action being heard by virtue of a commission granted by Archbishop Hamilton occurred around eight months after Mary Stewart's return to Scotland. The action was brought by Hugh Montgomerie, Earl of Eglinton, against his first countess, Jane Hamilton, the pursuer seeking his marriage to be decerned null *ab initio* on the ground of the impediment of consanguinity. The judges in the case were three canons of Glasgow cathedral, John Houston, John Hamilton and Archibald Crawford, who had been commissioned on 1 April 1562 to hear the case by 'a reverend father in Christ, John, by divine mercy Archbishop of St Andrews, primate of all Scotland, legate with the power of a legate *a latere* of the Apostolic See'.[39] Such a commission appears to have been required because 'Mr Robert Herbertson, commissary general of

---

[39] Fraser, *Memorials*, ii, 166–167 (commission), 163 (commission accepted 2 April 1562).

Glasgow, and Henry Sinclair, Bishop of Ross, then vicar general of Glasgow, had refused to entertain the case'.[40] On 13 April 1562 the principal judge in the case, Master John Houston, styled himself 'commissary and judge subdelegate of the apostolic see'.[41] Process having been led before the judges, sentence definitive was pronounced at Glasgow cathedral on 30 May 1562, annulling the marriage between Eglinton and his countess since they were attingent in the fourth degree of consanguinity, and granting both parties licence to remarry *in Domino*.[42]

As a Catholic nobleman, the Earl of Eglinton was required to obtain such an annulment by virtue of lawful Catholic authority and in conformity with Canon law should he wish to remarry and produce legitimate issue under Canon law. During the course of 1562 the earl had also been active in restoring the Mass within his earldom, an attempt in which the Archbishop of St Andrews had been intimately involved, and for which activities, as already noted in Chapter 2, various 'mass mongers' had been convict criminally by assize for violating the Proclamation of Leith. The earl's first wife, however, may be presumed to have been of the Protestant faith, since at an unknown date she procured from the Privy Council a commission first to the 'minister and elders of Glasgow', and second to the minister and kirk session of Edinburgh, for declarator of Scottish Protestant divorce on the ground of the earl's adultery, conform not to Canon law, but to the 'ewangel and law of God'. The date of the Privy Council commission, and of the subsequent process before the kirk session of Edinburgh, are no longer known, although it would appear from the commission's internal evidence that it was issued by the Privy Council active between the Reformation Parliament and the commencement of Mary's personal reign.[43] In any event, those so commissioned to take cognisance of the process found in the countess's favour on 25 June 1562. It is therefore unclear whether the countess's proceedings were already being led in Edinburgh by the time the earl procured his own commission from the Archbishop of St Andrews. Notwithstanding these problems of chronology, it is clear from the extract made from the no-longer-extant 'book and register of the kirk of Edinburgh' of the final judgement in the countess's process that a very full process had occurred, and that the 'judges' in the action included John Knox, superintendent John Spottiswoode, John Spens of Condie and Clement Litill (by virtue of their office of eldership or deaconship in the kirk of Edinburgh), together with James MacGill of Nether Rankeillour. In this respect, unique light is shone on to the confusion which pertained prior to the appointment of the Commissaries of Edinburgh, with two litigants from the same marriage availing themselves of two types of divorce available from two different authorities according to two bodies of law, both of whose proceedings occurred within a period of constitutional

---

[40] Smith, 'Spiritual Jurisdiction', 9.
[41] Fraser, *Memorials*, ii, 164.
[42] Ibid., ii, 163–181, 166–167 (commission), 179–180 (sentence definitive).
[43] Further thoughts as to the dating of this Privy Council commission are offered in Chapter 4.

dislocation. On the one hand, the annulment proceeded by virtue of an exercise of papal legatine authority by the Archbishop of St Andrews and was decided in conformity with Canon law, notwithstanding the fact that the forbidden degrees of consanguinity and affinity had already been denigrated by that time in the court of the superintendent of Fife, Fotherick and Strathearn as 'papistical traditions' not forbidden by the 'Word and law of God'.[44] On the other hand, the involvement of the Privy Council, the new church court at Edinburgh, and a striking combination not only of Protestant reformers but also of officers of state and lawyers who would go on to be intimately involved in the creation of the commissary courts was brought to bear in an action for the new Scottish Protestant divorce on the ground of adultery. By virtue of the annulment both the earl and the countess were free to remarry according to Canon law; by virtue of the divorce on the ground of adultery the countess was certainly free to remarry, while the adulterous earl was debarred from remarrying during the lifetime of his innocent spouse.[45]

The Earl of Eglinton and the Archbishop of St Andrews conformed their actions subsequent to the sentence of annulment to Canon law. Thus on 8 June 1562 the Earl of Eglinton entered into a marriage contract with the Earl and the Countess-dowager of Huntly for the hand of the earl's sister, Agnes Drummond.[46] The couple were related within the forbidden degrees of affinity and as such required a papal dispensation from the impediment in order to contract a valid marriage. A dispensation was granted by Hamilton at Paisley on 19 August 1562, apparently after the couple had already solemnised marriage.[47]

THE RESTORATION OF SPIRITUAL JURISDICTION TO ARCHBISHOP HAMILTON

As is discussed at length in Chapters 5 and 6, the new order of the commissary courts created from February 1563/4 was in part a temporary expedient capable of being superseded by either a restoration of the suppressed courts spiritual, or by some more assertive and organised Protestant ascendancy. Given both the continued consistorial activity of Archbishop Hamilton and the on-going commitment of the Queen of Scots to the Catholic faith, the assumption of the new commissary system into a restored Catholic ascendancy was not out of the question, and could be justified within the context of the narrative of both the Court of Session's assumption of the spiritual jurisdiction in December 1560 and the charter of constitution of the Commissaries of Edinburgh in February

---

[44] *St Andrews*, i, 133–135, *Cunningham v. Wood*, 10 December 1561. The forbidden degrees were declared to have been reformed in conformity with the 'law of God' from 8 March 1558/9 by the Marriage Act 1567.
[45] That this was the law of the Church of Scotland, and later the Commissaries of Edinburgh, see Green, *Consistorial Decisions*, lv–lxii.
[46] Fraser, *Memorials*, ii, 185–187.
[47] Ibid., ii, 189–190.

1563/4: the old courts spiritual could cease to be absent or inactive. The ease with which the new dispensation in the administration of the spiritual jurisdiction by the new commissary courts could be set aside in law was directly demonstrated by the restoration of Archbishop Hamilton to his spiritual jurisdictions in December 1566, with an attendant and explicit discharging of the Commissaries of Edinburgh within the diocese of St Andrews. This restoration of jurisdiction was concerned primarily with episcopal, rather than papal, authority and jurisdiction.

The immediate reasons for the restoration of Hamilton's jurisdiction are much disputed. By December 1566 the problem of Mary's second marriage to Lord Darnley was being contemplated in earnest and a formal restoration of jurisdiction to the Archbishop of St Andrews ahead of an action of annulment of the marriage of Mary and Darnley may have formed part of the range of possible solutions, although such a course of action brought with it both a potential difficulty relative to the legitimacy of the couple's son, the future James VI, and a greater difficulty in that the impediment of consanguinity standing between the couple had been dispensed by Rome.[48] Allied to this possibility was the further potential for another annulment, namely of the marriage of James Hepburn, fourth Earl of Bothwell, and his countess, Jane Gordon, as a prelude to Hepburn's marriage to the Queen of Scots. In the event, the marital difficulties in respect of Lord Darnley were elided via the brutal expedient of his murder in February 1566/7, a course of action which may already have been in play before the archbishop's restoration, and one which also elided any potential difficulty surrounding the legitimacy of the issue of Mary's second marriage. The Hepburn thesis is also not compelling, since in the event the archbishop's formal restoration was soon rescinded, a move which nevertheless did not preclude him from commissioning judges to take cognisance of the Earl of Bothwell's action for annulment, in much the same way as judges had been commissioned to annul the marriage of the Earl of Eglinton in 1562. On the other hand, by December 1566 it may have been the case that there were no 'well beloved and trust councillors' reminding the queen of the imperative nature of maintaining the legal structures created by the Proclamation of Leith and the Act of Oblivion: certainly Henry and John Sinclair had both gone to their rest, on 2 January 1564/5 and 9 April 1566 respectively,[49] and while William Maitland of Lethington had initially proposed the queen's policy of toleration in 1561, Herkless and Hannay entertained the suggestion 'that it was Lethington, on behalf of Bothwell, who advocated the re-establishment of the prelate's court'.[50] Within the context of an increasingly aggressive and

---

[48] Obtaining this papal dispensation at Rome in 1565 was apparently done most quietly (Stuart, *Lost Chapter*, 28; Robertson, *Concilia Scotiae*, i, clxxviii–clxix).
[49] Watt and Murray, *Fasti*, 351 and 56.
[50] Herkless and Hannay, *Archbishops*, v, 177.

conflicted court life, the queen may have ill-advisedly sought openly to effect an alteration of the state of religion as found universally standing at her return to Scotland.

Be that as it may, the fact remains that on 23 December 1566 Mary signed a writ which restored 'Johnne, Archbischop of Sanctandrois, primat and legat of Scotland, to all and sindrie his jurisdictionis alsweill upoun the south as the north sydis of the watter of Forth within the diocie of Sanctandrois ... dischairgeing be thir presentis all utheris commissaris, clerkis and utheris officiaris quhatsumevir now establischit thairintill of thair offices forder in that part'.[51] In this respect Hamilton's jurisdiction had been restored for his entire diocese, including the archdeaconry of Lothian, which in effect represented the bounds of the local jurisdiction of the by then new Commissaries of Edinburgh. It would not appear that the clause 'all and sundry his jurisdictions' was intended to be limited by later specific clauses contained within the writ concerning the confirmation of major testaments and the disposal of benefices. The extent to which the jurisdiction of the but recently appointed new Commissary of St Andrews and the local jurisdiction of the new Commissaries of Edinburgh would have been totally eclipsed by this restoration, and, more importantly, the extent to which the national jurisdictions of the Commissaries of Edinburgh would have suffered derogation within the diocese of St Andrews, remain matters for speculation, since the restoration never took effect, and even if it had, the registers for both the Commissaries of Edinburgh and for the Commissary of St Andrews are not extant for this particular period.[52] Derogation of the Commissaries of Edinburgh's national testamentary jurisdiction within the diocese of St Andrews was expressly to have occurred, on account of which the queen's writ stated explicitly that the proceeds of the confirmation of testaments already allocated to the College of Justice, namely £1600 per annum,[53] was to be paid *pro rata* by the archbishop. Derogation of the Commissaries' consistorial jurisdiction would appear to have been intended in so far as the theses concerning the annulments are to be accepted, and certainly such proceedings could readily have been brought within the compass of the general 'all and sundry his jurisdictions' clause deployed twice in the writ.

On 27 December 1566 the General Assembly resolved to petition the Privy Council 'anent the purported commission of jurisdiction granted to [John Hamilton], the bishop of St Andrews, to the effect that their honours stay the same, in respect that those causes, for the most part, judged by his usurped authority, pertain to the true Kirk; and, howbeit, that, for hope of good things, the Kirk overlooked the queen's majesty's commission given thereto to such men, who for the most part were our bretheren, yet the Kirk can in no wise

---

[51] For the text of the writ see *RSS*, v, 3145; Robertson, *Concilia Scotiae*, i, clxxviii–clxxix.
[52] For Edinburgh see Green, *Consistorial Decisions*, lxvii–lxix.
[53] For the details of which endowment see MacQueen (ed.), *College of Justice*, 79–89.

be content that the bishop of St Andrews, a common enemy of Christ, use that jurisdiction'.[54] The subsequent petition styled Hamilton 'that conspiring enemie of Jesus Christ, and cruel murderer of our dear brethren',[55] and narrated that 'his ancient jurisdiction was, that he, with certain of his collateral colleagues, might have damned of heresy as it pleased him and then to take all that were suspect of heresy . . . Our queen is probably not well informed; she ought not, nor may not, justly break the laws; and so consequently she may not set up against us, nor without our consent, that Roman anti-Christ again'.[56] Authorship of the petition has been attributed to Knox,[57] and certainly the rhetoric is redolent of Knox's *Appellation* of 1558, and possibly redolent of some of the tenor of the extant ordinance of the Protestant 'Lords of Council' issued against the consistory of Brechin in December 1559.

It is particularly striking that General Assembly's remonstrance held Mary's actions to have broken the law. That the queen had broken the law was certainly a potent argument, in so far as the archbishop's restoration was a clear breach of the Proclamation of Leith. While the General Assembly raised the issue of the necessity of the consent of the General Assembly to such an alteration of religion within the context of the 'lawes', without which the queen risked undermining the second legal framework created in response to the Reformation crisis, there was a deeper argument now in play once more. In this respect the General Assembly was now taking a harder line, and alongside the remonstrance's assertion that the archbishop's jurisdiction actually pertained to the Reformed Kirk, on account of which the appointment of the Commissaries of Edinburgh had simply been 'overlooked for the hope of good things', was a renewed assertion of the validity of the legislation of the Reformation Parliament: 'For in one lawful and most free parliament that ever was before in this realm, that odious beast was deprived of all jurisdiction, office, and authority within this realm'.[58]

As to constitutional theory, this polemical rhetoric clearly contained a direct association of the legislation of the Reformation Parliament with the overthrow of both papal and episcopal jurisdiction in Scotland. This constitutional position, however, appears to have found no resonance among either the deliberations of the Lords of Council and Session or of the Commissaries of Edinburgh, as is discussed in Chapters 5 and 6: within those contexts a more nuanced series of distinctions between native Scottish episcopal and Roman papal jurisdictions may be observed.

Knox was clearly conversant with the events surrounding Hamilton's restoration, incorporating a copy of the General Assembly's December 1566

---

[54] Shaw, *Acts and Proceedings*, i, 112–113.
[55] Hamilton was legally responsible for the execution of the aged Walter Myll (or Miln) for heresy in 1558 (Herkless and Hannay, *Archbishops*, v, 92), the last Protestant to have been martyred in Scotland (Dawson, 'Theatre of Martyrdom', 260, n.5).
[56] Shaw, *Acts and Proceedings*, i, 113–115.
[57] *Knox's History*, ii, 195–196; cf. Robertson, *Concilia Scotiae*, i, clxxix–clxxx, n.1.
[58] Shaw, *Acts and Proceedings*, i, 114.

remonstrance into his *History*. Therein Knox also noted that the archbishop's restoration entailed a discharging of the Commissaries of Edinburgh, on account of which in January 1566/7 the archbishop, 'having a company of one hundred horses, or more', came to Edinburgh to 'take possession' of his jurisdiction. In the event the prelate seems to have been dissuaded from entering the burgh by some members of the town council sent by the Provost 'for fear of trouble and sedition that might rise thereupon'.[59] The general furore occasioned by the archbishop's restoration must have impressed upon the queen the folly of the undertaking, for by 9 January an intelligence report sent from Berwick to William Cecil relayed that 'the "jurisdiction in dyvers cases according to canon lawes," lately obtained from the Queen by the bishop of St Andrews, who meant to erect his court at Edinburgh, being found contrary to religion and not liked by the townsmen, has been revoked by her at the suit of [the earl of Moray]'.[60] The damage occasioned by the restoration was clearly perceived by Mary's government, for on 14 April 1567 the three estates passed an 'Act concerning religion' in which it was asserted that 'hir hienes, sen hir foirsaid arryvall, hes attemptit na thing contrar the estait of religioun, quhilk hir majestie fand publictlie and universallie standing at hir arryvale foirsaid, quhairby hir majestie is maist worthy to be servit, honourit and obeyit . . .', with the remainder of the act going on to reassure the subjects of the realm, albeit in a roundabout way, that they could not be tried for heresy and would be defended against all foreign authorities whatsoever.[61]

Between the revocation of Hamilton's restoration and the Act of April 1567, the queen's personal reign in Scotland entered yet more troubled waters, with the murder of Lord Darnley by strangulation at the Kirk o' Fields on 10 February 1566/7. Amid the sequence of events by which the queen's personal reign in Scotland was overthrown, of which the breakdown of the second legal framework is a previously understated element, the Archbishop of St Andrews played one final part, annulling the marriage of James Hepburn, Earl of Bothwell, ahead of his marriage to the by then twice widowed Queen of Scots.

GORDON V. HEPBURN, HEPBURN V. GORDON

While the queen's difficulties in respect of her second marriage had been resolved without recourse to litigation, the suspected chief perpetrator of Darnley's murder, the Earl of Bothwell, was still married to his countess, Jane Gordon. The couple had married on 22 February 1565/6, having been dispensed from the impediment of consanguinity standing between them by the Archbishop of St Andrews on 17 February 1565/6 by a virtue of the archbishop's legatine authority.[62] Within the year the queen had been freed of her second marriage, and it became incumbent

---

[59] *Knox's History*, ii, 201.
[60] *CSP Scot.*, ii, no. 461; Donaldson, *James V–VII*, 125.
[61] *RPS*, 1567/4/6.
[62] Stuart, *Lost Chapter*, 7, 93–94.

upon Bothwell to obtain a Catholic annulment of his first marriage as a prelude to his marriage to the queen. Yet at the same time that the Earl of Bothwell sought an annulment, his countess, Jane Gordon, sought to obtain a sentence of Scottish Protestant divorce on the ground of adultery before the Commissaries of Edinburgh. The reason for this dual process, the one Catholic, the other Protestant, is unclear, although it may have been part of a collusive bargain struck between Hepburn and Gordon. Such a bargain is plausible, since, on the one hand, Gordon's collusion was required by her husband for a Catholic process of annulment, since the success of such a process depended upon the concealment and denial of the dispensation by virtue of which their marriage had proceed, while, on the other hand, Gordon may have been of the Protestant faith and as such desired to be divorced from her husband according to the laws of her religion, so as to be free in conscience and law to remarry.

Be that as it may, on 26 April 1567 an action for Scottish Protestant divorce on the ground of adultery was brought by Gordon against Hepburn before the Commissaries of Edinburgh.[63] While the registers of the Commissaries are no longer extant for this period on account of the clerkship of Sebastian Danelourt,[64] copies of parts of the process papers are still extant. On 30 April various depositions of witnesses were taken by the Commissaries at Edinburgh, from which the adultery of Bothwell with one Bessy Crawford was proven.[65] The Commissaries accordingly pronounced decreet in Gordon's favour on 3 May 1567.[66] Although this decreet is no longer extant, it would have contained an express licence for Gordon to remarry, which licence Gordon exercised in marrying the twelfth Earl of Sutherland following his own action for Protestant divorce on the ground of adultery before the Commissaries.[67]

The day after proceedings had been initiated before the Commissaries of Edinburgh, that is to say on 27 April 1567, the Archbishop of St Andrews issued a commission as primate and legate of Scotland to the bishops of Dunkeld and Dunblane, together with Archibald Crawford (one of the canons of Glasgow commissioned in *Eglinton v. Hamilton*), Alexander Crichton and George Cook, canons of Dunkeld, and John Manderstoun, canon of the collegiate church of Dunbar, to take cognisance of *Hepburn v. Gordon*. The commission appears to have been received on 3 May by John Manderstoun, albeit under protest and duress, by virtue of which Jane Gordon, together with various named witnesses, was summoned to appear before the commissioned judges in the cause on 5 May at St Giles' collegiate church in Edinburgh. St Giles' had previously been the seat of the Official of Lothian and, by 1567, the upper level of the

---

[63] As noted in William Cecil's diary *per* Keith, *History*, ii, 575, n.2.
[64] For the problem of 'Danelourt's Registers' see Green, *Consistorial Decisions*, lxvii–lxix.
[65] *Calendar of the Manuscripts of the Marquis of Salisbury*, part XIII, 79–82.
[66] Stuart, *Lost Chapter*, 16–17; Robertson, *Concilia Scotiae*, clxxxi, notes.
[67] Green, *Consistorial Decisions*, xliii–xliv; and note the author's previous failure to note the revocation of Hamilton's restoration.

west end of St Giles' housed the Over or Upper Tolbooth, wherein the Lords of Council and Session, and likely the Commissaries of Edinburgh, sat in judgement.[68] On 5 May only one of the commissioned judges, John Manderstoun, sat in judgement, before whom appeared Master Edmund Hay, procurator for the Earl of Bothwell, and Master Henry Kinross, procurator for the countess.[69] At that time Kinross not only was procurator fiscal in the Court of the Commissaries of Edinburgh but had been appointed by Gordon on 22 March 1566/7 as her procurator before the Commissaries of Edinburgh in respect both of her forthcoming action of divorce and of 'any other cause whatsoever'.[70] Hay produced various witnesses who were accordingly examined, with Manderstoun appointing the following day for the publication of their depositions. On 6 May Kinross appears to have 'raised general objections of law' and renounced further defence. At St Giles' on 7 May, John Manderstoun pronounced sentence of annulment in Hepburn's favour on the ground of the undispensed impediment of consanguinity according to Canon law.[71] By virtue of this process the Earl of Bothwell was freed to marry the Queen of Scots, which marriage was solemnised at Holyrood on 15 May in a Protestant rite officiated by the 'reforming' bishop of Galloway.

ORDINARY EPISCOPAL JURISDICTION FOLLOWING THE REFORMATION CRISIS

While there is no evidence of the continued exercise of ordinary episcopal jurisdiction by the suppressed courts spiritual in respect of litigation following the Reformation crisis, there are a number of examples of what may arguably be viewed as the direct exercise of such jurisdiction by the Scottish episcopate. Whatever the legality of the suppression of the old courts spiritual, the overwhelming evidence is that they remained suppressed until their theoretical restoration within the diocese of St Andrews in late 1566. During the period 1559 to 1566 the courts of the Church of Scotland, the Court of Session and other civil courts, and more formally the commissary courts, variously assimilated, assumed and administered the old prelatical jurisdictions which had previously been administered by the Catholic Commissaries and Officials. Yet at the same time, there is no evidence that the Protestant party intended the formal abolition of episcopacy in Scotland. As has been noted, it would be difficult to argue that the attempted abrogation of papal jurisdiction could have somehow abolished episcopacy, since bishops were expressly prohibited from exercising papal jurisdiction, and, while there can be no doubt that the Protestant party aimed at the overthrow of the hierarchy of the

---

[68] MacQueen, 'Two Visitors in the Session'.
[69] *Calendar of the Manuscripts of the Marquis of Salisbury*, part XIII, 75–76, and 82.
[70] Ibid., part XIII, 78.
[71] Ibid., part XIII, 78–79.

Catholic Church, there is no express evidence to the effect that bishops were to be effaced from the Scottish ecclesiastical polity.

In respect of episcopacy within Scotland following the Reformation crisis, a distinction must be drawn between continuing Catholic episcopacy and the authority of those Catholic bishops who converted to Protestantism, the 'reforming' bishops of the early Church of Scotland. Among the examples of the reforming bishops of Galloway, of Caithness, and of Orkney, there is evidence of the continuing association of bishops with the matrimonial jurisdiction, and also collation to benefices. The episcopal function of collating presentees to Scottish benefices touched upon the spiritual jurisdiction but indirectly, being part of the rationale by which disputes over rights and titles to benefices fell within the purview of the courts spiritual. Yet nevertheless, while collation remained a function of office holders within the Church of Scotland, jurisdiction in 'beneficial' causes went on to fall within the purview of the Court of the Commissaries of Edinburgh, which was on occassion a source of grievance for the Kirk.

As to the procedures surrounding titles to benefices, the episcopal collation of presentees to Scottish benefices appears to have continued to some extent prior to 1567. Thus on 12 August 1566 one sir William Struthers was presented by the Crown to the bishop of Dunkeld for collation to the parsonage and prebend of Moneydie, although the collation did not occurr.[72] In respect of the reforming bishop of Orkney, Donaldson has noted, albeit without supporting citation, that 'Bishop Gordon was, of course, entitled to give collation to benefices in his diocese and to provide to those which were at his own presentation'.[73] And in September 1565, the Archbishop of St Andrews is thought to have given collation to Alan Stewart in respect of his royal presentation to the abbey of Crossraguel, although Robertson held the collation to have proceeded by virtue of legatine authority.[74] Despite these known instances of continued episcopal activity in respect of collations, this power was being comprehensively undermined by the Scottish Crown towards the end of Mary's personal reign. This has been noted by Donaldson in respect of the Crown's right of presentation in respect of lesser benefices. Such powers of presentation for episcopal collation slowly changed into royal powers of provision during Mary's personal reign.[75] Shortly after Mary's return to Scotland she disposed of a benefice by simply gift and a little over a year later she acted likewise in respect of a vicarage 'nochtwithstanding that collatioun ordinare nevir follow thairupoun'. The gradual development of direct royal gifts of benefices continued throughout Mary's personal reign and from the spring of 1565 a 'steady stream . . . of gifts of all kinds of benefices' by the Crown began, and continued until the end of her reign. This process was part of what Donaldson termed 'the

---

[72] Green, 'Scottish Benefices', 48–52.
[73] Donaldson, *Reformed by Bishops*, 6.
[74] Robertson, *Concilia Scotiae*, clxxiv, n.1.
[75] For the distinction between presentations and provisions see Green, 'Scottish Benefices', 51, including n.32.

silent revolution whereby the crown, assuming papal, and more than papal, powers, took into its own hands the disposal of the ecclesiastical property'.[76] Yet in respect of the distribution of benefices by the Crown by way of simply gift during Mary's personal reign, it was probable that recipients of such gifts desired good, or at least enforceable, title to ecclesiastical revenues, and had little interest in any cure of souls which might happen to attach to a particular benefice; in this respect episcopal collation might be ridden over roughshod within the context of the revolutionary disintegration of the Catholic ascendancy.

That the function of collation in respect of the cure of souls was still nevertheless important – and required extricating from the general subversion of collation within the context of the division of the spoils of ecclesiastical wealth during Mary's personal reign – appears to have been acknowledged by the three estates in Parliament in December 1567. The Act concerning the admission of those that shall be presented to benefices, having cure of ministry,[77] in effect transferred the power of collation to the superintendents and to commissioners appointed by the General Assembly of the Church of Scotland. Commissioners could and did include reforming bishops, and in this respect there was some continued 'episcopal' collation after 1567, although the basis of its validity had become statutory law within the context of the establishment of the Church of Scotland.

By virtue of this Act the power of collation as a function of ordinary episcopal authority appears to have been for a time eclipsed by superintendents and commissioners of the Kirk. Almost immediately after the passage of the act, a minister of the Church of Scotland, Thomas McGibbon, was presented to the parsonage and prebend of Moneydie, for collation by the superintendent of Fife, Fotherick and Strathearn; whereas a year or so previously collation to the same benefice had been by the bishop of Dunkeld.[78] In this episcopacy appears for a time to have been stripped of the power of collation, only to have it restored by the General Assembly on 16 January 1571/2, when the office of archbishop and bishop was acknowledged as part of the polity of the Kirk. Nevertheless, those appointed to bishoprics from that time on were to 'exercise no further jurisdiction in spiritual function than the superintendents have and presently exercise, until the same be agreed upon; and that all archbishops and bishops be subject to the Kirk and the general assembly thereof *in spiritualibus* . . .'[79] As such, episcopal jurisdiction was defined at that time within the context of the reformation of the Church relative to the office of superintendent, and not to the pre-Reformation conception of ordinary episcopal jurisdiction.

---

[76] RSS, v, introduction (by Gordon Donaldson), viii–xii, and ii. Alterations in the order observed in respect of provisions to the greater benefices occasioned by the Reformation are also noted in *Balfour's Practicks*, ii, 655.

[77] RPS, A1567/12/6.

[78] Green, 'Scottish Benefices', 46–48.

[79] Shaw, *Acts and Proceedings*, i, 254.

Yet even this distinction was not as clear cut as might be expected. As is discussed at length in Chapter 7, both a consistorial and a disciplinary jurisdiction variously formed part of the jurisdiction of John Winram, superintendent of Fife, Fotherick and Strathearn at St Andrews between 1561 and 1571/2. Winram's superintendent's court appears to have sat for the last time two days before the consecration of John Douglas as Protestant Archbishop of St Andrews on 1571/2, and, while the Commissaries of Edinburgh were to directly assert in June 1572 not only their exclusive competence in all consistorial causes within the realm, but also the incompetence of superintendent Winram in such matters, Archbishop Douglas does not appear to have managed to extricate entirely the disciplinary jurisdiction of the new church courts at St Andrews from occasioning consistorial decisions.[80]

In respect of continued exercises of the matrimonial, or consistorial, jurisdiction by the Scottish episcopate, attention falls to the three 'reforming' bishops who conformed to the Reformation, namely Adam Bothwell, Bishop of Orkney, Alexander Gordon, Bishop of Galloway, and Robert Stewart, Bishop of Caithness.[81] Of these, certainly Bothwell, and probably Gordon, heard consistorial actions. As is discussed at more length in Chapter 4, Gordon, in his capacity as bishop of Orkney, took cognisance of a Protestant action for divorce on the ground of adultery, *Tulloch v. Sinclair*, along with the minister, elders and deacons of the kirk session of Orkney in 1562. This sentence was the subject of an appeal to the General Assembly held at Perth in 1563, among whose records it was noted simply as an '"appellation from the bishop of Orkney's sentence in a cause of divorce'.[82] The subsequent course of that appeal, which upheld the original sentence, together with its acceptance as valid by the Commissaries of Edinburgh, is discussed at more length in Chapter 6. The point of note here is that the General Assembly appears to have been at no pains to mention that the bishop had sat in judgement along with the kirk session of Orkney, although this appears, from the Commissaries' decreet, to have been the case. In this respect it would appear that the General Assembly took no specific issue with a reforming bishop hearing consistorial actions.

This impression appears to be confirmed by a complaint given in to the same General Assembly held at Perth in June 1563. The complaint stated that Alexander Gordon, Bishop of Galloway, and commissioner for appointing office bearers for the reformed Kirk within his bounds, 'had not ministered justice to Margaret Murray, complaining on her husband Golfride MacCulloch [of Ardwell] for non-adherence. But the commissioner could not satisfy the

---

[80] For example *St Andrews*, i, 368 (*Prat & Tullos*), 381 (*Neilson, Swan, Kinsman & Grig*), 387 (*Myllar & Donaldson*); although it may be noted that actual consistorial litigation before the church courts at St Andrews appears to have ended with the consecration of Archbishop Douglas.

[81] For a consideration of their reformed episcopates see Donaldson, *Reformed by Bishops*.

[82] Shaw, *Acts and Proceedings*, i, 44.

assembly with any sufficient excuse.'[83] From this it would appear that the bishop of Galloway was expected to take cognisance of actions for adherence, and, by extension, presumably other consistorial actions. This was the view taken by Donaldson, who read this evidence as demonstrating that 'he was regarded as the proper judge in matrimonial causes', having just noted among the list of the reforming bishop's duties 'the giving of judgment in matrimonial causes'.[84]

CONCLUSION

The status of Scottish episcopal and Roman papal jurisdiction in Scotland subsequent to the Reformation Parliament provides a mixed and sometimes chaotic picture. The old courts spiritual remained inactive, but at the same time those bishops who conformed to the Reformation appear to have retained competences in respect of matrimonial litigation. Episcopal collation to benefices also appears to have survived to a limited extent, although collation was being substantially undermined by the Scottish Crown. Thus the Catholic bishop of Dunkeld was expected to give collation to a benefice in 1566, while both superintendents and reforming bishops variously enjoyed powers of collation. The general sense conveyed by the evidence in respect of actual exercises of episcopal authority is one of fragmented survival in multiple contexts.

As to papal jurisdiction, it appears that lawyerly opinion held it not to have been abolished or abrogated in law, being a view variously apparent from the decisions and judgements of the Court of Session, and even reflected in the statutory provisions of the 1563 Act of Oblivion. Within this context Archbishop Hamilton repeatedly exercised his legatine authority within Scotland, on occasion even commissioning judges delegate to convene courts for the hearing of actions of annulment. Whether Hamilton's actions betokened defiance of the Protestant revolution, or mere indifference to its illegalities, his legatine and episcopal jurisdictions were overtly and officially countenanced by the queen in December 1566. The post-August 1560 activities of the Scottish episcopate, Catholic or Reformed, and the confused and fragmentary contexts in which they took place, are indicative of some of the practical failings of reform by 'lesser magistrates'. Beyond the evidence of actual exercises of episcopal and papal jurisdiction during this confused period lies a more salient point: the constitutional principles of episcopal and papal spiritual jurisdiction had not been extinguished by the Reformation crisis.

---

[83] Ibid., i, 39.
[84] Donaldson, *Reformed by Bishops*, 5–6.

Chapter 4

The Rise of the Courts of the Church of Scotland

One of the complicating factors in the history of the spiritual jurisdiction in Reformation Scotland is that it was variously assumed by the earliest courts of the Church of Scotland following the suppression of the courts of the Catholic Church. Although this aspect of the Reformation has been variously noted by earlier historians, it has not previously been described in full. The courts of the Church of Scotland developed spontaneously and rapidly during the period 1559–61, and became particularly active in consistorial (that is, matrimonial) actions previously heard by the suppressed courts spiritual. Various questions and difficulties attached to this phenomenon in respect of the lawyerly view. At the time, it was not clear by what authority the new legal system had been created or sanctioned, nor was it clear that the new system of church courts formed part of the Scottish legal system, a problem not resolved until they were expressly declared to be so by statute in December 1567. In addition to the constitutional status of these new courts, the question of their competent jurisdiction also remained vexed, even after 1567.

The early courts of the Church of Scotland certainly assumed and exercised aspects of the old spiritual jurisdiction. This was the understanding implicit in a petition given in by the General Assembly to Mary's Privy Council in December 1566, wherein it was stated that the causes previously judged by virtue of the 'usurped' authority of the Archbishop of St Andrews 'for the most part . . . pertain to the true Kirk'.[1] In respect of the jurisdictions routinely administered by the old courts spiritual, the earliest courts of the Church of Scotland were to some extent involved in proceedings concerning pre-Reformation sentences of heresy, but the point of central significance for this study was that the courts of the early Church of Scotland enjoyed a widespread consistorial jurisdiction. This assumption of the consistorial jurisdiction occurred prior to the Reformation Parliament, and developed rapidly during the period August 1560 to August 1561.

Prior to the Reformation Parliament, the extant evidence reveals the direct involvement of John Knox in hearing consistorial actions with the kirk sessions of St Andrews and Edinburgh. Following the Reformation Parliament, the provisional government of August 1560 to August 1561 was directly involved

---

[1] Shaw, *Acts and Proceedings*, i, 112–113.

in the appointment of superintendents within the Church of Scotland, which superintendents convened courts which heard consistorial actions. In addition to what appears to have been a spontaneous assumption of jurisdiction by the courts of the early Church of Scotland, the 'Privy Councils' active after October 1559 and after August 1560 also commissioned the new church courts to hear consistorial actions, and, on one occasion, a process for the reduction of a pre-Reformation sentence of heresy. This early phase of the development of the new church courts therefore occurred within the context of revolution during the years encompassed by the Act of Oblivion 1563. Consequently the subsequent legitimacy of the new Protestant church courts depended for a time upon the second legal framework created during Mary's personal reign in response to the Reformation crisis. That the Protestant Kirk's consistorial jurisdiction continued to be exercised and, to a limited extent, was countenanced within the second legal framework, then apparently transferred to the new commissary courts, and then, where specific reformed church courts proved resistant to a derogation of their jurisdiction, actively inhibited and suppressed, is the more complex theme within this history.

The assumption of aspects of the spiritual jurisdiction by the new church courts is all the more enigmatic because it does not seem to have been initially intended or acknowledged by either the Lords of the Congregation when they suppressed the courts of the Catholic Church in Scotland or by the extant legislation of the Reformation Parliament. The ordinance of autumn 1559 issued by the rebel Lords envisaged the transfer of the spiritual jurisdiction to the civil courts of Scotland, while the provisions of the Reformation Parliament in respect of papal jurisdiction likewise directed litigants to the civil courts. While some aspects of the old spiritual jurisdiction, including the consistorial jurisdiction, were assumed by the Court of Session and, arguably, other civil courts prior to the appointment of the Commissaries of Edinburgh,[2] the consistorial jurisdiction was also firmly assumed by the earliest courts of the Church of Scotland.

While ecclesiastical histories of the Protestant Kirk have from time to time noted this phenomenon, albeit briefly, and often in footnotes, Scottish legal historiography has a distinct tradition of considering the early Kirk's consistorial jurisdiction. This tradition may be traced through the works of John Riddell,[3] Joseph Robertson,[4] Gordon Donaldson[5] and David Smith,[6] and has its origins principally in the study of the early registers of the Acts and Decreets of the Commissaries of Edinburgh. The evidence of these registers has been augmented in part through the printed edition of *St Andrews* prepared by David

---

[2] For which see Chapter 5.
[3] Riddell, *Inquiry*, i, 390–555.
[4] Robertson, *Concilia Scotiae*, i, clxxiii–clxxxii.
[5] Donaldson, 'Church Courts'.
[6] Smith, 'Spiritual Jurisdiction'.

CONSISTORIAL ACTIONS BEFORE KIRK SESSIONS PRIOR TO THE REFORMATION PARLIAMENT

Hay Fleming,[7] which drew upon the works of Riddell and Robertson to a limited extent, but which stopped short of fully developing the significance of the evidence provided from the *St Andrews* material in relation to that of the Commissaries of Edinburgh, although this was in part rectified by Donaldson,[8] and brought to a fuller expression by Smith.[9]

The first consistorial process known to have been led before a kirk session in Scotland concerned an action for Scottish Protestant divorce on the ground of adultery brought before the kirk session of St Andrews on 1 February 1559/60,[10] within three months of the move to suppress the courts spiritual by the Lords of the Congregation. As has already been noted in Chapter 1, the suppression of the old church courts at St Andrews may have been part of the pre-October 1559 reform of St Andrews, and there is a clear sense from the evidence that the kirk session, or new 'consistory', at St Andrews replaced the consistorial courts of the Commissaries and Officials there. Thus on 1 February 1559/60 one William Renton gave in a petition of divorce to the 'minister and elders' of the kirk of St Andrews against his wife Elizabeth Geddes. While Adam Heriot was the first minister at St Andrews from an unknown point in 1559 until July 1560,[11] John Knox is also variously noted among the extant evidence as being at St Andrews, and continuously so between early to mid-November 1559 and the end of April 1560.[12] The minister sitting in judgement during *Renton v. Geddes* was likely Knox, as opposed to Heriot, since, while Knox was mentioned explicitly in relation to the case, Heriot was not. Process was led in *Renton v. Geddes* before the session from 10 February and sentence absolvitor pronounced in Geddes's favour on 21 March 1559/60. This sentence definitive was read publicly to the Protestant congregation at St Andrews by John Knox, minister, on Sunday 24 March, 'lykeas the samyn wes decerned and pronunced in the consistory, settand judges juditialie, upoun Thuirsday the xxj day of the samyne moneth of Marche, 1559[/60]'.[13]

While process was still being led in *Renton v. Geddes*, the minister and kirk session of St Andrews, in an exercise of their disciplinary jurisdiction, decerned a man to adhere to his wife.[14] Two weeks after sentence had been pronounced in *Renton v. Geddes*, the minister and kirk session took cognisance of a process for

---

[7] *St Andrews*, i, especially 268–269, n.2.
[8] Donaldson, 'Church Courts', 367, 371–373.
[9] Smith, 'Spiritual Jurisdiction'.
[10] *St Andrews*, i, 18.
[11] Ibid., i, 3, n.1.
[12] Ibid., i, 27, n.1.
[13] Ibid., i, 18–26 (process); 26–27 (sentence absolvitor).
[14] Ibid., i, 28, *Smyth & Lummisden*, 16 March 1559/60.

solemnisation, *Tweddell v. Ramsay*, on 4 April 1560. The petition sought solemnisation on the ground of promise of marriage and subsequent copulation. This was one of the ordinary grounds on which solemnisation was sought according to Canon law. Nevertheless, on 11 April 1560, the kirk session decerned the defender to solemnise marriage with the pursuer, declaring that this was in conformity with the law of God, 'because the said woman alleaget hir to haif beyne ane virgine or [i.e. before] he gat hir, and he culd say na thing in the contrare therof'.[15] This sentence of solemnisation therefore proceeded upon the basis of Exodus, chapter 22, verse 16, which enjoined that he who deflowered a virgin must marry her, unless the woman's father absolutely refused to let the man marry his daughter, in which case the deflowerer was to pay compensation. This principle was incorporated into the *First Book of Discipline* and was variously enforced by the kirk session and superintendent's court at St Andrews, and by the General Assembly of the Church of Scotland.[16]

The kirk session's reliance on the ground of deflowered virginity appears to have led to an avoidance of the acknowledgement of the Canon law doctrine of *sponsalia per verba de futuro cum copula subsequente* in *Tweddell v. Ramsay*. The question as to what law the kirk session might enforce where only promise and copula were relevantly libelled was tested in *Millar v. Adie* – brought the day judgement was given in *Tweddell v. Ramsay* – wherein the pursuer in effect attempted to stay the banns of the defender with a third party. It was alleged that the defender had promised to marry the pursuer, while in his answer the defender granted that he had copulated with the pursuer, but denied any promise of marriage. This answer was clearly thought to amount to a peremptory exception, in that it was admitted to the defender's probation, bringing with it an apparent, if tacit, acceptance of the Canon law principle of *sponsalia per verba de futuro cum copula subsequente*. Two witnesses were subsequently summoned before the kirk session, but their depositions appear to have been inconclusive.[17] At this point in the proceedings Knox is thought to have left St Andrews for Edinburgh, leaving Adam Heriot as sole minister at St Andrews, and, while on 2 May 1560 the minister and elders postponed pronouncing their sentence until 16 May, no final judgement appears to have been pronounced in the case. Adam Heriot's ministry is thought to have come to an end at St Andrews in July 1560, when he was translated to Aberdeen, being replaced at St Andrews by Christopher Goodman.

These cases demonstrate a significant assumption of the old consistorial jurisdiction by the kirk session of St Andrews between the suppression of the old courts spiritual and the Reformation Parliament, with clear evidence of litigation involving divorce, adherence, solemnisation and the staying of banns. Certainly this was Donaldson's understanding, who noted that 'the reformers had their candidates for

---

[15] Ibid., i, 29–30.
[16] Green, 'Authority of the Sources', 131–132.
[17] *St Andrews*, i, 31–33.

the consistorial jurisdiction',[18] and also Smith's understanding, who noted that the early kirk sessions 'operated in almost every sense as the spiritual successors to the Roman Church'.[19] The editor of the early registers of the kirk of St Andrews, David Hay Fleming, also held this to be the case, noting that the early kirk session of St Andrews did not hesitate 'to judge in claims of marriage and divorce. There was no feeling of usurpation in this, for the body of the citizens had voluntarily placed themselves on the side of the Reformation, and the Session naturally took up the work that had previously fallen to the ecclesiastical courts.'[20]

The kirk session of St Andrews on various occasions styled itself the 'consistoriall court' or 'consistory',[21] which brought with it connotations not only of the old courts spiritual, which were routinely referred to as consistories, but also the Consistory of Geneva. On the one hand, the Catholic consistories had heard litigation in all manner of matrimonial disputes and possessed the authority to pronounce judicial sentences accepted as valid and binding by the rest of the Scottish legal system. On the other hand, the Genevan Consistory enjoyed powers of inquiring into all manner of matrimonial disputes, and also of hearing what was in effect litigation between parties. If the Genevan Consistory could resolve matrimonial disputes through recourse to admonitions and councils, in effect procuring the consent of parties to the resolution of disputes, then such disputes could be brought to a conclusion without recourse to another court. Nevertheless, Genevan ecclesiastical ordinances stated that, if a matrimonial process before the Consistory resulted in the need for a judicial sentence to be pronounced, the process was to be remitted to the Small Council with a recommendation, so that a legally binding definitive sentence could be pronounced by a competent authority. In this respect, proceedings before the Genevan Consistory could be resolved through an exercise of a disciplinary, religious or moral jurisdiction, or such proceedings could have something akin to persuasive force when remitted to the Small Council so that judicial sentences could be pronounced.[22] The evidence for the development of the new church courts within Scotland suggests that they exercised both a disciplinary jurisdiction and also a consistorial jurisdiction, in the sense that they also held themselves to possess the authority to reach a final, legally binding judgement, being an authority not exercised by the Genevan Consistory.

While Canon law was never explicitly cited in litigation before the new church courts, some of its legal principles were tacitly accepted: the Lateran canons concerning banns and solemnisation *in facie ecclesiae* were observed,[23] and the

---

[18] Donaldson, 'Church Courts', 367.
[19] Smith, 'Spiritual Jurisdiction', 4.
[20] *St Andrews*, i, viii.
[21] Ibid., i, 42, 38.
[22] Witte and Kingdon, *Sex, Marriage and Family*, 61, 91, 71–79; Kingdon, *Adultery and Divorce*, 16, 13.
[23] The Fourth Lateran Council had prescribed the procedure to be followed in contracting regular marriages in 1215 (*Decrees of the Ecumenical Councils*, ed. Tanner, i, 258), a procedure adopted in Scotland and retained following the Reformation (e.g. *St Andrews*, i, 42).

Romano-canonical procedure of the old courts spiritual was regularly adopted in plenary processes.[24] Yet such retentions probably occurred more because they had become a deeply embedded part of the legal customs and 'practick' of Scotland rather than because they were consciously associated with Canon law.[25] The 'laws of Antichrist' were ostensibly shunned, and the reformers, having rejected the idea of a legislative competence delegated to the bishops of Rome by Christ, looked to the 'law of God' enacted by 'the eternal God in His parliament' and contained within the word of God.[26] Thus it was that William Renton had requested the kirk session at St Andrews to divorce him from his wife and to permit him to remarry 'according to Goddis law Christes Evangell and the richtuousnes therof',[27] and why in giving judgement the session had emphasised that they had deliberated in the presence of John Douglas and John Winram, 'men of singular eruditioun and understanding in the Scriptures and Word of God'.[28]

Knox's return to Edinburgh from St Andrews at the end of April 1560 presaged the first known consistorial process led before the kirk session of Edinburgh. Unlike those of St Andrews, the early registers of the kirk session of Edinburgh are no longer extant, and evidence as to the earliest examples of the kirk session there taking cognisance of consistorial actions would have perished, but for the subsequent production of consistorial sentences pronounced by the kirk session of Edinburgh before the Commissaries of Edinburgh. Thus on 22 June 1564 Jerome Hamilton produced a sentence of Scottish Protestant divorce on the ground of adultery before the Commissaries of Edinburgh, so that his wife, Elizabeth Sclater, against whom the sentence had been pronounced, might be determined to have forfeited her tocher and *donationes propter nuptias*.[29]

This sentence of divorce was stated in the Commissaries' decreet to have been pronounced on 25 July 1560 by the 'ministers, elders and deacons of Edinburgh'. The reference to the 'ministers' of Edinburgh suggests that John Knox had sat in judgement in *Hamilton v. Sclater* (1560) with John Willock. While Knox had been appointed as minister of Edinburgh on 7 July 1559 during the first occupation of Edinburgh by the Lords of the Congregation, it had been expedient for him to leave following Mary of Guise's re-entry to the burgh on 23 July 1559. The Protestant congregation of Edinburgh, in part safeguarded by the agreement reached between the Lords of the Congregation and Mary of Guise, was left under the charge of John Willock.[30] Willock is said still to have been ministering in Edinburgh at the time of the death of Mary of Guise during the second week of June 1560.[31]

---

[24] Green, 'Romano-canonical Procedure', 219.
[25] Green, 'Authority of the Sources', 139.
[26] Shaw, *Acts and Proceedings*, i, 27.
[27] *St Andrews*, i, 19.
[28] Ibid., i, 26.
[29] Green, *Consistorial Decisions*, item 9.
[30] According to *St Andrews*, i, 27, n.1.
[31] *Fasti*, I, 49–51.

Although Knox seems to have sat in judgement at St Andrews by virtue of his office of minister alone, at Edinburgh Knox and Willock had in fact been granted 'special licence' by the 'Lords of Secret Council' to take cognisance of *Hamilton v. Sclater* (1560). Frustratingly, neither the date of the granting of this 'special licence' nor the date upon which the process of divorce was first heard by the kirk session of Edinburgh is known. As has already been discussed in Chapters 1 and 2, the government of Scotland had been thrown into relative turmoil by the 'uproar for religion' and the authority of the Privy Council had been pressed into the service of the Lords of the Congregation following their deposition of Mary of Guise. By May 1560 those exercising the authority of the regent and Privy Council had felt sufficiently secure to summon the three estates in Parliament, and with the death of Mary of Guise in early June 1560 their position as the *de facto* government of Scotland following a successful rebellion must have seemed yet more secure. If the dating of the granting of the 'special licence' is therefore put at a date after Knox's return to Edinburgh from St Andrews, yet sufficiently before the pronouncing of the sentence of divorce (25 July 1560) which proceeded thereupon so as to have allowed probation to have been led in respect of the alleged adultery, this would give the 'special licence' an issue date of early May to early July 1560. In this respect, this is the earliest known example of the granting of a commission from the Privy Council to the courts of the Church of Scotland to take cognisance of a consistorial action, and that to two of the leading reformers of the Scottish Reformation, being granted by the Privy Council of the Lords of the Congregation prior to the enactment of any legislation by the Reformation Parliament.

The extent to which the pre-August 1560 kirk sessions were active in respect of the consistorial jurisdiction may not be recovered further as to particulars. Various of the 'privy kirks' which had met in secret during the 1550s had emerged into the public life of the kingdom by 1559 'complete with ministers, elders, and deacons, and with regular meetings or kirk sessions . . . in centres such as Dundee, St Andrews, Montrose and Ayr',[32] with 'reformed congregations with established ministers' also found at Edinburgh, Perth, Stirling and Brechin.[33] While the proceedings of most of these kirk sessions are unknown, the evidence from *St Andrews* demonstrates that actions for divorce, adherence and solemnisation were being heard, and it is unfortunate that only one other piece of evidence, from Edinburgh, has survived. Nevertheless, the general comment as to the predicament of the old courts spiritual in respect of the new kirk sessions provided by Archbishop Hamilton on 18 August 1560, as already noted in Chapter 2, suggests a more widespread assumption: 'the elderis callit of every town takis all the

---

[32] Cameron, 'Office of Superintendent', 240.
[33] Kirk, *Patterns of Reform*, 13. Kirk also notes the fact that Fife, Angus, Argyll, Strathearn and the Mearns are thought to have been already largely Protestant by this time, bringing the suggestion that other privy kirks must also have been well established in these areas.

causis of our ecclesiasticall jurisdiction, and intromettis with all our office'.[34] On a constitutional, or ecclesiological, level this was a radical development as to jurisdiction and law: within the context of the early kirk sessions there was limited scope for episcopal jurisdiction, and absolutely none for papal jurisdiction, with an attendant rejection of the Canon law of marriage. In succession to the old episcopal courts came sessions of ministers, elders and deacons administering what they understood to be the law of God.

CONSISTORIAL ACTIONS BEFORE SUPERINTENDENTS' COURTS AND KIRK SESSIONS FOLLOWING THE REFORMATION PARLIAMENT

Almost immediately in the aftermath of the Reformation Parliament, in a letter written by the chamberlain of the Archbishop of Glasgow dated 28 August 1560 and sent to the archbishop, by then at Paris, the enigmatic news was relayed that 'Johne Willokis is maid Bischop of Glasquo, now in zour Lordschipis absens, and placit in zour place of Glasquo'.[35] The chamberlain was mistaken in thinking Willock was made 'Bishop of Glasgow', but this evidence has been taken to indicate that by August 1560 Willock had been installed 'in Glasgow as preacher, presumably in the cathedral', was resident in the dean's house and was in receipt of an allowance from the archepiscopal revenues.[36]

As with Edinburgh, the registers for the early kirk session of Glasgow are no longer extant, and again evidence concerning the early consistorial jurisdiction in 'the West' would also have perished but for the production of consistorial sentences pronounced at Glasgow before the first Commissaries of Edinburgh. Yet, whereas the early evidence from St Andrews and Edinburgh concerned John Knox sitting in judgement with the elders, and sometimes deacons, of the kirks of both burghs, and joined at Edinburgh by Willock, the evidence from Glasgow concerns the earliest recorded working of a superintendent's court.

This first-known consistorial sentence from 'the West' was one of Scottish Protestant divorce on the ground of adultery, and is known from its subsequent production during the course of an action of annulment of the ground of 'unlicenced' remarriage before the Commissaries of Edinburgh in 1565. The sentence of divorce was accepted by the Commissaries, and it was stated in the Commissaries' decreet that a married couple, Janet Paterson and Constantine Stevenson, had been divorced by 'the superintendent and elders of Glasgow', on the ground of Stevenson's adultery (*Paterson v. Stevenson*, 1560/1), no mention being made of a minister at Glasgow. The date of this sentence of divorce was recorded as being 'the *blank* day of *blank* the zeir of God jaj cv lx zeris [i.e. 1560]' in the manuscript,

---

[34] Keith, *History*, iii, 5.
[35] Ibid., iii, 10.
[36] Kirk, *Patterns of Reform*, 181–182.

the clerk having failed to fill in the relevant day and month.[37] Prior to 1600 the Scottish year ended on the Feast of the Annunciation, that is on 25 March, and it therefore follows that this sentence was pronounced on or prior to 24 March 1560/1. That the sentence also held there to have been a superintendent at Glasgow, but no minister, clearly indicates that John Willock sat in judgement.

The date of Willock's nomination for the superintendency of Glasgow was reported by Knox as being around 19 July 1560,[38] but this is thought to be inaccurate,[39] principally because it predates the proposals for the creation of the office of superintendent in the *First Book of Discipline*, and the nomination and admission of the first superintendents is generally dated to a period subsequent to the Reformation Parliament. Knox's recollection is also contradicted by a report of Thomas Randolph to William Cecil, dated 5 March 1560/1, which stated that Willock was to be nominated to the superintendency of Glasgow 'Sunday next'.[40] Willock appears, therefore, to have been nominated on 9 March 1560/1, although he was not actually formally admitted to office until 14 September 1561.[41] This evidence would suggest that Willock pronounced the sentence of divorce in *Paterson v. Stevenson* as superintendent-nominate between 9 March and 24 March 1560/1.

Knox was left as sole minister of Edinburgh by Willock's departure to Glasgow, but continued to hear consistorial actions. Thus on 30 September 1560 the 'minister of Edinburgh' pronounced a sentence of Scottish Protestant divorce on the ground of adultery (*Hamilton v. Semple*), which again is known from its production before the first Commissaries of Edinburgh.[42] The administration of this jurisdiction was soon to be augmented within the burgh of Edinburgh, as well as the burghs of Haddington, Linlithgow and Stirling, by the appointment of the superintendent of Lothian.

Knox was clearly the natural choice for superintendent of Lothian, as the office tended to go the chief minister of the principal burgh within a lowland area. Although Knox was offered the office he declined the same[43] and in the event it went to John Spottiswoode. The date of Spottiswoode's nomination is unclear, but he was admitted on 9 March 1560/1 by Knox, who recorded the order of service used on that occasion in his *History*.[44] In conformity with the temporary expedient conceded in the *First Book of Discipline* that the Privy Council was to nominate ministers to the first superintendencies,[45] Spottiswoode had

---

[37] Green, *Consistorial Decisions*, item 20.
[38] *Knox's History*, i, 334.
[39] Dunbar, *Reforming the Scottish Church*, 65.
[40] *CSP Scot.*, i, no. 967.
[41] Ibid., i, no. 1023.
[42] NRS, CC8/2/2, fo. 419v, 3 April 1568, *Semple v. Hamilton*.
[43] Although on one occasion Knox is known to have been referred to as the 'superintendent of Edinburgh' (*Charters and Documents*, ed. Chambers, 275, 5 February 1561/2).
[44] For which see *Knox's History*, ii, 273 ff.
[45] *First Book of Discipline*, 123 ff.

been 'elected' by the Privy Council, and enjoined by them, among various duties, 'to take inquisition' as to which persons had broken the Mass Act 1560 – a clear indication that the legislation of the Reformation Parliament was being enforced by the provisional government prior to Mary's return.[46] It is likewise clear that the provisional government appointed by the Reformation Parliament continued to issue ordinances as the Privy Council in much the same way as had occurred following the deposition of Mary of Guise. On 19 March 1560/1, the Privy Council issued a commission to Spottiswoode, narrating that he had been appointed to the office of superintendent by virtue of the Lords' 'specialle nominatioun and admissioun'.[47]

This commission from the Lords of Secret Council further stated that, since 'thai ar daylie trublit and cummerit to grant commissionis to proceid in . . . actionis of divorce . . . for the cryme of adultre' and since 'thai ar nocht to continew and be of sufficient numer, quhill the parliament, to grant the samin commissionis, quhar throw the saidis actiones, to the greit hurt of the persones quhilkis ar offendit, salbe vndecidite, without sufficient remeid be providit thareffor', they were delegating their full power to Spottiswoode in regard of all actions of divorce which might arise within his 'diocesye' of Lothian until the next Parliament. No evidence for the exercise of this commission by Spottiswoode prior to Mary Stewart's return to Scotland in August 1561 has survived.

It is therefore known that the Privy Council active in Scotland prior to August 1561 were 'daylie trublit and cummerit' to grant commissions for the hearing of actions of divorce; yet unfortunately the Privy Council registers for this period are no longer extant. Had they survived, the full scale of the Protestant Kirk's early consistorial jurisdiction might well have been a long-established feature of Scottish legal and ecclesiastical historiography. Yet it has already been noted that the pre-August 1560 Privy Council had granted a commission to Knox and Willock at Edinburgh, and this process was clearly being continued and expanded following the Reformation Parliament. While it was a normal function of the Privy Council to remit actions to another court when petitioned by litigants unsure as to the court by which their causes should be heard,[48] the device of actual commissions may have been adopted in view of the uncertain position of the new church courts within the legal system. Beyond the granting of a general commission to Spottiswoode, only one other specific commission in a consistorial action is known to have been granted and exercised during the period August 1560 to August 1561, and that to the kirk session of St Andrews (*Lathrisk v. Simpson*). A further such commission also appears to have been granted to the kirk session at Edinburgh during this period, although it was not exercised until after Mary's return and is accordingly discussed below

---

[46] Donaldson, *Scottish Reformation*, 226–227.
[47] See Appendix, item 1.
[48] McNeill, 'Interference with the Court of Session', 255.

in respect of *Hamilton* v. *Eglinton* (1562).[49] This granting of commissions and special licences by the Privy Council is curious, since both the 'Privy Council' ordinance of 1559 and the legislation of the Reformation Parliament held the temporal courts to be competent to hear spiritual causes, yet the Privy Council is not known to have directed actions for divorce to the temporal courts.

The earliest consistorial actions at St Andrew have already been noted during Knox's time in that burgh and, following Knox's departure to Edinburgh, Adam Heriot took cognisance of a process for divorce, *Geddes* v. *Renton*, being a continuator of the earlier litigation *Renton* v. *Geddes*. While Geddes had been assoilzied from an action of divorce on 21 March 1559/60, this had been followed ten days later by a public confession of adultery by one Margaret Aidman, who named Renton as her paramour.[50] By early May 1560 Geddes had handed in a 'complaint' to the kirk session desiring a Scottish Protestant divorce on the ground of Renton's adultery, founding her action upon 'the law of God'.[51] In an apparently new development for this sort of litigation, Geddes also desired that a tocher, or dowry, of 200 marks (£133 6s 8d Scots) be restored to her by Renton. While the session took cognisance of the action of divorce, the parties selected four 'amicable compositors', with John Douglas and John Winram acting as 'ower men, for deciding of the matter of tocher gude'.[52] Among the compositors was Master William Skene, who had already been consulted in *Renton* v. *Geddes*,[53] and who went on to be the first post-Reformation Commissary of St Andrews. The litigation dragged on for more than half a year, until sentence was pronounced in Geddes' favour several months after the Reformation Parliament, on 3 January 1560/1, and read publicly before the congregation nine days later.[54]

By this time Adam Heriot had been translated to Aberdeen and his place at St Andrews had been taken by Christopher Goodman,[55] by whom sentence was therefore presumably pronounced in *Geddes* v. *Renton*. While process had been led in *Geddes* v. *Renton*, two further consistorial sentences had been pronounced by the minister and elders of St Andrews. On 29 August 1560 decreet was pronounced in *Beverriche* v. *Phenisone*, an action in which the defender had exchanged promises of marriage with both the pursuer and a third party. Goodman presumably sat in judgement, and, 'Mr Knox being consulted heirupoun', decerned the defender to be married to the pursuer and to adhere to the same.[56] On 7 November 1560

---

[49] The date of a further Privy Council commission to the kirk session of Jedburgh in respect of *Hardy* v. *Rutherford* (discussed below) cannot be dated more precisely than to the period July 1560 to December 1562.
[50] *St Andrews*, i, 27.
[51] Ibid., i, 37–38.
[52] Ibid., i, 38–39.
[53] Ibid., i, 26.
[54] Ibid., i, 59–60.
[55] Ibid., i, 3, n.1.
[56] Ibid., i, 48.

the minister and elders, 'judges in the actioun and caus of divorce' *Gudlawde v. Archbald*, pronounced a 'sentence diffinityve' of Scottish Protestant divorce on the ground of the defender's proven adultery.[57]

On 9 January 1560/1 a further sentence of divorce, *Lathrisk v. Simson*, was pronounced by the minister and elders of St Andrews,[58] but this time the session had taken cognisance of the action by virtue of a commission from the Privy Council. Remarkably the commission in part survives, since engrossed in the kirk session's register. The commission was dated at Edinburgh, 2 December 1560, and concerned an action of divorce being brought by one Alexander Lathrisk in Kirkcaldy. Lathrisk had initially petitioned the minister, elders and deacons of Kirkcaldy, but they had refused to 'tak the caus before them, without command of your lordschipes to them to tak tryall in the mater'. Lathrisk therefore petitioned the Lords of Secret Council, who issued a commission not to the kirk session of Kirkcaldy but to that of St Andrews. The names of the signatories of the commission survive, namely Chatelherault and Lord James Stewart, joined by the Lords Boyd and Ochiltree, John Erskine of Dun, Sir John Wishart of Pittarrow and William Cunningham of Cunninghamhead, all of whom are to be found among the list of 'regentis' appointed by the Reformation Parliament; and, in the citation subsequently issued by the kirk session of St Andrews, they were styled 'the Lordis of Christiane Congregatioun and Secrete Counsale'.[59] While a further sentence of divorce is known to have been pronounced at St Andrews during the initial period of Goodman's ministry,[60] neither that nor any subsequent consistorial sentence pronounced at St Andrews is known to have proceeded by virtue of Privy Council commissions.

The apparent absence of Privy Council commissions raises various questions about the inherent authority of the courts of the Protestant Kirk to hear consistorial actions. It might be argued that the Privy Council, when petitioned, directed litigants to their nearest kirk session or superintendent's court because the Protestant regime did acknowledge that the courts of the Kirk were the proper forum in which such actions should be heard; or it may have been the case that such litigants, already determined to have a case heard by a new church court, wished for such proceedings to have their legitimacy augmented by a commission or licence from the Privy Council. As is discussed in Chapter 6, the Commissaries of Edinburgh appear to have taken a different view, and appear to have been careful not to grant the inherent authority of the new church courts in consistorial actions, but rather to have in part emphasised the authority of the Privy Council in countenancing a temporary expedient. Nevertheless, a further development at St Andrews prior to Mary's return was to augment a tradition that the courts of

---

[57] Ibid., i, 49–50.
[58] Ibid., i, 58–59.
[59] Ibid., i, 50–53.
[60] *Clerk v. Schevez*, 23 February 1560/1 (ibid., i, 62).

the Kirk were inherently competent to hear consistorial actions, a tradition which endured even after the appointment of the Commissaries of Edinburgh, as is discussed at more length in Chapter 7.

That development was the nomination and admission of John Winram to the superintendency of Fife, Fotherick and Strathearn. Winram was nominated for this office on 9 March 1560/1, the same day on which John Spottiswoode had been admitted to the superintendency of Lothian, and Winram's own admission followed shortly thereafter, on 13 April 1561.[61] As part of the process of Winram's admission to office, an edict dated 20 March 1560/1 was issued by Christopher Goodman and the deacons of St Andrews, summoning Winram, together with all persons to whom a vote in the election 'of such chief ministers' appertained, to be present at Holy Trinity, St Andrews, at 9 am on Sunday 13 April 1561. This edict narrated that the Lords of Secret Council had charged all the ministers, elders and deacons of Lothian, Fife, the Mearns, Glasgow and Argyll to propone, by public edict, the names of those nominated for the offices of superintendent. While Spottiswoode and Willock have already been discussed, it should be noted that, by the time of the issuing of this edict from St Andrews on 20 March 1560/1, it is thought that John Carswell had been nominated for the superintendency of Argyll, and that John Erskine of Dun had been nominated for the superintendency of Brechin, or of Angus and the Mearns.[62] The actual admission to office of both Willock and Erskine of Dun did not occur until after Mary's return to Scotland, while the date of Carswell's admission cannot now be traced.[63]

Immediately following Winram's admission, Christopher Goodman and the elders of the kirk of St Andrews continued to hear actions for divorce. Thus on 14 May 1561 they pronounced a sentence of divorce in *Calland v. Alexander* 'be this owr sentence diffinityve . . . pronounced in owr consistoriall auditore'. While Winram had not sat as one of the 'judges in the accion and caws', the minister and elders had nevertheless communicated 'the secretis of the said accione and caws wyth Maister John Wynram, Superintendent of Sanctandrois' and had pronounced sentence 'wyth his avysement and consent';[64] as already noted, Winram, when still subprior of St Andrews, had been consulted in *Renton v. Geddes*.

It does not appear, however, that the kirk session of St Andrews was obliged to consult with Winram when hearing actions of divorce, and certainly the General Assembly did not move to reserve such actions to superintendents until December 1562.[65] Three days after pronouncing sentence in *Calland v. Alexander*, the 'ministerie of the reformed kyrk of St Andrews' issued an edict or summons of divorce

---

[61] Dunbar, *Reforming the Scottish Church*, 65–67.
[62] *St Andrews*, i, 73–75.
[63] Donaldson, *Scottish Reformation*, 65–66; Kirk, *Patterns of Reform*, 182.
[64] *St Andrews*, i, 70–72.
[65] Shaw, *Acts and Proceedings*, i, 38.

against James Martin at the instance of his spouse Elizabeth Thacker, and, probation having been led, the 'minister and eldaris' pronounced sentence in Thacker's favour on 23 July 1561, no mention being made of John Winram in the extant process.[66] This provides a curious contrast with Spottiswoode's roving commission from the Privy Council to hear all actions of divorce within the Lothians, sitting in conjunction with the kirk sessions of Haddington, Edinburgh, Linlithgow and Stirling. Rather, the kirk session of St Andrews appears to have continued to hear actions of divorce by its own authority, without any need to be directed by commissions from either their superintendent or the Privy Council. Neither does it appear that Winram was commissioned by the Privy Council to hear divorce actions during his early ministry, despite the example of Spottiswoode. As to other consistorial actions, Winram took cognisance of an action of adherence, *Forret v. Leslie*, around 2 July 1561, although decree absolvitor was not pronounced in the defender's favour until after Mary's return.[67]

While no further consistorial processes appear to have been led, or sentences pronounced, by either kirk sessions or superintendents prior to August 1561, there is one last Privy Council commission of note for that period. With the queen's return to Scotland imminent,[68] the provisional government issued a commission under the style 'the Lordis of our Soveran Ladeis Secreit Consayll' to the superintendent of Fife, Fotherick and Strathearn, and the minister, elders and deacons of St Andrews, to take cognisance of an action of reduction of a pre-Reformation sentence of heresy.[69] In the commission it was narrated that the sentence of heresy in question had been pronounced against Sir John Borthwick on 28 May 1540 by David Beaton and a phalanx of Scottish prelates and clerics, on the ground that Borthwick obstinately maintained various articles condemned as heretical.[70] The day Mary Stewart landed at Leith, Sir John Borthwick presented the Privy Council's commission to superintendent Winram and the kirk session of St Andrews, who proceeded to issue an edict summoning all who had interest to compear before them at St Andrews on 5 September 1561.[71] Thus on the day before Mary Stewart appointed her own Privy Council on 6 September 1561, superintendent Winram, sitting with Christopher Goodman and the elders and deacons of the kirk of St Andrews, reduced the sentence of heresy as having been pronounced by men 'ignorant of Godis Word and lawis',[72] and upheld the articles maintained

---

[66] *St Andrews*, i, 77–81, *Thecar v. Martyn*.

[67] Ibid., i, 112 (initial diet), 128 (decree absolvitor). This unsuccessful action of adherence in fact led on to a sentence of annulment on the ground of prior irregular marriage, but that is cited below.

[68] Mary Stewart embarked at Calais on 14 August 1561 and landed at Leith on 20 August according to Leslie, *History of Scotland*, 297.

[69] The commission, dated 12 August, is mentioned twice in the process, the second time more fully (*St Andrews*, i, 89, 101).

[70] The original sentence was coped into the edict issued by the Protestant ministry at St Andrews (Ibid., i, 91–101).

[71] Ibid., i, 89–91.

[72] Ibid., i, 101–104.

by Sir John, one of which held 'the laws of the Church, that is to say the sacred canons and the decreetals of the holy fathers approved by the holy, catholic and apostolic church, to be null and of no force, [having been] made and issued contrary to the law of God'.[73] Following Mary's return, the General Assembly held itself competent to issue commissions for the reduction of pre-Reformation sentences of heresy, as is discussed below in respect of the case of William Johnstone, advocate.

THE CONSISTORIAL JURISDICTION OF THE NEW CHURCH COURTS FOLLOWING THE QUEEN'S RETURN

By the time Mary, Queen of Scots, landed at Leith on 19 August 1561, the new church courts had already established a considerable claim to the consistorial jurisdiction. The kirk session of St Andrews and then that of Edinburgh had heard consistorial actions, and on occasion both received direct commissions so to proceed from the 'revolutionary' Privy Councils of October 1559 to August 1561. In Glasgow and 'the West' the superintendent-nominate had already heard at least one action for divorce, while in the Lothians the new superintendent enjoyed a general commission from the Privy Council to hear actions of divorce within his jurisdiction. At St Andrews the superintendent of Fife, Fotherick and Strathearn had been formally admitted to office, and was being both consulted in respect of consistorial causes being heard by the kirk session there, and being countenanced by commissions from the Privy Council. And while no evidence may now be recovered concerning the activities of the superintendents-nominate of Argyll and of Angus and the Mearns, the evidence from Glasgow suggests that lack of formal admission to office was no bar to taking cognisance of consistorial actions.

Those ministers and superintendents of the early Church of Scotland known to have heard consistorial actions prior to Mary's return were among the leading reformers of the Scottish Reformation: John Knox, John Willock, Christopher Goodman, John Winram, Adam Heriot and John Spottiswoode. Of these, at least Knox and Goodman are known to have heard not only actions for divorce but also actions for solemnisation and adherence: given that Knox and Goodman had been ministers together of the English exile congregation at Geneva,[74] this feature of the evidence carries considerable weight as to what these two leading Calvinist reformers thought the jurisdiction of a Reformed church court in Scotland ought to encompass. In addition, Knox, Willock, Winram and Spottiswoode were four of the six authors of the *Scots Confession of Faith* and the *First Book of Discipline*,[75] and

---

[73] See *St Andrews*, i, 96–97, for the original articles in Latin (relevant article paraphrased by the author of the present work); cf. Spottiswoode, *History*, i, 139.

[74] For the profound bonds of religion and friendship which existed between these two reformers during their exploits in Geneva and Scotland see Dawson, *John Knox*, 136 ff.

[75] *Knox's History*, i, 343; the phrase 'as well as they had done the Doctrine' has traditionally been understood as referring to the *Scots Confession of Faith*.

in this it would be difficult to argue that the Protestant Kirk's early assumption of the consistorial jurisdiction was unconsciously done as a chaotic and temporary expedient, which formed no part of the early polity of the Church of Scotland. The picture that emerges from the fragmentary evidence is rather one of a widespread assumption, implemented by many of the leading ministers and superintendents of the Kirk, often under the direction of the *de facto* government of Scotland through the agency of the Privy Council.

The progress of the early Church of Scotland up to Mary's return had, however, been carried through by way of revolution, apparent usurpation of a regent's authority, the issuing of Privy Council ordinances under a counterfeit signet, treasonable overtures to a foreign power, the irregular summoning of the three estates, the disregarding of the 'Concessions' subsequently offered by the queen and king of Scots to their subjects, the enacting of invalid statutes by the Reformation Parliament and the appointment of a government without the consent of the kingdom's sovereigns. Nevertheless, as has already been noted, it was the policy of the government of Mary's personal reign not to undo the progress of the Reformation but rather to offer legal protection to the same through the Proclamation of Leith 1561 and the Act of Oblivion 1563.

In respect of the courts of the Church of Scotland, it would appear that Mary's government held that the patterns established by the time of her return as to the involvement of the kirk sessions and superintendents in consistorial litigation were to be allowed to continue, at least for a time. As has already been mentioned, Mary appointed her own Privy Council on 6 September 1561, and from the fact that the Law of Oblivion enacted by the first Parliament of her personal reign was to encompass a period ending on 1 September 1561 it is reasonable to infer that contemporaneous opinion held the actions of the provisional government of August 1560 to August 1561 to require indemnification against legal prosecution, and that lawful government had been fully restored only by Mary's assumption of government from early September 1561. Mary's government clearly accepted the nominations of superintendents made by the Privy Council prior to her return, and Spottiswoode's roving commission may have been countenanced by Mary herself on one occasion. Nevertheless, there is no clear evidence to the effect that Mary's Privy Council granted new commissions or licences to the courts of the Church of Scotland in respect of consistorial actions, as had the Privy Councils active prior to her return. Rather, it would appear that Mary's privy councillors pursued a more circumspect line in respect of the Kirk compared to the period prior to the queen's return, withdrawing themselves from the 'conventions of the brethren' to the extent that it was rumoured that 'the queen and her secret council would have gladly have had all the assemblies of the godly discharged'.[76]

One of the first tests for Mary's Proclamation of Leith concerned the formal admission of John Willock to the superintendency of Glasgow. Willock's

---

[76] Shaw, *Acts and Proceedings*, i, 12-15 and 61–62; cf. Knox, *History*, ii, 25–28.

nomination, together with his involvement in the consistorial jurisdiction, have already been noted, as have the formal admissions of Spottiswoode and Winram at the direction of the pre-August 1561 Privy Council. While Willock, Carswell and Erskine of Dun had all been nominated by the time of Mary's return, neither Willock nor Erskine had been formally admitted to office.[77] In this respect Randolph reported to Cecil on 24 September 1561 that 'to approve the Queen's proclamation, upon the 14th instant Mr Wyllock was admitted superintendent of Glascowe – the Duke, Arran, Glencairn, Ruthven, Boyd and [Ochiltree] being present – little I assure you to the content of those that thought neither to have left Mr Knox or him in Scotland'.[78] The reference to the queen's proclamation was presumably a reference to the Proclamation of Leith of three week's earlier, and as such Willock's appointment, witnessed by many of the Lords of the Congregation, appears to have been a test of her sincerity. In this it would appear that, the nomination of the first five superintendents of the Church of Scotland having occurred prior to Mary's return, this aspect of the organisation of the early Church of Scotland was deemed to have already been in motion, and thus legitimated by Mary's Proclamation.

The date of John Erskine of Dun's admission is not known, but it probably occurred at 'the beginning of 1562',[79] since on 31 December 1561 the *Records of the Burgh of Edinburgh* narrate that 'the minister, Johnne Knox, is requyrit be the hale kirk to pas in the parttis of Angus and Mernys for electing of a superintendent thair . . .'.[80] There is an earlier reference to the 'superintendent of Angus' from a process of adherence, *Forret v. Leslie*, led before superintendent Winram from July 1561. However, Winram's apparent attempt to have some form of probation led by the superintendent of Angus in *Forret v. Leslie*, which would likely have involved taking the depositions of witnesses, seem to have been unsuccessful.[81]

The date of Carswell's admission to the superintendency of Argyll cannot be dated, but he is known to have been 'active in this capacity in the early 1560s'.[82] Whether Carswell was admitted before or after Mary's return matters little either way, since there is no extant evidence of his involvement in the consistorial jurisdiction.[83] But it is nevertheless reasonable to suppose that, by early 1562, the first

---

[77] The date of Carswell's admission is unknown, on account of the paucity of the records available for Argyll in this respect.
[78] *CSP Scot.*, i, 1023.
[79] Donaldson, *Scottish Reformation*, 65.
[80] *Extracts from the Records of the Burgh of Edinburgh*, ed. Marwick, iii, 129.
[81] This procedurally imprecise reference to the superintendent of Angus is at *St Andrews*, i, 113, and the obvious connection from the internal evidence of the process would have been to suppose that Erskine of Dun was to be commissioned to examine one Elizabeth Auchterlony. Yet her deposition, taken at Auchenleck on 18 September 1561, together with its attendant commission and summons, makes no mention of the superintendent of Angus (see *St Andrews*, i, 123–127).
[82] Kirk, *Patterns of Reform*, 182.
[83] Obtaining a detailed knowledge of various aspects of Carswell's superintendency is frustrated through a lack of extant evidence: for the fullest account see ibid., 280–304.

five superintendents of the Church of Scotland were all formally in office,[84] and that their positions had been rendered secure in law by the Proclamation of Leith. It is also noteworthy that beyond the five superintendents already nominated by the time of Mary's return, no further superintendents were ever appointed in the Church of Scotland. It has often been argued that the office of superintendent was a temporary expedient in the history of the ecclesiology of the Church of Scotland, but it may be the case that nominations for new superintendents were not forthcoming from her government. The *First Book of Discipline* had proposed the creation of ten superintendencies, and after Mary's return the General Assembly nominated various candidates for the superintendencies of Jedburgh and Aberdeen, and remitted further action on this head to Mary's Privy Council, but no action appears to have been taken. This must have been something of an impasse for the General Assembly, since, having explicitly acknowledged the authority of the pre-August 1561 Privy Council on 27 May 1561 ('your just authority, which, in the absence of our sovereign, we acknowledge to be in your hands'),[85] it could not bypass Mary's Privy Council in respect of the appointment of superintendents without risking undermining the functions of the earlier Privy Councils, and as such continued to refer the final selection of superintendents to the Privy Council after Mary's return.

The apparent failure to appoint the full compliment of superintendents did not pose an insuperable barrier to the continued development of the consistorial jurisdiction of the Church of Scotland. James Cameron has argued that superintendents represented a temporary development of an earlier principle in Scottish reformed ecclesiology that the chief minister and kirk session of the principal burgh within a reformed 'diocese' exercised a supervisory jurisdiction over the kirks scattered throughout their hinterlands. In this the contrast between the dioceses of the Catholic Church and the superintendencies of the Church of Scotland has been noted, in that the latter were centred upon principal burghs: St Andrews for Fife and beyond, Dundee for Angus and the Mearns, Glasgow for the West, Edinburgh for the Lothians, Jedburgh for the south-east, Aberdeen for the north-east, and so forth.[86] Cameron's thesis is borne out by the evidence of the post-August 1561 exercise of the consistorial jurisdiction by the Church of Scotland, particularly in respect of Adam Heriot at Aberdeen.

If some doubts remain as to the assertion that the early Church of Scotland was exercising a consistorial jurisdiction, rather than simply developing a new disciplinary jurisdiction which had been temporarily extended so as to enforce a new kind of divorce for adultery within Scotland, the post-August 1561 evidence, which is richer than the earlier evidence, removes these doubts. The prominence of sentences of divorce on the ground of adultery from the pre-Marian period is probably the result of the fact that the majority of these sentences are known only

---

[84] They were all certainly in office by 29 June 1562 (Shaw, *Acts and Proceedings*, i, 17).
[85] Ibid., i, 10.
[86] See generally Cameron, 'Office of Superintendent'; *First Book of Discipline*, 116–121; Donaldson, *Scottish Reformation*, 112–113.

because of their chance survival, in that they were produced in litigation before the first Commissaries of Edinburgh. In this respect, sentences of divorce were the most likely type of consistorial decision to be thus preserved, since they ordinarily brought with them consequences for property and the legitimacy of issue considerably in excess of other types of consistorial decisions. The new Protestant divorce required the redistribution of tocher goods and *donationes propter nuptias* on the basis of fault, and the granting of licences to remarry as a prerequisite of producing subsequent legitimate offspring, being matters of immediate and long-term importance to those affected. In particular, the St Andrews kirk session's treatment of the issue of tocher in *Geddes* v. *Renton* seems to have been the exception rather than the rule and, as such, following the appointment of the Commissaries of Edinburgh, various sentences of divorce pronounced by the courts of the Protestant Kirk were produced before the new Commissaries so that the party guilty of adultery might be decerned to have forfeited the various financial settlements made at the time of the contracting of the failed marriage. Within this context, the extant evidence from St Andrews that, during the pre-August 1561 period, actions for solemnisation of marriage and for adherence were being heard, suggests that other kirk sessions and superintendents' courts may have been hearing such actions, being now unknown merely for lack of extant evidence. Be that as it may, the evidence for the period of Mary's personal reign prior to the appointment of the Commissaries of Edinburgh demonstrates that the courts of the Church of Scotland were hearing the full range of consistorial actions. For the avoidance of doubt, these actions involved actual litigation between parties, and were not examples of direct exercises of discipline by the new church courts.

CONSISTORIAL ACTIONS BEFORE SUPERINTENDENTS' COURTS AND KIRK SESSIONS FOLLOWING THE QUEEN'S RETURN

Within the Lothians, John Spottiswoode's general commission from the Privy Council may be presumed to have continued in force until the stated period of its expiry, namely the next Parliament to be held, which came to pass in June 1563. While there is no direct evidence for Spottiswoode ever having exercised this commission, he was actively involved in the consistorial jurisdiction. The first evidence of his activity dates from December 1561, when Spottiswoode received a direct commission from Mary herself to take cognisance of what appears to have been a marital action. Although the precise type of action is not mentioned, beyond it being at the instance of a woman against 'hir pretendit spous', it is noteworthy that the queen directed Spottiswoode to determine the action 'according to God's word'.[87] Since this is the only known occasion on which Mary or her Privy Council may have acknowledged the consistorial jurisdiction of the new church

---

[87] For which see Appendix, item 2.

courts, it may have been the case that such a recognition could not be declined on account of Spottiswoode's general commission to hear divorce actions within the Lothians issued by the post-August 1560 Privy Council.

While Spottiswoode may be presumed to have had a dominant role in any divorce actions brought at Haddington, Linlithgow or Stirling, his role at Edinburgh may have been somewhat limited by the strength of Knox's position and reputation within that burgh. On 2 April 1562 the 'ministers, elders and deacons of Edinburgh' pronounced a sentence of divorce in favour of John Weston against his adulterous spouse Katherine Ewart, and, while the 'ministers' were presumably John Knox and John Craig,[88] there is no mention of Spottiswoode. Less than three months later however, Knox and Spottiswoode were sitting in Edinburgh, hearing an action of divorce which has already discussed in Chapter 3, *Hamilton v. Eglinton*, and which proceeded by virtue of a commission from the Privy Council.

Sentence was pronounced in *Hamilton v. Eglinton* on 25 June 1562, which brings with it the possibility that the Privy Council commission by virtue of which it proceeded had been issued by Mary's Privy Council. While the date of the issuing of the Privy Council commission is unknown, some of the details of the commission are known, and those details suggest that the commission was issued prior to Mary's return to Scotland. In the sentence of divorce pronounced by the kirk of Edinburgh in *Hamilton v. Eglinton*, it was narrated that the Lords of Secret Council had at first directed their commission to the 'minister' and kirk session of Glasgow, but that since the 'minister' was absent in England, the session at Glasgow would not take cognisance of the action. The reference to the minister of Glasgow must have been to John Willock. That his title of superintendent was not mentioned suggests that this commission was directed to him at some point between his first known ministry at Glasgow following the Reformation Parliament and his nomination as superintendent of the West on 9 March 1560/1. This suggestion may be confirmed by the fact that the commission was directed to Willock at a time when he was absent in England; he is known to have left Glasgow for London not long after the Reformation Parliament, and, although the date of his return is not known, the evidence from *Paterson v. Stevenson* suggests that he had returned to Glasgow by March 1560/1 at around the time he was nominated as superintendent of the West. Conversely, Willock was certainly back in Scotland by the time he was admitted to the office of superintendent on 14 September 1561, and is thought to have been in Scotland thereafter during 1561 and 1562.[89] It would therefore appear that the Privy Council commissioned Willock and the kirk session of Glasgow to take cognisance of *Hamilton v. Eglinton* at some point between October 1560 and February 1560/1, being the period of time when Willock would

---

[88] Although Craig was not formally translated from the Canongate until 2 July 1562 (according to *Fasti*, I, 23, 51).

[89] For the dates of Willock's absence in England subsequent to his arrival at Glasgow, together with his known presence in Scotland, see Shaw, 'John Willock', 61–63.

have been designated 'minister' rather than 'superintendent' and would have been absent in England. This would date the granting of this commission to a period prior to Mary's return to Scotland.

On account of Willock's absence in England, the Lords directed their commission to the 'ministers, elders and deacons of the kirk of Edinburgh', charging them to decide *Hamilton v. Eglinton* 'according to the ewangell and law of God'. It would be reasonable to suppose that the redirection of the commission from Glasgow to Edinburgh occurred timeously: if so, then the delay between the granting of this commission and its exercise by Jane Hamilton in pursing her husband before the kirk of Edinburgh may have been occasioned by Hamilton's unwillingness to pursue her husband for divorce until spurred into doing so by her husband's action of annulment during the course of April and May 1562.[90] In any event, the extant evidence from this case is of further value, since a full list of those who actually heard *Hamilton v. Eglinton* has survived. The list of judges began 'John Knox, minister, Mr John Spottiswod, superintendent of Louthiane', which has been taken to suggest that Knox had precedence over Spottiswoode.[91] The elders and deacons of the kirk were then listed, among whom were found John Spens of Condie, who was to sit on the commission which recommended the appointment of the first Commissaries of Edinburgh, and Clement Litill, one of the first four Commissaries of Edinburgh. The minister, superintendent, elders and deacons were also joined by James MacGill of Nether Rankeillour at the express command of the Privy Council.[92]

While John Willock had been unable to take cognisance of *Hamilton v. Eglinton* owing to an absence in England, he is known to have pronounced a sentence of divorce in *Maxwell v. Hamilton* on 5 or 6 August 1563. The action was a complex one, and was to be subsequently reduced by the Commissaries of Edinburgh on 16 March 1564/5,[93] which reduction is discussed at more length in Chapter 6. There is no further evidence for Glasgow and the West, but this fragment demonstrates the continued competence of Willock to hear such actions following Mary Stewart's return to Scotland.

To the evidence of Spottiswoode's and Willock's continued involvement in the consistorial jurisdiction may be added evidence for the activity of John Erskine of Dun and John Winram. As has already been noted, Erskine of Dun was admitted to the superintendency of Angus and the Mearns by John Knox at some point after 31 December 1561. Only two pieces of evidence survive concerning the exercise of Erskine of Dun's consistorial jurisdiction. One is from an incomplete action of reduction raised before the Commissaries of Edinburgh on 6 July 1564

---

[90] *Eglinton v. Hamilton*, which proceeded by virtue of a commission issued by the Archbishop of St Andrews exercising his legatine authority, has already been discussed in Chapter 3.
[91] Kirk, *Patterns of Reform*, 180, n.88.
[92] Fraser, *Memorials*, ii, 183–185.
[93] Green, *Consistorial Decisions*, item 12.

against a sentence of divorce, the other from the extant registers of the General Assembly. In respect of the first piece of evidence, a sentence of divorce, *Rollock v. Forrester*, had been pronounced at Dundee at an unknown date[94] by 'Cristofer Gudman minister, James Luvell, Robert Kid, Alexander Weddirburne, and the remanent eldaris and deaconis of the burgh of Dunde, and Johne Erskin of Dvn, superintendent of Angus'. The involvement of Christopher Goodman, already noted for his activity at St Andrews prior to Mary's return, is at once curious, for the very reason that he was minister of St Andrews, not Dundee, from 1560 to 1565. The minister of Dundee was rather William Christison, whose name is not recorded in the Commissaries of Edinburgh's register of acts and decreets. The sentence had clearly been one of Scottish Protestant divorce on the ground of adultery, since the pursuer from the original action had remarried while her first spouse was still alive; it was the first spouse who pursued for reduction before the Commissaries and, by extension, for the annulment of his sometime wife's subsequent marriage.[95]

From the second piece of evidence Erskine of Dun is known to have pronounced a declarator of freedom from a promise of marriage in favour of one Beatrix Livingston, on the ground that her promise had been exchanged with a man who was already married. The date of this consistorial sentence is not known, but, on 1 July 1563, Livingston presented the same 'for verification' before 'John Willock, superintendent of the West, Christopher Goodman [minister of St Andrews,] and Mr George Hay [minister of Rathven,] of the diet of Edinburgh'. It is not clear what this 'diet of Edinburgh' signified: no session of the General Assembly is known for that date, so it is possible that this was some sort of reference to the kirk session of Edinburgh, although the absence of Knox, and of the superintendent of Lothian, makes this interpretation problematic. It is also unclear what the 'process of verification' entailed, whether it was some sort of appeal, or whether Livingston simply desired to make absolutely certain that she was not engaged to be married, not so much as a matter of law, but of conscience. Apparently still not entirely satisfied, Livingston presented the 'decreet' to the General Assembly on 26 December 1564, which 'in one voice authorised and allowed the said decreet' and, apparently for the avoidance of doubt, made a further declarator of freedom from the problematic promise of marriage.[96] There does not appear to be a suggestion of the exercise of appellate jurisdiction in these proceedings, but rather of a repeated procedure of confirmation, and that at the desire of the party in whose favour the original declarator of freedom had been pronounced.

---

[94] The sentence was presumably pronounced at some point between Erskine of Dun's admission to office in around early 1562 and the appointment of the Commissaries of Edinburgh on 8 February 1563/4.
[95] For which see Appendix, item 4.
[96] Shaw, *Acts and Proceedings*, i, 75.

The curiosity of Christopher Goodman, minister of St Andrews, sitting in judgement at Dundee with the superintendent of Angus and the Mearns, and sitting at a diet at Edinburgh with the superintendent of the West (although in the latter example perhaps not in a judicial capacity), brings into view the continuing activity of the kirk session of St Andrews and of superintendent Winram. The final action which Winram appears to have been hearing prior to Mary's return was *Forret v. Leslie*,[97] an action of adherence from which the defender, Elizabeth Leslie, was assoilzied on account of the fact that the pursuer, John Forret of that Ilk, had married her bigamously. Decreet absolvitor was pronounced on 6 January 1561/2, and two days later Leslie raised an action for annulment on the ground of bigamy against Forret before the superintendent's court. Winram issued a libelled summons on 8 January, which stated that he would 'proceid in the said caws as we may and awcht of the law of God'. In the subsequent term of probation Leslie produced the superintendent's 'decreit absalvator' from the earlier action of adherence, and Winram accordingly pronounced a sentence of annulment on 21 January 1561/2. Winram was styled 'juge in the caws' in the sentence, which was pronounced 'wythin the parrochie kyrk and consistorie hows of the cite of Sanctandrois' in the presence of, among others, Christopher Goodman.[98]

The remaining evidence from *St Andrews* is particularly rich, and demonstrates that Winram and the kirk session of St Andrews continued to hear a full range of consistorial actions following Mary's return and prior to the appointment of the Commissaries of Edinburgh in February 1563/4. During this period somewhere in the region of around twenty consistorial processes were led before the court of superintendent Winram, including actions for annulment,[99] actions for divorce on the ground of adultery,[100] actions for solemnisation of marriage on the grounds both of prior exchanges of promises of marriage[101] and of deflowered virginity,[102] actions for adherence,[103] and an action probably arising out of the staying of banns.[104]

---

[97] Process was begun around 2 July 1561 (*St Andrews*, i, 112).

[98] Ibid., i, 128–131.

[99] *Leslie v. Forret*, 21 January 1561/2 (ibid., i, from 128 to 130–131); *Hyllok v. Gyb*, 23 June 1563 (ibid., i, 151–153).

[100] *Scrymgeor v. Dundas*, 7 January 1561/2 (*St Andrews*, i, 139–140); *Kaye v. Duncan*, 28 January 1561/2 (ibid., i, 140–141); *Philip v. Thomson*, 20 January 1562/3 (ibid., i, 150); *Hyllok v. Gyb*, 11 August 1563 (ibid., i, 155–156).

[101] *Swyntoun v. Robertson*, 20 May 1562 (*St Andrews*, i, 143–145); *Pawy v. Kynnisman*, 11 November 1562 (ibid., i, 174); *Duncan v. Wemyss*, 31 March 1563 (ibid., i, 181–182); *Malcolm v. Duncan*, 16 June 1563 (ibid., i, 182–183).

[102] *Steyson v. Brown*, 3 June 1562 (*St Andrews*, i, 145–146); *Turpy v. Lystar?*, 30 September 1562 (Ibid., i, 173; incomplete process); *Gray v. Johnstoun*, 3 to 10 February 1562/3 (ibid., i, 178–179; incomplete process); *Lyndesay v. Lyndesay*, 4 August 1563 (ibid., i, 184–185; incomplete action); *Kyd v. Jarden*, 29 September 1563 (ibid., i, 186–187).

[103] *Cunynghame v. Wod*, 10 December 1561 (*St Andrews*, i, 133–135); *Masterton v. Boyd*, 19 August to 17 December 1562 (ibid., i, 168–169; defender adhered prior to pronouncing of sentence).

[104] *Budge v. Jak*, 5 August 1562 – 27 January 1562/3 (ibid., i, 148–149, 177-178; incomplete process).

Three other processes before the superintendent, although decidedly consistorial in form, either may have arisen, or in fact did arise, out of an initial exercise of disciplinary jurisdiction, rather than litigation between parties.[105] The kirk session appears for the most part to have avoided hearing obviously consistorial actions at first instance during this period, although it did take cognisance of an action for declarator of legitimacy,[106] and, as is discussed in Chapter 7, the kirk session's disciplinary jurisdiction could lead it to pronounce what were in effect consistorial sentences, particularly in respect of solemnisation of marriage. To what extent such levels of activity were common among the other courts of the Church of Scotland cannot now be determined for want of extant evidence. The extent to which the example of St Andrews was exceptional is discussed in Chapter 7, as is the evidence concerning the consistorial activity of the church courts at St Andrews following the appointment of the Commissaries of Edinburgh, on account of the complex jurisdictional relations which may be observed between Edinburgh and St Andrews from that time.

As to those principal burghal kirks which lacked a superintendent, evidence has survived for Jedburgh and Aberdeen. A process of divorce, *Hardy v. Rutherford*, heard by the 'minister, elders and deacons of Jedburgh' is known from its production before the Commissaries of Edinburgh in 1565. This process had again proceeded upon a commission from the Privy Council, although the date of the commission and process of divorce are unknown. Various inferences as to the probable date of the granting of the commission may be drawn from the evidence of the decreet of divorce pronounced by the Commissaries on 11 April 1565 in conformity with the process. The official narrative in the Commissaries' decreet was that process had been led before the kirk session of Jedburgh up to the pronouncing of a final judgement, but that the process had then been remitted to the Commissaries by virtue of their appointment, which was held to have superseded the Privy Council's commission and the kirk session's competence in the matter.

Nevertheless, the fact that the Commissaries' decreet stated several times that the process had been heard at Jedburgh before a minister there suggests a different narrative. Paul Methven, the Dundee baker who had risen to prominence as the first public minister of the Church of Scotland prior to the outbreak of the Wars of the Congregation, had been translated to Jedburgh during July 1560. His ministry was engulfed in scandal by December 1562, and he was formally deposed from the ministry of the Church of Scotland in 1563 following a formal inquiry undertaken by John Knox. By the time Methven was formally deposed, he had already fled into England, and it is thought that Jedburgh was left without a minister until 1566. It therefore seems likely that the Privy Council had commissioned Methven

---

[105] *Henderson & Peebles*, 24 March 1562/3 (*St Andrews*, i, 182); *Howeson & Lyndesay*, 7 July 1563 (ibid., i, 184); *Sandelandis & Forbes*, 8 December 1563 (ibid., i, 156–157, 167–168).
[106] *Colt*, 8 July 1562 (ibid., i, 147–148).

and the kirk session of Jedburgh to hear *Hardy* v. *Rutherford*, and that process had been interrupted by the scandal.[107] This would date the commission to the period of Methven's active ministry at Jedburgh, that is to say at some point between July 1560 and December 1562.

It may therefore have been that the problem of how to proceed in *Hardy* v. *Rutherford* was not resolved until the solution afforded by the appointment of the Commissaries of Edinburgh presented itself from the spring of 1564. The General Assembly had desired that a superintendent of Jedburgh be appointed following Methven's departure, in that it put forward two nominees for the post on 29 December 1562, the day before Knox received his commission to inquire into Methven's conduct.[108] Nevertheless, following the nominations by the General Assembly, further action in respect of a formal admission to the superintendency of Jedburgh, together with various other superintendencies, was remitted to the Privy Council, which by December 1564 had still taken no action:[109] no superintendent of Jedburgh was ever appointed.

The apparent inaction of Mary's Privy Council in respect of the appointment of ministers nominated for superintendencies following her return is also to be found at Aberdeen. The minister of the kirk of Aberdeen was Adam Heriot from the time of his translation from St Andrews in 1560. Heriot's activity at St Andrews in respect of the consistorial jurisdiction has already been noted, and at Aberdeen he appears to have exercised the function of the chief minister of the principal burgh within the north east, which functions have been noted by Cameron as the precursor of the office of superintendent.[110] There is some evidence from the fragmentary survival of the register of the kirk session of Aberdeen that actions for divorce were being heard there from at least 10 December 1562, as noted below. Heriot was shortlisted for nomination to the superintendency of Aberdeen by the General Assembly on 29 December 1562, but again no election or appointment appears to have taken place.[111] Nevertheless, in a chance survival in a decreet pronounced by the Lords of Council and Session on 19 February 1562/3 in *Ogilvy* v. *Birnie*, it was mentioned that the pursuer, Janet Ogilvy, had been abducted by her husband, James Birnie, on 27 December 1562, at which time it was alleged that an action of divorce was pending before 'the superintendand and minister of Abirdene' and that the process was 'neir proceidit to an end'.[112]

This evidence is, regrettably, open to a range of interpretations. It may be the case that there was some error in the recollection of the date of the abduction, and that the process of divorce should be dated to a period after Heriot's nomination as superintendent. This is unlikely because Heriot was one of three ministers

---

[107] Green, *Consistorial Decisions*, item 15.
[108] Shaw, *Acts and Proceedings*, i, 34–35.
[109] Ibid., i, 37–38, and 73–74.
[110] Cameron, 'Office of Superintendent'.
[111] Shaw, *Acts and Proceedings*, i, 34 and 73.
[112] First noted by Smith, 'Spiritual Jurisdiction', 6, citing NRS, CS7/25, fo. 353r, 19 February 1562/3.

nominated for the office by the General Assembly, and it would have been too presumptive to have held Heriot to have been sole superintendent-nominate in the way John Willock had been in Glasgow in March 1560/1. If the phrase 'superintendent and minister of Aberdeen' is accurate, it could be that two different persons were thereby designated, one Adam Heriot, minister of Aberdeen, the other a superintendent already in office, the most likely candidates being Erskine of Dun or Winram, both of whom had been charged by the General Assembly to inaugurate whichever nominee for the superintendency of Aberdeen might happen to be elected.[113]

Be that as it may, Heriot was active in some capacity analogous to that of a superintendent, namely that of chief minister of the principal burgh of a region. Evidence for such activity comes not from a kirk session register but from the production of a sentence of annulment on 9 April 1565 before the justiciary court in Edinburgh,[114] where Master John Craig, parson of Kincardine, and Margaret Mowat, alleged spouse to John Craig of Craig Fintray, stood accused of the crimes of adultery and incest. While the details of the case are complex, Mowat's defence effectively hinged upon her assertion that she had never been lawfully married to Craig of Craig Fintray, since their marriage had been annulled on the ground of the latter's impotence. The alleged sentence of annulment on the ground of impotence in question had in fact been pronounced by Master John Ramsay, minister of Aberdour, and Thomas Christison, minister of Gamrie, 'with the consent of our elders, deacons, and ministers assembled' at Gamrie on 28 November 1562. The action of annulment had proceeded not by virtue of a Privy Council commission, but by virtue of a summons directed by Adam Heriot, minister of Aberdeen, to Ramsay and Christison, at the request of Margaret Mowat against her impotent husband. Ramsay and Christison judged that Craig of Craig Fintray had been impotent since birth, and accordingly annulled his marriage to Mowat. This sentence was accepted as valid by the justiciary court and copied into the court's books.

Shortly after Heriot had commissioned Ramsay and Christison, the kirk session of Aberdeen prescribed some procedure in respect of divorce actions on 10 December 1562. Among a list of acts and statutes concerning, among other issues, adultery, irregular marriages, and the baptising of bastards, the kirk session of Aberdeen ordained 'that the minister nor the clerk gife na summondis of diuorce furth aganis ony persoun without the avise of the Assemblie'. The context of these acts and statutes demonstrates that the reference to 'the Assemblie' was to the kirk session, and not to the General Assembly.[115] That the activity of the minster and clerk of session in respect of issuing summons of divorce was sufficiently common as to require regulation is noteworthy.

---

[113] Shaw, *Acts and Proceedings*, i, 34.

[114] A transcription of the justiciary court proceedings, together with a copy of the Kirk's sentence of annulment, is printed in Pitcairn, *Ancient Criminal Trials*, i, 459–461.

[115] *Selections from the Records of Aberdeen*, ed. Stuart, 11; cf. NRS, CH2/448/1, 9 to 13.

From the foregoing evidence arising for the period subsequent to Mary's return to Scotland, a clear picture emerges of the continued exercise of the consistorial jurisdiction by the courts of the Church of Scotland, with the on-going involvement of Knox, Willock, Spottiswoode, Winram, Goodman and Heriot, and with the addition of the previously unnoted activity at Dundee of Erskine of Dun, and at Jedburgh during the ministry of Methven. Sometimes these reformers appear to have acted by virtue of their own office, be it that of superintendent, or of chief minister of a principal burgh, or of minister sitting with a kirk session, and on other occasions by virtue of commissions and licences from the Privy Council, albeit commissions probably all granted prior to Mary's return. While the evidence continues to be dominated by actions for Scottish Protestant divorce on the ground of adultery, there is also direct evidence of actions of adherence, of solemnisation, of annulment on the ground of bigamy, of annulment on the ground of impotence, and of declarator of freedom. Taking all of this evidence together, every type of consistorial action heard either by the old courts spiritual or by the Commissaries of Edinburgh is found to have been heard by the courts of the Church of Scotland.

THE GENERAL ASSEMBLIES OF THE KIRKS OF SCOTLAND

To the evidence already considered concerning the consistorial jurisdiction of the superintendents, chief ministers and kirk sessions of the Church Scotland at Aberdeen and Gamrie, Dundee, St Andrews and Fife, Edinburgh and the Lothians, Jedburgh and Glasgow, one more aspect of the courts of the early Church of Scotland falls to be considered in this chapter, namely the jurisdiction of the General Assemblies of the kirks of Scotland. While general remarks as to the matrimonial jurisdiction of the bishops of the Catholic Church who conformed to the Reformation have already been offered in Chapter 3, one particular case involving a 'reforming' bishop brings into view the jurisdiction of the General Assembly.

Adam Bothwell, Bishop of Orkney, is known to have exercised a consistorial jurisdiction in conjunction with 'the minister, elders and deacons of the kirk of Orkney', by whom a sentence of Protestant divorce for adultery, *Tulloch v. Sinclair*, was pronounced on 8 August 1562. A precept of reduction was subsequently raised against this sentence before the General Assembly on 27 June 1563, the General Assembly having defined the 'order of appellation' within the courts of the Church of Scotland the preceding day. Thus on 26 June the Assembly had 'statute and ordained, that if any person finds himself hurt by a sentence given by any ministers, elders, or deacons of the Kirk, it shall be lawful for the party so hurt to appeal to the superintendent of the diocese and his synodical convention . . . and if the party yet alleged himself hurt by the superintendent and his convention, it shall be lawful to appeal to the general assembly of the Kirk', the General Assembly being final forum of appeal.[116] Curiously, the precise issue of an appeal

---

[116] Shaw, *Acts and Proceedings*, i, 41.

from the sentence of a reforming bishop and kirk session was not touched upon, but the General Assembly, in taking cognisance of such an appeal, must have taken the view that it was the proper court of appeal in such instances.

In response to the appeal in *Tulloch* v. *Sinclair* the General Assembly appointed superintendent Spottiswoode, the ministers, elders and deacons of the kirk of Edinburgh, together with various officers of state and advocates, to hear the cause of appellation. The ministers were presumably John Knox and John Craig,[117] while among the officers of state and advocates were to be found James MacGill of Nether Rankeillour, John Spens of Condie and Clement Litill, one of the first Commissaries of Edinburgh.[118] On 27 April 1564 the original sentence was confirmed, the outcome of the appeal being known from the subsequent production of the original sentence of divorce and process of reduction before the Commissaries of Edinburgh.[119]

This sequence of litigation brings into view the only recorded exercise of such an appellate jurisdiction of the General Assembly of the Church of Scotland in respect of consistorial actions. As is discussed in Chapter 6, procurators pleading before the Commissaries of Edinburgh variously contested the on-going validity of the General Assembly's appellate jurisdiction in consistorial actions in respect of sentences pronounced by courts of the Church of Scotland prior to the appointment of the Commissaries of Edinburgh.

The General Assembly's appellate jurisdiction also appears to have been observed by the Assembly in the sense that it declined to hear first instance consistorial actions. When petitioned on 29 December 1563 by John Baron, minister of Galston, who narrated that his wife, Anne Goodacre, had deserted him and passed into England, the General Assembly ordained that letters be directed to the Archbishops of Canterbury and York, requesting that they serve summons upon Goodacre.[120] The General Assembly does not appear to have regarded itself as the proper court for an action of adherence at first instance, since the case was directed to the superintendent of Lothian and kirk session of Edinburgh. On 31 December 1563, the General Assembly was asked whether one Thomas Duncanson, schoolmaster and reader in Stirling, having made public repentance for fornication, should be restored to his office in the Kirk. The Assembly ordained that he should be restored only following a request from the kirk session of Stirling to the local superintendent, adding in passing that, if the woman he had committed fornication with had been a virgin, he should marry her if she required the same. In this respect the General Assembly appears to have done no more than highlight the law of the Kirk in respect of those who deflowered virgins; the facts of the case were

---

[117] Ibid., i, 22; *Fasti*, I, 23, 49–52.
[118] Shaw, *Acts and Proceedings*, i, 44. In this version the commission was entrusted to the 'ministers of the *kirks* of Edinburgh', but this is at variance with the evidence from the Commissaries of Edinburgh's later decreet.
[119] Green, *Consistorial Decisions*, item 13.
[120] Shaw, *Acts and Proceedings*, i, 55–56.

not to be determined in process before the General Assembly.[121] In these respects it might be ventured that the General Assembly neither heard first instance cases, nor commissioned first instance consistorial litigation before inferior courts of the Kirk.[122] Rather, this commissioning function appears to have been exercised by the Privy Councils of October 1559 to August 1561. This apparent division of powers between the General Assembly and the Privy Council in respect of appellate jurisdiction on the one hand, and commissioning the new church courts on the other, may have arisen out of the fact that the General Assembly could redirect first instance consistorial actions to inferior church courts by simple remit, while the Privy Council's commissioning activities were simply the result of *ad hoc* petitions submitted by litigants who had doubts or uncertainties as to the court by which their case should be heard, and as such may be considered to have been a temporary expedient, rather than an integral part of the Kirk's consistorial jurisdiction.

The apparent division of appellate and commissioning powers in respect of consistorial causes between the General Assembly and the Privy Council does not appear to have been carried over into processes concerning heresy. On the one hand, the Privy Council's commissioning of the kirk session of St Andrews concerning Sir John Borthwick has already been noted. On the other hand, the General Assembly itself reduced a pre-Reformation sentence of heresy on 27 June 1563,[123] while on 29 December 1563 the General Assembly was petitioned by Mr Andrew Johnstone, brother of the late Mr William Johnstone, advocate, who 'humbly required process for the reduction of the sentences pronounced by the late James [Beaton], archbishop of St Andrews, and his commissioner against him and his brother, for alleged heresies . . . The assembly ordained the superintendent of Lothian, with the assistance of the session of Edinburgh, to take cognition in the premisses, to give and lead process therein . . . and after summary process therein, to pronounce and give final sentence.'[124]

The kirk sessions of the principal Scottish burghs, together with the courts of the superintendents, and apparently the courts of the reforming bishops, were understood to be the competent forums for first and second instance consistorial litigation. When such courts were commissioned or licensed to hear consistorial actions by the Privy Council, it may have been the case that the church courts so commissioned held such commissions to have proceeded upon an acknowledgement of the Kirk's jurisdiction, rather than being construed as a constitutionally valid creation of the same.[125] In this respect the General Assembly's

---

[121] Ibid., i, 59.
[122] Shaw discussed this briefly, highlighting the appeal in *Tulloch* v. *Sinclair* and the Commission appointed in 1572 to discuss divorce for malicious desertion in respect of the fifth Earl of Argyll's marital difficulties (*General Assemblies*, 210), although neither example involved the General Assembly disposing of a new case.
[123] Shaw, *Acts and Proceedings*, i, 44.
[124] Ibid., i, 55; and for further relevant proceedings see 76–77.
[125] Although the significance of the Privy Council's commissions appears to have taken on a different significance for the Commissaries of Edinburgh, as is discussed at more length in Chapter 6.

lack of commissioning activity in respect of consistorial actions appears normal, since it was simply the final court of appeal in actions heard by kirk sessions, superintendents' courts and reforming bishops' courts.

CONCLUSION

During the period between the suppression of the courts of the Catholic Church in Scotland from the autumn of 1559 and the appointment of the Commissaries of Edinburgh during the winter of 1563/4, the Church of Scotland developed an extensive consistorial jurisdiction. This development was not supervised by the supervening authority of Parliament or Privy Council in the first instance, but arose spontaneously among the early kirk sessions of the Church of Scotland as they emerged into the public life of the kingdom by virtue of the protection against persecution afforded by the militant Lords of the Congregation. While the evidence indicates that the primary focus of this jurisdiction was Scottish Protestant divorce on the ground of adultery, it also included the full range of other consistorial actions, with the sole exception of any actual litigation in respect of legitimacy, although the kirk session of St Andrews did pronounce one declarator of legitimacy.

The development of the internal structures of government within the early Church of Scotland following the Reformation Parliament witnessed the introduction of the office of superintendent into the polity of the Kirk, and, of the five superintendents actually appointed, four are known to have joined kirk sessions in the exercise of a consistorial jurisdiction. The Privy Councils of the era of revolution, that is to say of the years encompassed by the Act of Oblivion 1563, not only supervised the appointment of the superintendents but also acknowledged the consistorial jurisdiction of the courts of the Church of Scotland by repeatedly commissioning them to hear actions for divorce. Following Mary's return to Scotland, her own Privy Council did not nominate further superintendents, and there is no clear evidence that they issued new commissions or licences to the new church courts in respect of consistorial actions.

Where regions lacked a superintendent, it appears that either the minister of the principal burgh of a region developed the right to commission provincial kirk sessions to hear consistorial actions, or reforming bishops sat with their kirk sessions in judgement. The unifying theme in this group of eclectic courts was the kirk session, either on its own, as part of a superintendent's court, or sitting with a reforming bishop. In this respect it is cogent that appeal lay from these courts to the General Assembly of the Church of Scotland, which in itself derived much of its jurisdiction and legislative competence from its representation of the regional kirks by which the Reformed Church in Scotland was constituted.

Chapter 5

The Lords of Council and Session

While several aspects of the old Scottish polity of the Catholic ascendancy had received rough treatment during the Reformation crisis, the legitimacy of the Lords of Council and Session appears to have survived the revolution intact. While the legitimacy of the Privy Council had been compromised through its apparent appropriation by the Lords of the Congregation as the executive arm of the rebel government from the time of the deposition of Mary of Guise in October 1559, and while the legitimacy of the three estates in Parliament had been compromised through the Lords' attempt to legitimate their revolution through the enactments of an irregularly summoned and irregularly constituted Parliament in July and August 1560, evidence from the records of the Court of Session indicate that Scotland's central court of civil justice had not been pressed into the service of the Protestant revolution. The on-going credibility of the Lords of Council and Session in the midst of the collapse of the Catholic ascendancy was to have enduring consequences for the history of the spiritual jurisdiction in Scotland, and in particular for the new commissary courts and the jurisdiction of the courts of the Church of Scotland.

Before entering upon the details surrounding the assumption of the spiritual jurisdiction by the Court of Session, it is perhaps expedient to briefly rehearse the distinction between the Lords of Council, who sat as the Privy Council, and the Lords of Council and Session, who sat as the Court of Session. During the fifteenth century a distinct King's Council had developed within the Scottish polity, which Council assumed various legal jurisdictions previously exercised by the sovereign in Parliament. The Lords of Council and Session were at first an undifferentiated part of the King's Council, and tended to deal with litigation. During the course of the late fifteenth and early sixteenth centuries, the Lords of Council of Session developed as a distinct part of the Scottish polity, in effect the Court of Session, which began to assume the features of a centralised court of civil justice, a kind of suprafeudal expression of royal justice capable of assuming civil jurisdictions once administered by older parts of the legal system. In 1532 the full institutional separation of the Court of Session from the earlier King's Council was put on a statutory basis, while provision was made for the remuneration of the judges of Scotland's supreme civil court through the papal foundation of a college endowed with ecclesiastical revenues, the College of Justice.[1] Within the Court of Session the ordinary fifteen Lords of Council and Session were appointed senators of the College of Justice, while other judges could be admitted to the court as unremunerated extraordinary

---

[1] For a full consideration of the history and development of the Court of Session see Godfrey, *Civil Justice*.

Lords of Council and Session. The remaining part of what had been the King's Council in effect retained wide-ranging executive powers as the sovereign's Privy Council, whose members were styled Lords of Council, or Lords of Secret Council. These Lords were in theory to sit in Council with the sovereign and manage the affairs of the kingdom, and, while they continued to exercise residual legal functions, their powers were for the most part executive and legislative.[2] Both the Court of Session and the Privy Council derived their authority and jurisdiction from the sovereign. This relatively clear institutional differentiation of Council from Session has sometimes been conflated by historians,[3] since the same officers of state, nobles, jurists and ecclesiastics could often be members of both bodies; but such a conflation would be a mistake by the period presently under consideration. Yet even by the era of the Reformation, the judges of the Court of Session could still be referred to simply as 'Lords of Council', on which occasions particular care must be taken to establish the context in which the term was used, so as to differentiate judges sitting in the Court of Session from privy councillors sitting in the Privy Council.

The relative stability of Scotland's supreme civil court in the years immediately prior to Mary's return to Scotland was possibly unique when compared to the uncertainties which attached to the other 'candidates for the consistorial jurisdiction' in Scotland.[4] The constitutional and actual position of the old courts spiritual was incongruous, except for those who held the revolution to have been entirely legitimate and lawful. Added to this was the uncertain position not only of the earliest courts of the Church of Scotland but of the Church of Scotland itself. There could be no doubt that the new religion, enjoying widespread devotion throughout much of lowland Scotland, in addition to the military protection of the Lords of the Congregation, and, from February 1559/60, the implicit protection of the Protestant regime of Elizabeth I, was a *de facto* force within Scottish society, which had the potency to capture or overthrow any aspect of the Scottish polity which opposed its advance. There could also be little room for doubt that the new kirk sessions enjoyed an extensive disciplinary jurisdiction over the Protestant faithful of Scotland, who consented to be governed in their moral lives by the ministers, elders and deacons of the parishes in which they lived. Yet what was more doubtful was the extent to which the disciplinary and consistorial judgements of the courts of the Church of Scotland enjoyed binding legal force within the realm in the same manner as had the judgements of the old courts spiritual. This was not simply a technical distinction for Scottish jurists to fret over: the husband or wife who put away an adulterous spouse with the sanction of the Kirk and who subsequently remarried needed to know not only that such proceedings were acceptable to their co-religionists, but that they would be acknowledged by the Scottish legal system. Failure to obtain a judgement capable of being recognised and enforced

---

[2] For a history of which see McNeill, 'Jurisdiction of the Scottish Privy Council'.
[3] Including, it may be noted in the interests of transparency, by the present author in his own doctoral thesis.
[4] The phrase is Gordon Donaldson's, for which see 'Church Courts', 367.

in respect of issues such as property and the legitimacy of offspring was a central concern in a society where the transmission of property, heritage, honours, various legal jurisdictions and the Scottish Crown itself depended upon lawful marriage and legitimate issue.

Such anxieties were clearly apparent during the uncertain years of 1559 to 1563, and on occasion the legal authority of the proceedings of kirk sessions and superintendents was certainly augmented by the authority of the Privy Councils active during the years encompassed by the Act of Oblivion 1563.[5] Yet while historians of earlier generations have usually satisfied themselves as to the regularity of the Church of Scotland's conduct during these years because of the involvement of the Privy Council, failure to consider how the Privy Council was actually constituted between October 1559 and September 1561 has resulted in a failure to appreciate just how tenuous the Protestant Kirk's consistorial proceedings could have proved to be, even when authorised by the Privy Council. Such proceedings potentially counted for nothing in law until accepted by some legitimate constituent part of the legal system within the context of litigation.

In addition to legal uncertainties surrounding the Church of Scotland's spontaneous assumption of various aspects of the spiritual jurisdiction, the general provision, or at least intention, behind both the autumn 1559 ordinance of the Privy Council of the Lords of the Congregation and the legislation of the Reformation Parliament in respect of the spiritual jurisdiction was that it be transferred to temporal courts. While this intention sits uneasily with the realities of the Church of Scotland's activities, it at least purported to authorise the assumption of the spiritual jurisdiction at least by the Court of Session, and potentially by any 'temporal ordinary judge' within the kingdom. Even where doubts were entertained as to the legality of such revolutionary ordinances and statutes, it may be presumed that at least the Protestant faction could not be heard to object in the event of the assumption of the spiritual jurisdiction by civil judicatures. In the event it came to pass that during the same period that the early Church of Scotland was being organised into superintendancies and consolidating its hold upon various aspects of the spiritual jurisdiction in the wake of the Reformation Parliament, a parallel process of assumption of jurisdiction was taking place within the Court of Session as the Lords of Council and Session asserted their competence to hear those spiritual causes accustomed to be heard by the suppressed courts spiritual.

THE CIRCUMSPECTION OF THE LORDS OF COUNCIL AND SESSION DURING THE REFORMATION CRISIS

As already intimated, the legitimacy of the Lords of Council and Session had been relatively unimpaired by the Protestant rebellion and its attendant revolutions in the years 1559 and 1560. While the Lords of Council and Session's administration

---

[5] As has been discussed at length in Chapter 4.

of justice had been interrupted by the various occupations of Edinburgh by revolutionary forces during the Wars of the Congregation, such interruptions appear to have betokened a desire on the part of the judges of the Court of Session to avoid entanglement with the revolutionary faction. The first occupation of Edinburgh had begun on or around 28 June 1559,[6] and the Lords of Council and Session ceased to sit after 27 June.[7] This occupation was brought to an end following the appointment made between the revolutionaries and Mary of Guise, the regent re-entering Edinburgh on 23 July 1559.[8] The harvest vacation usually occurred between 1 August and 19 October each year,[9] but the Lords nevertheless sat on 2 August, 6-7 September and 25–6 September 1559.[10] The normal pattern of sitting in judgement was not resumed after the end of the harvest vacation, presumably because the second occupation of Edinburgh began on 18 October, immediately prior to the deposition of Mary of Guise. This occupation came to an end on 6 November 1559, but there are no sederunts for the Lords until after the Christmas vacation, which ran between 20 December 1559 and 7 January 1559/60.[11] On 9 January the Lords resumed sitting in judgement once again,[12] and continued to sit regularly until 23 March 1559/60.[13] On 30 March 1560 an English army entered Scotland in support of the Lords of the Congregation, and on 1 April Mary of Guise entered Edinburgh castle from Holyrood to await the impending siege of Leith.[14] Following the death of Mary of Guise shortly after midnight on 11 June and the subsequent truce, which ensued around 17 June 1560,[15] the Lords of Session resumed sitting in judgement on 26 June.[16] Nevertheless, the harvest vacation once again intervened, although the Lords did sit once on 21 August,[17] while the Reformation Parliament was still in progress. They did not resume sitting again until a month after the end of the harvest vacation, on 20 November 1560,[18] from which time their normal pattern of holding court may be observed. As such, during the period from the first occupation of Edinburgh by the rebel Lords of the Congregation in June 1559 down to 20 November 1560, the Lords of Council and Session sat regularly in the months of January, February and March only; of all the other months during this period they sat not at all, saving one day each in June and August, and four days in September, 1560. Yet despite the disruption of the

---

[6] *Diurnal*, 53.
[7] NRS, CS7/20, fo. 51r.
[8] *Diurnal*, 53.
[9] The harvest vacation began on the Feast of St Peter and ended on 19 October (*RPS*, 1532/6).
[10] NRS, CS7/17, fos 297r, 301r, 302v, 304r, 307v (red ink pagination).
[11] The Christmas vacation began on the eve of the Feast of St Thomas and ended on the morning after Epiphany Day, which usually fell on 6 or 7 January (*RPS*, 1532/6).
[12] NRS, CS7/20, fo. 61r.
[13] NRS, CS7/20, fo. 175r.
[14] *Diurnal*, 56.
[15] Ibid., 59.
[16] NRS, CS7/20, fo. 179r.
[17] NRS, CS7/20, fo. 182r.
[18] NRS, CS7/20, fo. 183r.

Court of Session during the Wars of the Congregation, it is clear that the Lords of Council and Session declined to sit regularly in Edinburgh during periods of occupation by the Lords of the Congregation prior to the conclusion of the wars with the Treaties of Leith and of Edinburgh. This strongly suggests that Scotland's supreme civil judges did not desire to countenance such occupations with their continued presence in Edinburgh, but rather saw fit to adjourn their proceedings until such times as the authority of Regent Guise was reasserted over the capital. In the relatively more settled, although as yet uncertain, times following the Reformation Parliament, the Lords of Council and Session clearly determined to resume their normal pattern of sitting in judgement from 20 November 1560. At that point in proceedings the return of Mary Stewart to her native realm was still a remote possibility, her husband Francis II not dying until 5 December that year. Within that context, the Lords of Council and Session may have determined that the rebellion was over, and that whatever the problems attending the legality of the government of the 'Council of the Realm' appointed solely by the Reformation Parliament, a degree of order had been restored to the realm. With as then no prospect of a clear reassertion of royal authority from Mary and Francis, it may have seemed best to the Lords to resume the administration of justice entrusted to them by the Crown, and in so doing ensure both that their supreme civil jurisdiction continued to be administered and that some thought was given to the crisis within the legal system occasioned by the suppression of the courts spiritual.

While these thoughts must remain speculative, they are consonant with the general context in which the Lords of Council and Session found themselves, and with the course of action they adopted in respect of the spiritual jurisdiction within a month of resuming their usual pattern of sitting in judgement in late November 1560. While some litigants with spiritual causes had already petitioned the Privy Council, which, under normal circumstances, was the competent court to which litigants ought to turn when the competent tribunal for hearing their action was in doubt, other litigants with spiritual causes began to petition the Lords of Council and Session from December 1560.

LITIGANTS PETITIONING THE COURT OF SESSION WITH SPIRITUAL CAUSES

The composition of the Lords of Council and Session was determined by the constituting documents of the Court of Session and College of Justice. Of the fifteen senators of the College of Justice, seven were appointed from the spiritual estate, seven from the temporal, with the Lord President always appointed from the prelates of the Catholic Church. This continued to be the case during the first phase of the Reformation. In this respect, although the Court of Session was a civil court, there was a strong, if not dominant, presence of churchmen in the court. There was, moreover, a long tradition of what Ollivant has termed the 'easy interchange' of judges between the spiritual and civil jurisdictions in Scotland. Most striking was the association of the Officials of Lothian with the Court of Session: 'of the eight men who served as officials of Lothian during the sixteenth century, three served concurrently as judges in the central courts', while a further two became senators of the College of Justice after demitting office.[19] Somewhat famously, James Balfour served as last Official of Lothian, was appointed an extraordinary Lord of Council and Session in 1561, an ordinary Lord in 1563, the first 'chief' Commissary of Edinburgh in 1563/4, and Lord President in 1567.

The first petition known to have been received by the Lords of Council and Session from a litigant seeking to have a spiritual action heard by them was that presented by John Chalmer of Fintry on 19 December 1560,[20] a month after the Lords had resumed their regular pattern of sitting in judgement following the Wars of the Congregation, and 14 days after the death of Francis II. The record keeping for sederunts seems quite poor during this period, which makes it difficult to establish with certainty which Lords were present on 19 December; nevertheless, the plain reading of the sederunts creates the presumption that the judges listed as present on 9 December 1560 were also present on 19 December, with the exception of Gavin Hamilton, Abbot of Kilwinning.[21] If this was the case, the judges who actually pronounced sentence in *Chalmer v. Lumisdene* were: John Sinclair, dean of Restalrig, brother of the then Lord President, Henry Sinclair; Abraham Crichton, provost of Dunglass collegiate church, a former Official of Lothian and sometime papal judge delegate;[22] John Stevenson, precentor of Glasgow, provost of Biggar collegiate church; James Scott, provost of Corstorphine collegiate church; John Spens of Condie, Queen's Advocate; James MacGill of Nether Rankeillour, Clerk Register; Sir Robert Carnegie of Kinnaird; and Master John Gledstanes, doctor in the laws.[23]

Of these Lords of Council and Session, Spens and MacGill have already been noted in respect of their involvement in the 1559/60 Inquiry undertaken by La Brosse and Cleutin, Spens having framed the interrogatories used by the same, and MacGill, along with another Lord of Council and Session, Bellenden of Auchnoul, having prepared the French translations of the proceedings of the Inquiry and authored the *Discours Particulier d'Ecosse*. Within this context, Spens and MacGill certainly knew about the issuing of Privy Council ordinances under a counterfeit signet during the autumn of 1559. To what extent it was known with certainty by the judges on the bench that one such ordinance had been the instrument by which the courts spiritual had been suppressed cannot now be ascertained, although the breadth of connections between the judges of the Court of Session and the courts of the Catholic Church makes it at least a possibility that it was known. Be that as it may, the judges, in being petitioned by

---

[19] Ollivant, *Court of the Official*, 51.
[20] *Chalmer v. Lumisdene*, Smith, 'Spiritual Jurisdiction', 11.
[21] For the detailed reasoning on this head, see Appendix, item 3.
[22] Green, *Consistorial Decisions*, item 137.
[23] Styles and titles for these judges, in addition to those found in the indirect sederunt, have been added from Brunton and Haig, *Historical Account*, and from Watt and Murray, *Fasti*, 422, 462, 453, 207, 445.

litigants with spiritual actions, had no doubt that the courts spiritual were no longer functioning. Had the ordinance been known to them, it is difficult to imagine how they could have accepted it as a valid royal ordinance upon which to found their subsequent assumption of the spiritual jurisdiction. In respect of provisions made by the Reformation Parliament in respect of the spiritual jurisdiction, such provisions focused on papal, rather than ordinary episcopal, jurisdiction, and in any event similar considerations as to validity applied. As discussed in Chapter 3, John Sinclair is known to have argued openly that the legislation of the Reformation Parliament was invalid, and MacGill's opinion that the Reformation Parliament could not move to ratify the Treaty of Berwick while also enacting a law of oblivion to indemnify against prosecution those who had entered into the Treaty has already been noted in Chapter 2.

Among the Lords of Council and Session who may be presumed to have sat in judgement on 19 December 1560, half were of the spiritual estate, half of the temporal, and it seems reasonable to suppose that at least the ecclesiastical Lords of Session, together with MacGill and Spens, were unlikely to have taken the view that the Court of Session might assume the spiritual jurisdiction of the Catholic Church in Scotland on the basis either of the ordinance of 1559 directed against the courts spiritual, or of the statutes of the Reformation Parliament touching upon the spiritual jurisdiction, both of which had asserted that civil judicatures had succeeded to the courts spiritual. This presumption appears to be confirmed by a consideration of the extant evidence from *Chalmer v. Lumisdene*.

In the letters purchased by the pursuer in *Chalmer v. Lumisdene* it was argued that 'becaus thair is na consistoreis instant and the office of the spirituale juge, quhilkis of befoir wes wont to cognosche in siclike causis, now ceisis, thairfoir necessar it is that the Lordis of Counsale put remeid thairto',[24] there being no mention of the cause of the cessation of the courts spiritual. The basis upon which the Lords proceeded to hear the action was included by James Balfour in his *Practicks*: 'The Lordis of Counsall hes powar to cognosce and decide upon spiritual causes, gif the consistorie, or ecclesiastical jurisdictioun ceissis, or be stopt be civil wars or utherwayis'.[25] The variation in wording suggests that the Lords' reasoning was not simply copied from the letters purchased by the pursuer, but was their own considered response to the problem of the spiritual jurisdiction. The sense of the Lords' reasoning in *Chalmer v. Lumisdene* was that the Lords could hear spiritual actions, but only in lieu of the consistories 'if they be stopped by civil wars or otherwise', a reasonable enough expedient given the presence of many churchmen and spiritual judges within the Court of Session. The sense of the inaction of the courts spiritual due to extenuating circumstances was no more than a simple statement of the *de facto* suppression of those courts during the Wars of the Congregation. It will also be noted that the reasoning in *Chalmer v. Lumisdene* was limited to a consideration of causes formerly heard by

[24] See Appendix, item 3, for a full transcription of this act.
[25] *Balfour's Practicks*, i, 269.

spiritual judges in 'consistories'. From this it would appear that the native Scottish spiritual courts only were being considered, and that papal jurisdiction fell outwith the purview of the problem considered by the Lords in this case. That the judgement reached by the Lords in this case did not contain a judgement as to the on-going validity of papal jurisdiction in Scotland, but was limited in scope to spiritual causes formerly heard by native consistories, appears to be confirmed by the Lord's subsequent considerations of various appeals pending before papal judges delegate, as discussed below. From these observations it would appear that the Lords of Council and Session determined to formulate their own reason for hearing spiritual causes formerly accustomed to be heard by native Scottish courts spiritual, rather than justifying their actions through reference to the ordinances and statutes of a revolutionary group which had directed litigants with spiritual actions to civil courts. The sense of the Lords' explanation was that their assumption was a valid practical expedient, that is concerned causes falling within the competence of Scottish Commissaries and Officials, and that there was nothing in law to say that it was permanent, or the result of some permanent alteration in the constitution of the realm. As is discussed at more length in Chapter 6, this understanding found expression in the constituting charter of Court of the Commissaries of Edinburgh, which was issued following the recommendations of a commission headed by Henry Sinclair, and whose number included MacGill, Spens and Bellenden.

Having assumed the ordinary spiritual jurisdiction of the suppressed courts spiritual in *Chalmer v. Lumisdene*, the Lords of Council and Session proceeded to hear spiritual causes until the appointment of the Commissaries of Edinburgh in February 1563/4. In this, the Lords of Council and Session first assumed the spiritual jurisdiction at a time when there was no obvious legal framework within which to work following the actions of the Reformation Parliament, but then continued their administration of the same following the Proclamation of Leith down to the erection of a new system of commissary courts by which spiritual actions previously decided by 'the prelates of this realm' could be heard. This principal and enduring development within the spiritual jurisdiction may accordingly be seen to have commenced during a time of revolution and to have subsequently fallen within the compass of the provisions of the Proclamation of Leith. The manner in which this development culminated in the creation of the commissary system without disturbing the terms of the Proclamation of Leith is discussed in Chapter 6.

The spiritual causes heard by the Court of Session between 1560 and 1563/4 have been brought fully to light by the research of David Smith among the manuscript Acts of the Lords of Council and Session for the period in question. Smith's research has demonstrated that *Chalmer v. Lumisdene* was the first spiritual action to be heard by the Court of Session, and has provided details of, or references to, all the subsequent actions heard by the Lords prior to the appointment of the Commissaries of Edinburgh. In all there were in excess of twenty known spiritual actions brought before the Court of Session between August 1560 and April 1564, among which are found consistorial, executry and ecclesiastical actions.[26] Through a combination of access to Smith's unpublished research and of revisiting the references provided in his published work, further details about the Court of Session's administration of the spiritual jurisdiction may be offered.

Chalmer v. Lumisdene was a matrimonial action for adherence on the ground of desertion, and the only other consistorial action heard by the Court of Session, *Logane v. Wod* (1561), was also one of adherence.[27] Both these matrimonial sentences were included by Balfour in his *Practicks*,[28] and it may be noted in passing that there is no evidence of the reform of marriage law in Scotland by the Court of Session during the era of the Reformation.[29] Other spiritual actions concerned: the confirmation of the appointment of an executor by the Court of Session, following further process, subsequent to the raising of edicts of executry before both the sheriff of Edinburgh and the 'dean thereof';[30] the advocation before the Court of Session of an action concerning executry raised before the sheriff of Fife, whose competence to hear the same was in doubt;[31] the pronouncing of a definitive sentence in an action of executry, conform to a process led before the Commissary of Dunblane;[32] the execution of a sentence of the Official of Lothian in an executry action,[33] and in two debt actions;[34] the enforcement of the terms of acts registered with various Commissaries and Officials;[35] and a petition made to the Court of Session in respect of letters in four forms which they had issued subsequent to letters of cursing issued by the Commissary of Dunblane following upon a debt action.[36]

PAPAL JURISDICTION

In addition to these actions, three supplications involving appeals pending before papal judges delegate were given in to the Lords. On one of these occasions the Lords of Council and Session appear to have been prepared to hear an appeal

---

[26] Smith, 'Spiritual Jurisdiction, 11–15.
[27] NRS, CS7/21/1, fo. 66r–v, 26 March 1561, *Logane v. Wod*, in which the pursuer sought to have the defender compelled to adhere 'as the ward of god and lawis maid for keping of lauchfull matrimonie commandis . . .'
[28] *Balfour's Practicks*, i, 269 and 99; both cases involved consideration of the defence of adultery in actions for adherence.
[29] A significant point not made explicit in Green, 'Authority of the Sources'.
[30] NRS, CS7/26. fo. 255r–v, 3 April 1563, *Leirmonth v. Leirmonth*.
[31] NRS, CS7/23, fos 318r–319r, 20 March 1561/2, *Leslie & Grant v. Crichtoun et al*.
[32] NRS, CS7/23, fos 252v–253v, 12 March 1561/2, *Stewart v. Stewart & Doig*.
[33] NRS, CS7/27, fos 324v–325v, 28 July 1563, *Heslop v. Borthwick*.
[34] NRS, CS7/28, fo. 306r–v, 31 January 1563/4, *Abercrumby v. Creychtoun*; NRS, CS7/29, fos 64r–65r, 14 March 1563/4, *Scott v. Earl of Argyll*.
[35] NRS, CS7/23, fos 307v–309r, 19 March 1561/2, *Bishop of Dunblane v. divers*. Cf. NRS, CS7/26, fos 232v–234r, 31 March 1563; NRS, CS7/27, fo. 109r–v, 7 July 1563, *Wylsoun v. Symynton*; NRS, CS7/27, fos 130r–131r, 6 July 1563, *Scrmgeour v. Ramsay*; NRS, CS7/27, fos 202r–203r, 19 July 1563, *Franche v. Graden*; NRS, CS7/29, fo. 258r–v, 15 April 1564 (being the date of sentence, process having been commenced prior to the appointment of the Commissaries of Edinburgh), *Spittall v. Gillespy & Spittall*.
[36] NRS, CS7/23, fo. 307r–v, 19 March 1561/2, *Home v. Grahame*.

which was pending before papal judges delegate. In *Blacader & Blacader* v. *Bishop of Dunblane* (1563), in respect of a supplication for the continuation of an appeal pending before papal judges delegate against a sentence pronounced by the Official Principal of St Andrews concerning ecclesiastical revenues, the complainer narrated that the appeal had reached interlocutor 'before the abolishing of the consistorial jurisdiction', at which point, the appeal having 'stopit & restit'", the complainer could get no further process. In response 'the lordis of counsale, for certane causis & considerationis moving tham, fyndis that thai will tak the said mater to them selfis & that thai will proceid & do justice to bayth the saidis parteis as accordis quhair it left befor the saidis Juges delegatis'.[37] It would appear that among these 'certain causes and considerations' was not an acceptance that papal jurisdiction had been abolished in Scotland by statute, and certainly the case involved no recorded arguments to that effect. Rather, the internal evidence of this judgement points in one direction only, namely that the appellant could not get further process in the appeal, and on that basis the Lords of Council of Session continued to hear the appeal. That the Lords of Council and Session did not proceed on the basis that papal jurisdiction had been abolished is directly confirmed by the other two supplications they received involving appeals pending before papal judges delegate.

In one case noted by Smith concerning a payment of money, *Crichton of Anstruther* v. *Melville* (1562/3), the Lords of Council and Session 'suspended letters of poinding [which had been issued by themselves] on a sentence of the Official of St Andrews because the suspender had produced an appeal to Rome and an act remitting it to judges delegate and further proof that the action was still dependent before them'.[38] In another similar case noted by Smith, *Sempil & Campbell* v. *Sempil* (1563/4), the Official of Glasgow had pronounced a sentence compelling the payment of a certain sum of money and letters of poinding had been obtained thereupon from the Lords of Council and Session. Nevertheless, on 21 February 1563/4, almost two weeks after the appointment of the first Commissaries of Edinburgh, it was argued before the Lords of Council and Session that their letters of poinding ought to be suspended because there was an appeal pending against the sentence of the Official of Glasgow before papal judges delegate, which process of appeal had reached decreet, although decreet had not actually been pronounced 'be ressoun of the cummeris quhilkis raises within the realme anent the religioun and the acclesticall [sic] Jurisdictioun'. This narrative concerning the interruption of the appeal does not appear to have been aimed at persuading the Lords of Council and Session to continue to hear the appeal themselves, but rather to have been offered by way of an explanation as to why the appeal had been in dependence for so long. The judges of the Session certainly did not hold the appeal to have been deserted and, whatever practical difficulties had beset the process of appeal during the 'uproar for religion', by 1563/4 the Lords must have adjudged

---

[37] NRS, CS7/26, fos 212v–213r, 26 March 1563, *Blacader & Blacader* v. *Bishop of Dunblane*.
[38] Smith, 'Spiritual Jurisdiction', 15, citing NRS, CS7/26, fo. 25, 7 March 1562/3, *Crichton of Anstruther* v. *Melville*.

the papal judges delegate in question to once again be in a position to continue to hear the appeal, for the Lords found the appeal still to be in dependence before the papal judges delegate commissioned by Rome and duly suspended their letters of poinding during the dependence of the appeal.[39] It also seems significant that John Stevenson was among the papal judges delegate in question, and although the sederunt has been left blank in the register for the day *Sempil & Campbell v. Sempil* was decided in the Court of Session, Stevenson was one of the Lords of Council and Session likely to have sat in judgement in *Chalmer v. Lumisdene*.

Given that the Reformation Parliament had undoubtedly intended to abrogate papal authority and jurisdiction in Scotland, and moreover is thought to have enacted the 'Jurisdiction of Rome' Act whereby appeals pending before Rome or before papal judges delegate were transferred to the Court of Session or other 'temporal ordinary judges', it follows that the Lords of Council and Session did not accept as valid the legislation of that Parliament. From the two instances of the judges of the Court of Session suspending their letters of poinding in 1562/3 and 1563/4 because of appeals then pending before papal judges delegate appointed by Rome, it is apparent that they did not have recourse to the legislation of the Reformation Parliament. Had they accepted that legislation as valid, they would have been bound by statute law to continue to hear such appeals themselves, or at the very least to have stated that such appeals could no longer be heard by virtue of papal authority and jurisdiction. Rather, the Lords of Council and Session accepted the continued validity of papal jurisdiction following 1560, allowing appeals pending before papal judges delegate to continue to be heard where it was clear that the judges delegate were in a position, practically speaking, so to proceed, and continuing to hear one such appeal themselves where it was clear that the appellant could get no further process before the papal judge delegate in question, because process had been 'stopped'. In this latter instance, there is to be found the same practical response or remedy provided by the Lords of Council and Session where jurisdiction had simply been interrupted and could not be resumed, as contained in the reasoning in *Chalmer v. Lumisdene*.

If the ordinances and legislation concerning the spiritual jurisdiction of the period October 1559 to August 1560 are simply set to one side as invalid, the actions of the judges of the Court of Session are rendered comprehensible and consistent. Neither episcopal nor papal jurisdiction had been abolished. Yet the 'consistories' had ceased to function, and it was accordingly incumbent upon the Court of Session to hear spiritual causes previously heard by those Scottish church courts. Appeals against the judgements of those courts being heard by papal judges delegate appointed by Rome were to be left alone, except if the practical problems attending the Scottish church courts also applied to a particular papal judge, or judges, delegate hearing a particular appeal. Where such judges delegate were in a position, practically speaking, to continue to hear such appeals, the Lords of Council and Session would await the outcome of such appeals. Pragmatism in

---

[39] NRS, CS7/28, fo. 389r–v, 21 February 1563/4, *Sempil & Campbell v. Sempil*.

the wake of revolution, rather than a lawful alteration of the constitution of the kingdom, appears to have guided the interventions of the judges of the Court of Session within the spiritual jurisdiction.

LITIGANTS' UNDERSTANDING OF WHAT HAD BEFALLEN THE OLD COURTS SPIRITUAL

A further feature of note among these cases are the phrases used by litigants in justifying their petitioning of the Lords of Council and Session with reference to what had befallen the courts spiritual. None of them made any mention of the ordinances issued by the 'Privy Council' in 1559, or of the legislation of the Reformation Parliament, but rather echoed the straight statement of fact found in *Chalmer v. Lumisdene*, namely that the consistorial courts had 'ceased'. This general tenor was expressed in a range of specific phrases, with many petitions narrating that 'thair is na consistories instant and the office of spirituale juge . . . now ceisis',[40] that 'the consistoriall lawis hes cessit',[41] that 'the consistorial lawis now ceisis and takis na effect',[42] that 'the consistoriall law ceisses now',[43] that 'the consistorie iurisdictioun ceissis',[44] that 'the consistoriall at this present ceissis',[45] and that 'in place of the consistorie now ceissand, the Lordis of Counsale ar maist competent juges'.[46] Nevertheless, in other cases the sense that the courts spiritual had been 'abolished' was narrated, with supplications stating that 'the consistoriall jurisdictioun is abolescit',[47] that actions could not be brought since 'the abolessing of the consistoriall jurisdictioun',[48] that 'the consistorie is abolischit',[49] that 'the consistorie is now obleist',[50] and that 'the consistorie sittis nocht and the jurisdictioun thairof [is] abolischit'.[51]

These two main narratives may be suggestive of two distinct views circulating during this period: the first that the courts spiritual had 'ceased', or even 'ceased at this present time', bringing with it a sense of a temporary cessation of function, which appears to have been the view adopted by the Lords of Council and Session in *Chalmer v Lumisdene* and which found resonance in the charter of constitution of the Commissaries of Edinburgh; the second that the courts spiritual had

---

[40] NRS, CS7/20, fo. 219r–v, 19 December 1560, *Chalmer v. Lumisdene*.
[41] NRS, CS7/23 fos 252v–253v, 12 March 1561/2.
[42] NRS, CS7/26, fos 232v–234r, 31 March 1563.
[43] NRS, CS7/27, fos 202r–203r, 19 July 1563, *Franche v. Graden*.
[44] I.e. NRS, CS7/23, fo. 307r–v, 19 March 1561/2, *Home v. Grahame*; NRS, CS7/27, fos 130r–131r, 6 July 1563, *Scrymgeour v. Ramsay*; NRS, CS7/29, fo. 258r–v, 15 April 1564, *Spitall v. Gillespy & Spitall*.
[45] NRS, CS7/27, fos 324v–325v, 28 July 1563, *Heslip v. Borthwick*.
[46] NRS, CS7/23, fos 318r–319r, 20 March 1561/2, *Leslie & Grant v. Crichtoun et al.*; Smith, 'Spiritual Jurisdiction', 13.
[47] NRS, CS7/23, fos 307v–309r, 19 March 1561/2, *Bishop of Dunblane v. divers*.
[48] NRS, CS7/26, fos 212v–213r, 26 March 1563, *Blacader & Blacader v. Bishop of Dunblane*.
[49] NRS, CS7/29, fos 64r–65r, 14 March 1563/4.
[50] NRS, CS7/27, fo. 109r–v, 7 July 1563, *Wylsoun v. Symyntoun*.
[51] NRS, CS7/28, fo. 306r–v, 31 January 1563/4.

indeed been 'abolished', possibly reflecting the view based upon an acceptance of the legality of the actions of the Lords of the Congregation and possibly of the Reformation Parliament. This latter view, however, is difficult to sustain. While it ought to be borne in mind that the provisional government of August 1560 to August 1561 did enforce the legislation of the Reformation Parliament, and was almost certainly inclined towards an acceptance of the activities of the 'Privy Council' from October 1559, this does not appear to underpin the narrative that the courts spiritual had been 'abolished'. On the one hand, in July 1563 the Protestant superintendent of Angus and the Mearns, John Erskine of Dun, petitioned the Lords of Council and Session in relation to executry business 'be ressoun of the spiritual jurisdictioun now ceisses, quhill forther ordour be vniversale takin'.[52] It will be recalled that a copy of the ordinance issued by the 'Lords of Secret Council' against the court of the Commissary of Brechin in December 1559 survived among the papers of John Erskine of Dun. In this respect Erskine may be presumed to have been conversant with the events of the autumn of 1559, yet in 1563 made no assertion that the courts spiritual had been 'abolished'; rather, they had 'ceased, until further order be taken'. On the other hand, when the bishop of Dunblane petitioned the Lords of Council and Session in March 1561/2 concerning the payment of the price of certain victuals, conform to acts made by sir John Hume by virtue of a commission from the Commissary of Dunblane, the petition narrated that the consistorial jurisdiction had been abolished.[53] In these regards it appears difficult to place too much weight upon the use of 'abolished' within the narratives noted above, and to draw firm conclusions from them. It may be that a full-scale analysis of the cases noted by Smith, in terms of preparing full transcriptions and undertaking analysis of all the judges, litigants and men of law involved in all such cases, may provide some deeper insights into the narratives used to explain what had befallen the courts spiritual, but such an involved undertaking has fallen beyond the scope of this present work.

Beyond these considerations, two final cases provide perhaps fuller, and certainly more vivid, descriptions of what had befallen the old courts spiritual. In *Leirmonth v. Leirmonth* (1563) the supplicant explained that she had sought an edict of executry from the sheriff and dean of Edinburgh on the narrative that 'becaus of the alteratioun of the relegioun and lawis of this realm, it wes dowtsum quha had power to do the same . . .'.[54] In *Sempil & Campbell v. Sempill* (1563/4), which has already been discussed above in respect of the on-going validity of appeals pending before papal judges delegate, it was narrated that 'be ressoun of the cummeris quhilkis raisis within the realme anent the religioun and the acclesticall [sic] Jurisdictioun, the pronunceing of ane decreit in the said caus of appellatioun hes ceissit and wes nocht gewin furth . . .'[55] The narrative in

---

[52] Smith, 'Spiritual Jurisdiction', 12–13, citing NRS, CS7/27, fo. 370.
[53] NRS, CS7/23, fos 307v–309r, 19 March 1561/2, *Bishop of Dunblane v. divers*.
[54] NRS, CS7/26. fo. 255r–v, 3 April 1563, *Leirmonth v. Leirmonth*; Smith, 'Spiritual Jurisdiction', 12.
[55] NRS, CS7/28, fo. 389r–v, 21 February 1563/4, *Sempill & Campbell v. Sempill*.

Leirmonth v. *Leirmonth* suggests that the alterations in religion and law which Scotland was experiencing were not ordered, since it gave rise to doubt as to which authority was competent to issue an edict of executry. The narrative in *Sempil & Campbell* v. *Sempill* attests to the disorderly interruption of an appeal pending before papal judges delegate on account of the troubles and disturbances which had arisen in the realm concerning religion and the ecclesiastical jurisdiction. The fact that the Lords found that appeal still to be in dependence before papal judges delegate suggests that the narrative offered by the supplicant was intended to explain why the appeal had been in dependence for so long, thereby eliding any argument that the appeal had been deserted. Both cases indicate that the litigants involved were not aware of any of the attempted provisions made by the Protestant faction either during the Wars of the Congregation or by the Reformation Parliament. Rather, just as the judges of the Court of Session appear to have decided to administer the spiritual jurisdiction in lieu of the courts spiritual, recourse appears to have been had to them by litigants with spiritual causes, at least on occasion, because 'in place of the consistory . . . the Lords of Council and Session are most competent judges to hear the same'.[56]

COURT OF SESSION COMMISSIONS AND THE PREFIGURATION OF THE COURT OF THE COMMISSARIES OF EDINBURGH

In almost all of the spiritual actions brought before the Lords of Council and Session between 1560 and 1563/4, with the notable exception of the two cases in which they deferred to appeals pending before papal judges delegate, the judges of Scotland's supreme civil court proceeded to provide a remedy to the practical problems which attended the suppression of the courts spiritual, either hearing the cases themselves or granting commissions. The granting of commissions by which the Lords of Council and Session delegated their assumed authority in particular spiritual actions was apparently a needful device, in view of the practical constraints upon the judges' time and resources; 'the lordis of council havand consideration of the multitude of actionis dependent befoir thaim'.[57] Such commissions were granted to groups of advocates to sit in St Giles' collegiate church or generally within the burgh of Edinburgh.

David Smith has previously considered these commissions and highlighted the fact that many of the advocates named in them went on to be involved in the Court of the Commissaries of Edinburgh.[58] One such extant commission was granted on 12 March 1561/2 to 'Masteris John Abircrumby, Clement Litill, John Marioribankis, Alexander Sym, Robert Creytoun, Eduart Henrisoun [and] Alexander Mauchane'

---

[56] NRS, CS7/23, fos 318r–319r, 20 March 1561/2, *Leslie & Grant* v. *Crichtoun et al.*
[57] Smith, 'Spiritual Jurisdiction', 13–14; NRS, CS7/23, fos 252v–253v, 12 March 1561/2, *Stewart* v. *Stewart & Doig*.
[58] Smith, 'Spiritual Jurisdiction', 13–14.

to sit in the 'kirk of sanctgeill',[59] with another being granted on 20 March 1561/2 to 'Maister Alexander Sym, Maister Alexander Mauchane, Maister Henrie Kinross, Maister Edward Hendirsoun [i.e. Henrysoun], Maister John Scharp [and] Maister Richard Strang . . . to sitt in the burgh of Edinburgh'.[60] Of those so commissioned, Clement Litill and Edward Henryson went on to be two of the first four Commissaries of Edinburgh appointed in February 1563/4, while Alexander Sim replaced James Balfour on the same bench in October 1565.[61] Henry Kinross was the first procurator fiscal of the Court of the Commissaries of Edinburgh,[62] while Richard Strang, John Shairp, John Marjoribanks and John Abircrumby were all admitted as procurators before the first Commissaries of Edinburgh.[63] It is noteworthy that these groups of lawyers were directed to sit in St Giles' or generally within the burgh of Edinburgh, in so far as the Official of Lothian had sat in St Giles', while the Commissaries of Edinburgh were in the event commissioned to sit generally within the burgh of Edinburgh. There can be no real doubt that the groups of advocates to whom the Lords of Council and Session delegated their assumed jurisdiction in spiritual causes presaged the Court of Commissaries of Edinburgh. Beyond the similarities already noted, the entire concept of judges appointed to hear actions formerly pertaining to the courts spiritual of the Catholic Church and enjoying a jurisdiction delegated from the Lords of Council and Session was reflected in many of the practical arrangements attending the appointment of the Commissaries of Edinburgh in 1563/4, as is discussed in the next chapter.[64]

It is more than a century since David Baird Smith noted that the Court of the Commissaries of Edinburgh was 'to a large extent the creature of the Court of Session'[65] and, without anticipating the contents of the next chapter, some reflection upon this observation may be used to draw out several points of note concerning the continued involvement of the Court of Session with the spiritual jurisdiction following the winter of 1563/4. When from that time the new commissary system was created, appeal lay from the inferior commissaries to the Commissaries of Edinburgh, and then to the Lords of Council and Session. The Court of Session never lost this appellate jurisdiction, even during periods when the commissary system was integrated into the episcopal forms of government of the Church of Scotland during the seventeenth century.[66]

In addition to this enduring appellate superiority, summonses and sentences issued and pronounced by the commissary courts were enforced by the Court of Session. Thus in those instances where the ordinary authority of a post-1563

---

[59] NRS, CS7/23. fos 252v–253v, 12 March 1561/2, *Stewart v. Stewart & Doig*.
[60] NRS, CS7/23, fos 318r–319r, 20 March 1561/2, *Leslie & Grant v. Crichton et al.*
[61] The earliest Commissaries of Edinburgh are discussed in Chapter 6.
[62] Green, 'Court of the Commissaries', 45–46.
[63] Ibid., 323 ff.
[64] This paragraph is a lightly revised version of one already contained in Green, 'Court of the Commissaries', 22–23.
[65] Smith, 'Reformers and Divorce', 18.
[66] *Balfour's Practicks*, ii, 659, item xix; RPS, 1609/4/20.

Commissaries in enforcing summonses and sentences was exhausted, recourse was had to the authority of the Court of Session.[67] In respect of sentences, this continued a pattern which had developed in respect of the Catholic courts spiritual. It is a noteworthy feature of some of the spiritual actions dealt with by the Court of Session during the period 1560 to 1563/4 that they involved letters issued by the Court of Session by virtue of the sentences of Officials and Commissaries of the old courts spiritual. In this respect, the Court of Session's involvement in the spiritual jurisdiction predated the Reformation crisis. Ollivant has noted that, prior to the Reformation, 'the state was also ready to lend its assistance to the enforcement of ecclesiastical censures when an official invoked the "secular arm"' and that 'there is no doubt that the church courts were often dependent upon the civil power' in respect of the enforcement of their sentences.[68] This remained as true following the creation of the commissary system from 1563/4 as it had been prior to 1559. Yet, in respect of the censures available directly to the new commissary courts, the power to excommunicate passed to the courts of the Church of Scotland.

Pre-1559 and post-1563 continuities may also be seen in respect of the 'easy interchange' of judges between the spiritual and civil jurisdictions in Scotland which, as already noted, had been a marked feature of the administration of justice in pre-Reformation Scotland. Of the first four Commissaries of Edinburgh, three were concurrently Lords of Council and Session. James Balfour was already a senator of the College of Justice when appointed the first 'chief' Commissary of Edinburgh; Robert Maitland became a senator in December 1564; and Edward Henryson became an extraordinary Lord of Council and Session in January 1566/7. Thus while Balfour resigned from the office of Commissary of Edinburgh in 1565, prior to his appointment as Lord President of the Court of Session in 1567, the level of overlap between the bench of the Commissaries of Edinburgh and that of the Lords of Council and Session was pronounced. The Court of Session also rapidly obtained the right to appoint judges to the new commissary system at the expense of the Commissaries of Edinburgh,[69] although this power was subsequently transferred from the Court of Session to the Jacobean Scottish episcopate in 1609.[70] In addition, both the Court of Session and the Court of the Commissaries of Edinburgh sat within the Tolbooth of Edinburgh, quite possibly in adjoining rooms.[71]

A final, although a more general and imperfect, theme of comparison between the Court of Session, the pre-Reformation Church and the post-1563 commissary system concerns the endowment of the College of Justice. As had already been noted, the College of Justice was a papal foundation, and functioned in much the same way as a collegiate church or a university college. That is to say, it was a college of the pre-Reformation Church to which ecclesiastical revenues were

---

[67] Green, 'Court of the Commissaries', 74–75.
[68] Ollivant, *Court of the Official*, 134–135.
[69] Green, 'Court of the Commissaries', 75–76.
[70] RPS, 1609/4/20.
[71] Green, 'Court of the Commissaries', 44–45, esp. n.171.

assigned for the primary purpose of providing emoluments to the members of the college. Quite which revenues of the pre-Reformation Church had been assigned to the College of Justice remains a subject for further research, but the intermittent problems experienced by senators of the College of Justice in respect of their emoluments appear to have become acute by 1562.[72] Whether or not this proceeded upon a relative decline in the ingathering of ecclesiastical revenues following the suppression of the courts spiritual is not here determined, although ecclesiastical litigation before the first Commissaries of Edinburgh suggests that 1559 to1563 were difficult years for titulars of benefices.[73] The solution fixed upon following the creation of the commissary system from 1563/4 was to use the profits of justice arising from the confirmation of testaments through the levying of 'quots' to endow the College of Justice with £1600 a year. The system was not initially a success and necessitated the granting of a general supervisory power, at the expense of the Commissaries of Edinburgh, to the Chancellor and senators of the College of Justice in respect of the 'quot collectory' from 1566.[74] The initial attempt of the Court of Session to remain institutionally distinct from the new commissary system appears once more to have broken down.

CONCLUSION

While the assumption of the spiritual jurisdiction by the Lords of Council and Session in 1560 was to prove definitive in respect of the creation of the commissary system from February 1563/4, it was a parallel development to the rise of the courts of the Church of Scotland and their own assumption of the consistorial jurisdiction. While the Privy Council countenanced the latter, there is no evidence that they directed litigants to the Court of Session. There is also no evidence that the Lords of Council and Session ever countenanced consistorial processes and sentences led before and pronounced by the courts of the Church of Scotland, or commissioned the same to hear spiritual actions. Nevertheless, the number of consistorial actions heard by the Lords of Council and Session between December 1560 and February 1563/4 appears to have been limited to two actions for adherence. In this respect there is no indication that the alterations in marriage law then occurring within the new church courts were ever subject to judgement by the Court of Session. Yet at the same time, the relative absence of consistorial litigation before the Court of Session brings with it the suggestion that the majority of such cases were indeed being heard by the new church courts between the suppression of the old courts spiritual and the creation of the new commissary system. In this respect it may have been the case that the Lords of Council and Session did not assume the spiritual jurisdiction with a view to arresting the development of the jurisdiction of the new church courts, but

---

[72] MacQueen (ed.), *College of Justice*, 81.
[73] As is discussed at more length in Chapter 6.
[74] Green, 'Court of the Commissaries', 47 ff.

rather with a view to attempting to restore order to the Scottish legal system. Yet be that as it may, the narrative adopted by the judges of the Court of Session in *Chalmer v. Lumisdene* expressly linked the jurisdiction they had assumed to the old courts spiritual, and moreover conveyed a sense of a temporary expedient. That the spiritual jurisdiction thereby remained conceptually linked to the courts of the Catholic Church, rather than to those of the Church of Scotland, ensured that the two parallel developments within the spiritual jurisdiction down to February 1563/4 remained conceptually and constitutionally distinct. The new commissary system, in that it conformed to the narrative adopted by the Court of Session, was thereby to contain within it the potential to eclipse the consistorial jurisdiction of the courts of the Church of Scotland.

Chapter 6

The Court of the Commissaries of Edinburgh

The administration of the spiritual jurisdiction by the Lords of Council and Session, together with the legal framework of toleration and indemnity created during the first years of Mary's personal rule in response to the revolution of 1559 to 1561, provided the context within which the commissary courts, and most notably the superior court of that system at Edinburgh, were conceived and established. Just as leading jurists and officers of state within the College of Justice had charted the careful course adopted by the Court of Session during the uncertain period between the Reformation Parliament and Mary Stewart's return, the same group were to the fore in advising the queen to appoint the Commissaries of Edinburgh in February 1563/4 as the primary inheritors of the spiritual jurisdiction of the Catholic Church in Scotland.

As has already been discussed in the preceding chapter, various Lords of Council and Session, including John Sinclair, MacGill of Nether Rankeillour and Spens of Condie, had adopted a subtle line in respect of the Court of Session's assumption of the spiritual jurisdiction. They clearly accepted that the courts spiritual had been rendered inactive by the Reformation crisis of 1559–60, but declined to enter upon the details of this inactivity. Nothing was said or done that might countenance either the proceedings of the Lords of the Congregation following the deposition of Mary of Guise or the legislation of the Reformation Parliament. Not only did the legislation of 1560 pass without mention in any proceedings before, or judgements pronounced by, the Lords of Council and Session, but they in fact acknowledged two appeals from Scottish Officials pending before papal judges delegate appointed by Rome in 1562/3 and 1563/4, although in a third case they had continued to hear such an appeal for apparently practical 'causes and considerations'. In this respect the legislation of 1560 appears to have had no obvious or direct bearing on these judges' deliberations; rather, their deliberations appear to have been guided by considerations surrounding the fact that the Scottish courts spiritual were no longer functioning, and that as such the Lords might proceed to hear spiritual causes formerly falling within the competence of those 'inactive' courts. In addition, the Lords of Council and Session appear to have had no desire to directly challenge the growth of the consistorial jurisdiction of the courts of the Church of Scotland, or to interfere in the organisation of the early Kirk during the provisional government of the Lords of the Congregation triumphant between August 1560 and August 1561. Yet at the same time there is no evidence that the Court of Session either countenanced the courts of the Church of Scotland or ever had occasion to accept as valid a matrimonial judgement pronounced by them.

With Mary's return to Scotland in August 1561 lawful government was resumed in Scotland. The central policy of her early personal government centred upon the Proclamation of Leith. The precise origins of this policy are not known, but, since the policy was congruent with the approach taken by the Lords of Council and Session from December 1560, it seems reasonable to suppose that judges like the brothers Sinclair and officers of state like MacGill, Spens and Bellenden were among those who supported the queen's policy. The primacy of the maintenance of the Proclamation of Leith was a pronounced feature of Mary's personal reign, which broke down only after the ill-advised restoration of Archbishop Hamilton's spiritual jurisdiction in December 1566.

Following Mary's return, the Court of Session is not known to have heard further consistorial (i.e. matrimonial) actions, having heard actions of adherence in December 1560 and March 1560/1. In this respect it would seem that the policy which began to take shape during the first years of Mary's personal reign was one in which consistorial actions were heard by the courts of the Church of Scotland, while executry and beneficial causes, together with debt actions and the enforcement of deeds and obligations recorded in the registers of the old courts spiritual, were heard by the Court of Session. As has already been noted in Chapter 4, the courts of the Church of Scotland's consistorial jurisdiction continued to be exercised following Mary's return, although there are no clear examples of these courts being commissioned *de novo* by Mary's Privy Council in such causes. At the same time, the Court of Session's temporary administration of the spiritual jurisdiction appears to have been accepted to the point that both the Catholic Bishop of Dunblane and Protestant superintendent of Angus and the Mearns petitioned the Lords of Council and Session with actions formerly heard by the native courts spiritual.[1] This division of the spiritual jurisdiction between the courts of the Church of Scotland and the Court of Session does not appear to have been the result of a formal or comprehensive policy orchestrated by a central authority. While the distinction may have been created to some extent by litigants themselves, and although the Privy Councils active during the years encompassed by the Law of Oblivion had repeatedly directed litigants to the courts of the Church of Scotland in consistorial causes, the differentiation appears to have been fundamentally occasioned by the direct actions of the judges both of the courts of the Church of Scotland and of the Court of Session.

THE NEED FOR A MORE SUSTAINABLE ORDER

This dual succession to, or administration of, the spiritual jurisdiction may in time have assumed a more permanent and formal status, but for one significant problem. It has already been noted in Chapter 5 that, during the early years of

---

[1] CS7/23, fos 307v–309r, 19 March 1561/2, *Bishop of Dunblane v. divers*; Smith, 'Spiritual Jurisdiction', 12–13, citing CS7/27, fo. 370, July 1563.

Mary's personal reign, the Lords of Council and Session, 'having consideration of the multitude of actions dependent before them', began to commission groups of advocates to hear spiritual actions. This brings with it a suggestion that the Lords of Council and Session did not always have sufficient time to hear spiritual actions at first instance. In respect of the courts of the Church of Scotland during the same period, the consistorial case load which fell to them appears to have become a considerable burden among the multitude of other pressing business to which they were obliged to attend. On 4 July 1562 the General Assembly resolved to petition Mary's Privy Council that 'either they give up universally the judgement of divorce to the Kirk and their sessions, or else establish men of good lives, knowledge and judgment, to take the order thereof'.[2] It is not clear to what extent the General Assembly was aware of the activity of the Court of Session in respect of the spiritual jurisdiction,[3] and to what extent they considered the possibility that divorce actions might be assigned to the Lords of Council and Session; but it may have been with this possibility in mind that among the other proposed matters to be presented in the supplication was a request 'that papists be excluded from place in council and session'. In the resultant supplication presented to Mary and her Privy Council by superintendents Spottiswoode and Winram, no mention of Catholic Lords of Council and Session was made; and the proposed 'either or' option initially discussed by the General Assembly in respect of divorce actions took on the more direct form 'that judges be appointed to hear the causes of divorcement; for the Kirk can no longer sustain that burden'.[4] This sense that the volume of spiritual causes being brought before both the Court of Session and the courts of the Church of Scotland was burdensome is redolent of the general commission granted to the superintendent of Lothian in respect of divorce actions by the Privy Council on 19 March 1560/1, wherein they too had narrated 'that thai ar daylie trublit and cummerit to grant commissionis to proceid in sik causes'.[5]

From this it would appear that both the Court of Session and the General Assembly of the Church of Scotland were open to some further order being taken in respect of the spiritual jurisdiction. Perhaps with this in view, on 31 December 1562 the General Assembly commissioned superintendents Erskine, Spottiswoode, Willock and Winram to 'to travail with the lords of secret council to know what causes shall come in judgment to the Kirk'.[6] The consent of the General Assembly in respect of some further order being taken, in so far as it may be taken to have spoken for all the Protestant congregations of Scotland, was particularly important in view of the terms of the Proclamation

---

[2] Shaw, Acts and Proceedings, i, 25.
[3] Although the General Assembly of May 1561 knew of the Court of Session's involvement in respect of the revenues pertaining to the patrimony of the Church (ibid., i, 9–10).
[4] Ibid., i, 29.
[5] See Appendix, item 1.
[6] Shaw, Acts and Proceedings, i, 36–37.

of Leith: taking further order in respect of the spiritual jurisdiction would be to make an 'alteration or innovation in the state of religion'. There is evidence that not all of the judges who presided over courts of the Church of Scotland were in the event content with the eventual response of Mary's Privy Council; and such discontent may have arisen because the General Assembly's petition made reference to actions of divorce only, whereas the Privy Council's subsequent response dealt with the native spiritual jurisdiction entire, including all consistorial actions. This distinction may be an important one: Duncan Shaw has drawn attention to the fact that the constitution of the Genevan Church held divorce actions in particular to pertain to the civil authority, as distinct from matters concerning separation, non-adherence and the like.[7] Be that as it may, the General Assembly's petition of July 1562 appears to have been taken as authorising Mary's Privy Council, within the context of the Proclamation of Leith, to take further action in respect of the spiritual jurisdiction as a whole.

The Privy Council appears to have been slow to devise some more permanent order in respect of the spiritual jurisdiction. While there is no evidence indicating the cause of such delay, various plausible reasons present themselves for consideration. Taking a more permanent order in respect of the spiritual jurisdiction would involve some sort of response to the manifest fact that the courts of the Catholic Church in Scotland had been suppressed. How, then, ought this fact to be recognised in law? A full consideration by Mary's Privy Council of the suppression of the courts spiritual during the Wars of the Congregation could be fraught with potential difficulties. A principal difficulty was that some sort of judgement as to the validity of that suppression might have to be made. On the one hand, the Privy Council could state that the suppression had been lawful, which would bring with it an acceptance that regents might be deposed from office without sovereign consent, and that royal ordinances might be issued under a counterfeit signet. On the other hand, the suppression could be deemed invalid, but this would bring with it the logical conclusion that the old church courts must be restored. With this problem in mind, it is probably significant that no action was taken by the Privy Council until after the passage of the Act of Oblivion on 4 June 1563. The comprehensive language employed in that Act precluded any judges or officers of whatsoever estate taking cognisance of anything done by any person 'contrary to the laws of this realm, statutes, ordinances, constitutions thereof' between 6 March 1558/9 and 1 September 1561, with the memory of such deeds being 'expired, buried and extinct forever, even as if the same had never been made, done, counselled, thought, pretended or assisted to . . .'[8] More generally, the Parliament of 1563 had also apparently resolved another vexing problem with which Mary's Privy Council might have been faced, namely the validity of the statutes of the Reformation Parliament. As discussed at length in Chapter 3, the view that the 1560 statutes were invalid in law had been maintained openly

---

[7] Shaw, *General Assemblies*, 207–208.
[8] RPS, A1563/6/1.

during the course of the 1563 Parliament, and had moreover been countenanced directly in the Act of Oblivion.

In these respects, following the Parliament of 1563, Mary's Privy Council, in taking further order within the spiritual jurisdiction, was expressly prohibited from deliberating upon questions concerning the legality of, or even the details of, the manner in which the courts spiritual had come to be suppressed, while at the same time it was freed from an obligation to take the legislation of the Reformation Parliament into direct consideration. Protestant privy councillors may well have been content to let such matters pass, since the expedients of deposing Regent Guise and of summoning the Reformation Parliament had achieved their ends at the time, and within the fundamentally altered context of Mary's personal rule the achievements of such actions had been protected in law without reference to those earlier aspects of the Reformation. In addition, the 1563 Parliament had also criminalised adultery, to which end the General Assembly ordained on 26 June 1563 that supplications 'be made to the superior powers, for constituting judges in every province, to hear complaints of parties alleging adultery to have been committed by the husband or the wife'.[9] While this was, strictly speaking, a criminal matter, the link between adultery and the new form of Protestant divorce in Scotland was a direct one, and the suggestion that new judges required to be constituted for the trial of allegations of adultery may have fed into the idea of the new commissary system.

The General Assembly may be presumed to have had sufficient confidence in those by whom Mary's Privy Council was comprised to petition them in respect of jurisdiction in actions of divorce. During this period the Lords of Secret Council included many of the leading Lords of the Congregation, including Chatelherault, Argyll, Glencairn and Lord James Stewart (by then the Earl of Moray). Their number also included the oft-mentioned officers of state, MacGill of Nether Rankeillour and Bellenden of Auchnoul.[10]

THE CREATION OF THE COMMISSARY SYSTEM

On 28 December 1563 the Lords of Secret Council moved to commission a number of distinguished jurists and officers of state to consider the erection of jurisdictions in sundry parts of the realm by which would be discussed 'the caussis quhilkis the prelattis of this realme had decidit in the consistoriis of befoir'.[11] In this respect the commissioners were limited to a consideration of the causes formerly heard in Scottish consistories, that is to say by judges appointed by Scottish prelates, with no direct mention being made of papal jurisdiction, although a new provision as to the former would have consequences for the latter. Of the Lords of Council who were present when this commission was issued, all were Protestants and many of

---

[9] Shaw, *Acts and Proceedings*, i, 43.
[10] RPC, i, 157–158.
[11] RPC, i, 252.

them had been Lords of the Congregation and members of the Council appointed for the government of Scotland by the Reformation Parliament: Chatelherault, Argyll, Moray, Glencairn, Ruthven, Wishart of Pittarrow and William Maitland of Lethington, together with the Earls of Morton[12] and Marischal[13] and MacGill of Nether Rankeillour.[14] In this respect, the issuing of this commission can be considered to have enjoyed not only the full and valid authority of the Privy Council, but to have been issued by Lords of Council with very strong, and in various instances almost impeccable, Protestant credentials.

The head of the commission thus appointed was the Catholic Bishop of Ross, Henry Sinclair, Lord President of the Court of Session, who was joined by Sir Richard Maitland of Lethington and his son William Maitland of Lethington, Secretary, James MacGill of Nether Rankeillour, Lord Clerk Register, Sir John Bellenden of Auchnoul, Lord Justice Clerk, and John Spens of Condie, Queen's Advocate. All those appointed to the commission were senators of the College of Justice by December 1563, with the exception of William Maitland, who was nevertheless an extra-ordinary Lord of Council and Session.[15] To this group of judges and officers of state was entrusted the devising of a new order in respect of the spiritual jurisdiction, their commission explicitly stating that the Lords of Council could 'not gudlie await upoun the devising of the hale ordour of the saidis jurisdictionis'.[16]

An apparent difficulty concerning Henry Sinclair's actual presence in Scotland at this time ought first to be resolved, prior to discussing the various qualities and experiences of these commissioners. Sinclair suffered from ill-health by this time, apparently from gallstones or kidney stones, and was granted a licence from the queen on 2 May 1563 to pass to France 'for the recovery of his health and remedy thereof'.[17] The author of the *Diurnal* records that Sinclair passed to France on 2 July 1563, was 'schorne of the stane in Pareis' over a year later on 28 September 1564, and died at Paris on 2 January 1564/5.[18] Naturally, if this were accurate, it would mean that Sinclair could not have headed the commission concerning the commissary courts. However, an examination of the *Diurnal* for the years 1563 to 1564 suggests that the transcriber of the extant manuscript conflated the two years together, moving directly from an entry for 22 September 1563 to an entry for 23 September 1564 but one entry after that concerning Sinclair's departure

---

[12] Morton was one of the signatories of the 'first band' of 1557 (*Knox's History*, i, 137).

[13] Marischal was a Protestant, but provided no military support to the Protestant faction during the Wars of the Congregation, and declined to subscribe to the Treaty of Berwick (Michael Wasser, 'Keith, William, third Earl Marischal (c.1510–1581)' in ODNB (accessed January 2017)).

[14] MacGill was a Protestant, but there is no evidence that he 'threw his lot in with the lords of the congregation late in 1559' ('Michael Lynch, 'MacGill, James, of Nether Rankeillour (d. 1579)' in ODNB (accessed January 2017).

[15] Brunton and Haig, *Historical Account*, xii.

[16] RPC, i, 252, 28 December 1563; Smith, 'Spiritual Jurisdiction', 16–17.

[17] RSS, v, 1304.

[18] *Diurnal*, 77–79.

for France.[19] This brings with it the possibility that the no-longer-extant original manuscript of the *Diurnal* recorded that Sinclair departed for France on 2 July 1564, and was operated on at Paris in September 1564. Quite when Henry Sinclair departed for France has not here been determined, but an examination of the sederunts of the registers of the Court of Session confirm that he did not depart for France on 2 July 1563. During the period when he was heading the commission appointed by the Privy Council from December 1563 to February 1563/4, he was explicitly recorded in sederunts as sitting in judgement in Edinburgh on no fewer than eight occasions.[20]

The combined experience and insights of these commissioners in respect both of the history of the spiritual jurisdiction between 1559 and 1563 and of the legal framework created during Mary's personal reign in response to the revolution of 1559 to 1561 was remarkable. In respect of the suppression of the courts spiritual, it is possible that William Maitland had been present when the ordinance directed against the courts spiritual by the 'Privy Council' had been issued during the autumn of 1559. By virtue of their direct involvement in the 1559/60 Inquiry conducted by La Brosse and Cleutin, MacGill, Bellenden and Spens were in possession of a fairly specific knowledge of the deposition of Mary of Guise, and the attendant assumption of the title and authority of the Privy Council by the Lords of the Congregation, together with the procurement by the Lords of a counterfeit signet for the issuing of Privy Council ordinances. In addition, the proceedings of the Reformation Parliament, the tenor of the Treaty of Edinburgh and the contents of the ancillary 'Concessions' must have been known and understood to at least some members of the commission, from which knowledge proceeded the widely held view among lawyers that the statutes of the Reformation Parliament were invalid in law.

As to the assumption of the spiritual jurisdiction by the Lords of Council and Session, both MacGill and Spens appear to have sat in judgement on the day *Chalmer v. Lumisdene* was decided. Lord President Sinclair and Sir Richard Maitland may be presumed to have had a detailed knowledge of the Court of Session's assumption and administration of the spiritual jurisdiction during the period 1560–1563/4, both being recorded in sederunts in respect of various spiritual actions.[21] Of particular note is the fact that Sir Richard Maitland appears to

---

[19] Ibid., 77.
[20] NRS, CS7/28, fo. 89r (7 December 1563), fo. 135r (17 December 1563), fo. 168r (20 December 1563), fo. 213r (8 January 1563/4), fo. 265r (20 January 1563/4), fo. 272r (22 January 1563/4), fo. 276r (24 January 1563/4), fo. 370r (23 February 1563/4). A cursory inspection of subsequent sederunts suggests that Sinclair never sat in judgement again in the Court of Session after February 1563/4.
[21] For example 'Rossenis', denoting Henry Sinclair, Bishop of Ross, is recorded for NRS, CS7/26, fo. 255r–v, 3 April 1563, *Leirmonth v. Leirmonth* (per sederunt for 2 April); Lethington is recorded for NRS, CS7/27, fos 324v–325v, 28 July 1563, *Heslop v. Borthwick*; and both judges are recorded for NRS, CS7/23, fos 318r–319r, 20 March 1561/2, *Leslie & Grant v. Crichtoun et al.* and NRS, CS7/27, fos 202r–203r, 19 July 1563, *Franche v. Graden*, among others.

have sat in judgement both in *Blacader & Blacader* v. *Bishop of Dunblane* (1563), in which the Lords of Council and Session took to themselves an appeal pending before a papal judge delegate,[22] and in *Crichton of Anstruther* v. *Melville* (1562/3), when the Lords of Council and Session accepted the on-going validity on an appeal pending before papal judges delegate.[23] In this it seems yet more likely that the 1563 commissioners did not consider papal authority to have been abrogated in Scotland in 1560, which in turn brought with it the potential for the new commissary courts at least to continue to administer Canon law entire as an authoritative body of law – a potential for the most part realised – in pronounced contrast to the rejection of Canon law by the courts of the Church of Scotland.

In respect of the 'second legal framework' created in response to the revolution of 1559 to 1561, William Maitland had advocated Mary's policy of toleration towards Protestantism upon her return to Scotland, notwithstanding the fact that he appears to have undermined the same in December 1566 in respect of Archbishop Hamilton's 'restoration'. Henry Sinclair's moderation in respect of his often scrupulous maintenance of this policy has been noted in Chapter 3, while Sir Richard Maitland has been remembered for his 'instincts for reconciliation, practical tolerance, and moderation'.[24] It therefore seems most likely that the 1563 commissioners understood that they were not to make detailed inquiry into the actual events surrounding the suppression of the courts spiritual. As to the consistorial jurisdiction of the courts of the early Church of Scotland, and the acceptance of the same by the Privy Council, Spens had been among the elders and deacons of the kirk session of Edinburgh who had been commissioned by the Privy Council, along with John Knox, superintendent Spottiswoode and James MacGill, to determine the action of Protestant divorce, *Hamilton* v. *Eglinton* (1562).[25]

The commissioning of these judges and officers of state by the Privy Council was a defining moment in the history of the spiritual jurisdiction in Reformation Scotland. On the one hand, the very act of the Privy Council commissioning the Lord President of the Court of Session together with various Lords of Council and Session united two of the central developments witnessed since the suppression of the Catholic courts spiritual. On the one hand, the Privy Council represented the executive agency by whose authority both the courts spiritual had first been suppressed and the first superintendents of the Protestant Kirk had been appointed, and through which the courts of the Church of Scotland's assumption of the consistorial jurisdiction had been countenanced and possibly even encouraged. Notwithstanding the problems surrounding the legitimacy of such proceedings, the Protestant party could hardly resist the authority of the Privy Council within the context of Mary's personal reign, having earlier pressed

---

[22] NRS, CS7/26, fos 212v–213r, 26 March 1563 (per the sederunt for 24 March on fo. 163r).
[23] NRS, CS7/26, fo. 25, 7 March 1562/3 (per the sederunt for 1 March on fo. 1).
[24] Michael R. G. Spiller, 'Maitland, Sir Richard, of Lethington (1496–1586)' in *ODNB* (accessed January 2017.)
[25] Fraser, *Memorials*, ii, 183–185.

the same authority into the service of Protestant reform. On the other hand, the commissioning of the Lord President and other judges of the Court of Session in effect brought within the compass of these proceedings the Court of Session's administration of the spiritual jurisdiction from December 1560. This was a deft constitutional arrangement, in effect uniting in the one commission the authority of the Lords of Secret Council and the authority of the Lords of Council and Session.

Nevertheless, and notwithstanding Spens's and MacGill's direct knowledge of the Privy Council's acknowledgment of the consistorial jurisdiction of the minister and kirk session of Edinburgh, together with the superintendent of Lothian, there was a pronounced absence on the commission of December 1563: not a single superintendent or minister of the Church of Scotland was appointed to the same. Such an omission did not occur on account of a lack of quality among the early ministry of the Church of Scotland. Neither the appointment of superintendent Winram, nor that of superintendent Spottiswoode, may be regarded as having been out of the question in this respect. Other candidates might also have been found. For example, John Row, minister of Kennoway in Fife, held a doctorate in both laws from the University of Padua, had procured before the papal court for the confirmation and extension of the legatine powers of Archbishop Hamilton, and was one of the authors of the *Scots Confession of Faith* and the *First Book of Discipline*;[26] while Robert Pont, a prominent elder among the earliest kirk session of St Andrews, variously minister of Dunblane and Elgin and commissioner of Moray, went on to be appointed a senator of the College of Justice in 1572.[27] With these considerations in mind, the omission of ministers of the early Church of Scotland from the December 1563 commission appears to have been a deliberate policy.

Yet notwithstanding the absence of a direct influence of any ministers or superintendents who had sat in judgement in consistorial actions from 1559/60, or of other Scottish reformers, upon the deliberations of the commission, the religious and political realities which pertained in 1563 could not lightly be set aside by the commissioners. Even if so minded to recommend the restoration of the old church courts, the commissioners were precluded by the terms of their commission from such a recommendation, being limited to advising on the erection of jurisdictions by which the spiritual causes previously discussed by the prelates of Scotland might be heard. In any event, given that the commissioners were moderates, they would have had no desire to recommend a direct restoration of the old system, which would have served only to wreck the queen's policy of toleration and unbridle once more the forces of radical reform. It also seems reasonable to infer that the commissioners, as moderates, held the suppression of the courts spiritual, and the outright rejection of Canon law by the courts of the Church of Scotland, to have

---

[26] Richard L. Greaves, 'Row, John (c.1526–1580)' in *ODNB* (accessed January 2017).
[27] James Kirk, 'Pont, Robert (1524–1606)' in *ODNB* (accessed January 2017); Shaw, *Acts and Proceedings*, i, 68–69.

been too radical. From the recommendations of the commission it appears that the commissioners sought to chart a course between 'Catholic restoration' on the one hand and 'radical Protestantism' on the other. This was achieved through an emphasis on Scottish episcopal, or prelatical, jurisdiction, something not directly assailed or rejected by the Scottish reformers during the Reformation Parliament. This differentiation of native Scottish spiritual jurisdiction and papal jurisdiction appears to have allowed the commissioners to maintain that the ordinary jurisdiction of the Scottish episcopate remained an uncompromised part of the Scottish constitution, which, in light of the events of the Reformation crisis, now required to be administered by a new system of courts. By contrast, while papal jurisdiction remained valid in law as far as the Lords of Council and Session were concerned, any insistence by the commissioners that it be acknowledged within the new commissary system would have brought the new system into direct and open conflict with the Protestant reformers. In this respect papal jurisdiction was excluded from the new system, presumably as a pragmatic concession to the religious realities evidenced by the Reformation crisis. Yet even then, and within the context of the private proceedings of the Court of the Commissaries of Edinburgh, Canon law was retained to the extent that explicit references could be made to the Decretals of Pope Gregory IX during the course of consistorial litigation before the new judges.[28] A careful handling of the emotive issue of papal jurisdiction appears to have allowed Canon law to quietly endure, and to have allowed the concept of the spiritual jurisdiction of the old Commissaries and Officials to be differentiated from papal jurisdiction, notwithstanding developments within the legal system of the Church of Scotland. The survival of the tenable concept of episcopal, or prelatical, spiritual jurisdiction in Scottish constitutional thought appears to have provided the constitutional basis from which the creation of the commissary courts proceeded, and allowed the commissioners to recommend a new system of courts which restored order to the legal system, retained the functionality of the suppressed courts spiritual and created a context within which Canon law could continue to be enforced. Thus while radical Protestants or Catholic 'restorationists' would not have approved the course adopted by the commission, the course adopted was calculated to be an at least tolerable *via media*.

As to the actual deliberations of the commissioners as they took place, nothing is known directly, other than that they were brief as to duration: just over six weeks later on 8 February 1563/4 the first four Commissaries of Edinburgh, by whom many of the higher functions of the spiritual jurisdiction were to be administered, were appointed directly by royal charter. The charter of constitution of the Commissaries of Edinburgh narrated that 'by reason of the inaction or absence of the ecclesiastical jurisdiction of the Officials and Commissaries within this our realm, all consistorial actions and causes which used to be discussed and decided in the consistories' have become a pronounced problem 'through long

---

[28] Green, *Consistorial Decisions*, items 11 and 23, xliv–xlv.

delay of justice', many such actions having been postponed 'through a lack of order'.[29] This brief narrative was the only explanation offered in respect of what had befallen the courts of the Catholic Church in Scotland, no mention being made as to how they came to be suppressed. Rather, in stating that the courts spiritual were merely absent or inactive, a sense was conveyed that these courts might yet become active once more. This sense reflects the reasoning offered by the Lords of Council and Session in December 1560 in *Chalmer v. Lumisdene*, that they could hear spiritual actions 'gif the consistorie, or ecclesiastical jurisdictioun ceissis, or be stopt be civil wars or utherwayis': a sense of a potentially temporary interruption was conveyed, and the need to inquire too closely as to the cause of that interruption duly elided. In this respect, the reasoning both of the judges of the Court of Session and of the framers of the Commissaries' charter of constitution was that the jurisdiction of the old Commissaries and Officials had not in fact been lawfully abolished in respect of the Scottish constitution: it had simply ceased to be administered, and as such some provision had to be made for its ongoing administration in the interests of order and justice.

On the one hand, this sense of a potentially temporary solution to the problem of the spiritual jurisdiction brought with it the possibility of the renewed activity of the suppressed courts spiritual, a possibility realised at least in part in December 1566 in respect of the Archbishop of St Andrews, as already discussed in Chapter 3. On the other hand, this sense of a temporary arrangement must also have had some appeal for the Scottish reformers, in that it brought with it the suggestion that some better order might be established in the fullness of time, an order which sat more easily with the initial development of the jurisdictions of the courts of the Church of Scotland. Something of this sense still enjoyed currency in 1575, when Regent Morton and the Privy Council, contemplating a reform of the commissary system, held it to have been created by Mary 'quhill a mair perfyte ordour mycht be providit for and establissit'.[30] In these respects, the basis upon which the 1563 commissioners proceeded to create the commissary courts can be considered to have been a most prudent hedge against the various potential ecclesiastical and constitutional futures open to Scotland during Mary's personal reign.

Proceeding upon the basis of the constitutional understanding first adopted by the Lords of Council and Session, the charter stated that the queen willingly undertook to relieve her subjects from the 'great damage and skaith' which had arisen on account of the inaction of the courts spiritual, by establishing 'certain good ordinance' within Scotland 'so that justice may be ministered and done exactly, reasonably and with all due diligence hereafter to all'. Accordingly, the queen, with the advice of the Lords of Council, appointed four Commissaries of Edinburgh, and granted to them her full power and special commission within the

---

[29] An English translation of the *Carta constitutionis Commissariorum Edinburgi* has been provided in Green, 'Court of the Commissaries', 254 ff.

[30] *RPC*, ii, 455–456.

burgh of Edinburgh, by virtue of which they might take cognisance of a range of spiritual actions 'formerly accustomed to be judged and decided' in the courts of the Catholic Commissaries and Officials.[31] In this respect, and not withstanding the deep-seated historical, jurisdiction and personal bonds between the Lords of Council and Session and the Commissaries of Edinburgh, the fundamental basis of the authority by which the Commissaries were authorised to administer the spiritual jurisdiction was predicated upon a direct grant of power from the sovereign. This direct grant of authority superseded the authority of the Lords of Secret Council and the Lords of Council and Session, emanating as it did from the source of both bodies' authority, namely the sovereignty of the Scottish Crown vested in the person of the queen. The presence of Mary in her native realm was of course a factor which had been lacking during the years consigned to oblivion by statute, when both the Privy Council and the Court of Session had variously intervened in the spiritual jurisdiction: now that the queen was present, it was possible for the supervening authority of the Crown to be brought directly to bear upon the problem of the spiritual jurisdiction, in a manner which subsumed and superseded the earlier actions of the Privy Council and Court of the Session, and which in effect sanctioned and consummated the most legitimate development within the spiritual jurisdiction following the suppression of the courts spiritual, namely the assumption of jurisdiction by the Lords of Council and Session.

The charter stated in considerable detail all the types of spiritual actions which were now to be determined by the Commissaries of Edinburgh. On the one hand, they were entrusted with three principal national jurisdictions, namely in 'all benefice, matrimony, divorce and bastardry causes and actions, brought or to be brought by whatsoever person or persons within any parts or dwelling places of this our realm' together with the confirmation of the testaments 'of whatever person or persons dwelling or residing within any other part of this our realm, of which the dead's part shall exceed the sum of fifty pounds'.[32] These national jurisdictions in respect of first instance litigation concerning rights and titles to Scottish benefices, consistorial actions, and the confirmation of the greater testaments 'represented the centralisation of many of the higher jurisdictions of the pre-Reformation courts of the Officials',[33] to the extent that it would have been more apposite to have designated the new judges the 'Officials of Edinburgh'; although perhaps this nomenclature would have risked too direct an association with the old Catholic courts in the minds of radical Protestants. The Commissaries' exercise of their national consistorial jurisdiction has already been the subject of a detailed study,[34] while the exercise of their 'beneficial' jurisdiction has also recently been discussed in print.[35]

---

[31] Green, 'Court of the Commissaries', 256–258.
[32] Ibid., 258, 262.
[33] Green, *Consistorial Decisions*, xviii.
[34] Green, *Consistorial Decisions*; Green, 'Court of the Commissaries'.
[35] Green, 'Scottish Benefices'.

On the other hand, the Court of the Commissaries of Edinburgh also constituted a local commissary court within what was effectively the old archdeaconry of Lothian, being the southern part of the diocese of St Andrews. Its local jurisdiction may be understood to have been the template upon which the jurisdictions of other local commissary courts were based, although the erection of these inferior jurisdictions appears to have proceeded on an *ad hoc* basis after the appointment of the Commissaries of Edinburgh.[36] These local jurisdictions concerned 'the payment of tithes and other ecclesiastical revenues, executry business relating to lesser testaments, slander and defamation, the appointment of curators, and many small debt actions'.[37]

As to appellate jurisdiction, the new Commissaries of Edinburgh were authorised to hear 'all appellations interponed or depending from any other Commissary or Commissaries or other ecclesiastical judge whatsoever within this our realm in times gone by, [and] also appellations or reductions interponed hereafter from any Commissary whatsoever within this our realm'.[38] This authority extended to continuing to hear actions which had been pending before the courts spiritual at the time they were rendered 'inactive'.[39] While on-going exercises of papal jurisdiction formed no part of the new commissary system, it does not appear that papal jurisdiction was thereby extinguished from the Scottish constitution. Within two weeks of the appointment of the Commissaries of Edinburgh the Lords of Council and Session held an appeal still to be in dependence before papal judges delegate (*Sempil & Campbell* v. *Sempil*), as already discussed in Chapter 5. On the only occasion when the Commissaries of Edinburgh were obliged to deliberate on the issue of papal jurisdiction, it would appear that they accepted as valid, at least tacitly, a sentence pronounced by a papal judge delegate within the diocese of Ross in 1565.

The example of the judge delegate in Ross is not, however, as clear as could be wished. On 23 January 1567/8, some five weeks after the ratification of the Papal Jurisdiction Act in December 1567, the Commissaries of Edinburgh were petitioned by one Steven Kincaid, sacristan of the collegiate church of Tain within the diocese of Ross. Kincaid had had a sentence pronounced in his favour in an action heard by one Master John Cairncross, canon of Ross cathedral, 'Juge Deligait of the paip'. Cairncross thus appears to have heard this action at first instance, though whether by virtue of a commission issued by Rome, or by virtue of an exercise of Archbishop Hamilton's legatine authority, is not known. Appeal had subsequently been made against the sentence, presumably to Rome, and Kincaid desired the Commissaries of Edinburgh to decern the appeal to have been deserted. While the date of the original sentence pronounced by the papal judge delegate was not recorded, the appeal was stated to have occurred 'befoir the feist

---

[36] For the inferior commissary courts see Green, 'Court of the Commissaries', 59 ff.
[37] Green, *Consistorial Decisions*, xviii.
[38] Green, 'Court of the Commissaries', 258.
[39] Green, *Consistorial Decisions*, xix and xlii.

of Witsonday the zeir of God jai vc lxv zeris',[40] which fell on 10 June in 1565.[41] Since appeals ordinarily had to be made within ten days of the pronouncing of a sentence,[42] it seems reasonable to suppose that Cairncross had pronounced his original sentence during the summer of 1565. By January 1567/8 the appeal had therefore apparently been pending for more than two-and-a-half years, and it is perhaps significant that Kincaid did not petition the Commissaries until after the ratification of the Papal Jurisdiction Act. Regrettably the outcome of this action before the Commissaries is unknown, whether because the action was abandoned by Kincaid or because the relevant entries are simply no longer extant, or because the Commissaries wished to avoid a detailed engagement with the subject of post-August 1560 papal jurisdiction. What is known, however, is that the Commissaries were prepared to hear Kincaid's action, and that no arguments are known to have been advanced before the Commissaries concerning the validity of the original sentence, which brings with it the suggestion that the Commissaries were content to consider the matter of the appeal, and therefore to accept, at least tacitly, Cairncross's original sentence, pronounced by virtue of papal jurisdiction in 1565.[43] Thus while papal jurisdiction survived during the reign of Mary even following the appointment of the Commissaries of Edinburgh, the ratification of the Papal Jurisdiction Act in December 1567 finally resolved that aspect of the crisis within the spiritual jurisdiction.

Returning to the charter of constitution, the use of the phrase 'other ecclesiastical judges whatsoever' might conceivably have been intended to include the judges of the courts of the Church of Scotland. While the role of the Church of Scotland in relation to the spiritual jurisdiction passed without explicit mention in the charter, the Commissaries of Edinburgh certainly proceeded both to continue to hear consistorial actions which had been pending before the courts of the Church of Scotland at the time of their appointment, and to hear appeals against consistorial sentences previously pronounced by the new church courts. The superiority of the Court of Session in respect of the Commissaries of Edinburgh also passed without mention in the charter, although this was made explicitly clear in an ancillary set of instructions passed by the first 'chief' Commissary of Edinburgh, James Balfour, to his colleagues on the new commissary bench on 12 March 1563/4.[44] On the one hand, the Court of Session's appellate superiority made sense within the context of the temporary assumption of spiritual jurisdiction by the Court of Session. Yet, on the other hand, the new commissary courts, although constitutionally administering the old spiritual jurisdiction of the Scottish Church and enforcing for the most part the Canon law of that jurisdiction, were a system in which any on-going relation with Rome, either as to jurisdiction

---

[40] NRS, CC8/2/2, fo. 283r, 23 January 1567/8, *Kinnaid v. Vduard*.
[41] Cheney, *Handbook of Dates*, 146–147.
[42] Ollivant, *Court of the Official*, 121–122.
[43] For an earlier consideration of this case see Green, 'Court of the Commissaries', 71–73.
[44] *Balfour's Practicks*, ii, 659, item xix.

or as to new Canon law, was precluded. In addition, the instructions transmitted by Balfour also directed the Commissaries of Edinburgh to adopt the Romano-canonical procedure of the Court of Session, which was itself in effect the procedure of the old courts spiritual.[45]

The new system of commissary courts can therefore be understood in constitutional terms to have succeeded to the courts of the old Officials and Commissaries and to have inherited the majority of the jurisdictions which had pertained to them. In terms of the Reformation crisis and the development of the matrimonial jurisdiction of the Church of Scotland, the new system also succeeded, albeit quietly, to the consistorial jurisdiction of the kirk sessions, superintendents' courts and General Assembly. From the perspective of the restoration of order following a revolution, the new system represented a comprehensive intervention by the Scottish Crown in respect of the spiritual jurisdiction, whereby a new system of courts effectively replicated the functions of the old courts spiritual within the Scottish legal system.

THE COMMISSARIES OF EDINBURGH

The four lawyers appointed as the first Commissaries of Edinburgh were named in the charter as 'Masters James Balfour, parson of Flisk, Edward Henryson, doctor in the laws, Clement Litill, advocate and Robert Maitland'. Their qualifications and suitability for these new judicial offices have already been discussed at length, with supporting citations, in the author's *Consistorial Decisions*,[46] although the following salient features may be recapitulated here. Henryson, a noted civilist and a senator of the College of Justice from 1565 to 1567, together with Litill, a pillar of the early Protestant kirk in Edinburgh, are known to have been part of a circle of lawyers closely associated with Henry Sinclair, and their friendships with Sinclair appear to have survived the religious divisions occasioned by the Reformation. Litill had been among the elders and deacons of the kirk of Edinburgh who had taken cognisance of the Protestant divorce action *Hamilton v. Eglinton* in 1562 by virtue of a Privy Council commission, among whose number were also to be found John Spens and James MacGill. At the time of his appointment as a Commissary of Edinburgh, Litill was hearing the appeal made against a judgement of the reforming bishop of Orkney to the General Assembly in *Tulloch v. Sinclair*, along with Spens and MacGill. In addition, Litill may have served his legal apprenticeship in the court of the Official of Lothian, at a time when that office had been held by Abraham Crichton, one of the Lords of Council and Session who had likely taken cognisance of *Chalmer v. Lumisdene* in December 1560.

Balfour had sat as the last Official of Lothian prior to the suppression of the courts spiritual during the Wars of the Congregation, and as such may be presumed to have had an intimate knowledge of what had befallen the old church

---

[45] For which see Green, 'Romano-canonical Procedure'.
[46] Green, *Consistorial Decisions*, xxxi–xxxvi.

courts; he had also been an extra-ordinary Lord of Council and Session from 1561, and a ordinary Lord since 1563, in which respect he may be presumed to have enjoyed a working knowledge of the Court of Session's assumption and administration of the spiritual jurisdiction from 1560, being oft-recorded in sederunts in respect of various spiritual actions.[47] Balfour resigned as 'chief' Commissary in 1565, and was appointed Lord President in 1567. Balfour is particularly interesting in that it is likely that he was conversant with the Lutheran treatment of Canon law during the 1520s and 1530s, having studied at Wittenberg during the 1540s. During the first phase of the Lutheran Reformation, Canon law had been rejected out of hand on account of its direct associations with papal authority and jurisdiction; yet within a decade Canon law had been readopted, being too comprehensive a body of jurisprudence to simply replace.[48] Balfour's adherence to Calvinism and association with John Knox during the 1540s also meant that he was well placed to understand the rejection of Canon law by the courts of the early Church of Scotland, and as the last Official of Lothian he was well placed to understand the inherent value of Canon law as a highly developed body of law. As a senator of the College of Justice he would have been well placed to understand that Canon law was a central pillar of the European *ius commune* to which the Lords of Council and Session often referred in determining civil actions. In these respects, it may well have been the case that a new system of commissary courts in which Canon law continued to be enforced was deemed preferable to a new system of church courts in which it was rejected. At the same time, should the new church courts remain in possession of their consistorial jurisdiction, the marriage law of Scotland would be created *de novo* through the decisions of the kirk sessions and superintendents' courts, and through the legislative acts of the General Assembly of the Church of Scotland: this brought with it a potential for radical law reform, and for the fusing of disciplinary and consistorial jurisdictions within those courts. This potential radicalism may have been in the minds of those by whom the new commissary courts were conceived and constituted: certainly there is no doubt that the Commissaries of Edinburgh succeeded in place of the new Protestant church courts in consistorial causes, and in so doing steered the marriage law of Scotland towards a conservative retention of almost all aspects of the old Canon law.[49]

Balfour's religious convictions have long been a subject of uncertainty, and while he had almost certainly been a Calvinist in his youth, and possibly held Lutheran beliefs for a time, he tends to be remembered as a careerist for whom

---

[47] 'Flisk', denoting Balfour's ecclesiastical designation as parson of Flisk, is recorded in numerous relevant sederunts, for example: NRS, CS7/23 fos 252v–253v, 12 March 1561/2, *Stewart v. Stewart & Doig* (per sederunt for 10 March); NRS, CS7/23, fos 318r–319r, 20 March 1561/2, *Leslie & Grant v. Crichtoun et al.*; NRS, CS7/26. fo. 255r–v, 3 April 1563, *Leirmonth v. Leirmonth* (per sederunt for 2 April); NRS, CS7/27, fos 202r–203r, 19 July 1563, *Franche v. Graden*.

[48] For a full consideration of the Lutheran example see Witte, *Law and Protestantism*.

[49] For the consistorial law of the earliest Commissaries see Green, *Consistorial Decisions*, xlv ff. and Green, 'Authority of the Sources'.

religious considerations came to have only a secondary importance. The religious beliefs of the other Commissaries of Edinburgh, Henryson, Litill and Maitland, together with those of Alexander Sim who replaced Balfour in 1565, are easier to determine, in that they were all Protestants. Robert Maitland, about whom relatively little is known, may have been Sir Richard Maitland's brother, and was appointed a senator of the College of Justice ten months after his appointment as a Commissary of Edinburgh. Litill and Alexander Sim, neither of whom became senators of the College of Justice, were both involved in the legal affairs of the Church of Scotland over many years: both were appointed procurators of the Church of Scotland in 1567, and both were members of yet another committee appointed by the General Assembly in 1576 to define the jurisdiction of the Kirk.[50]

Within this group of judges may be observed a complex network of associations with the Court of Session, the old courts spiritual and the new church courts, in addition to varying degrees of familiarity with the December 1563 commissioners. Whatever may be said as to their religion, these judges were moderates, and were just as well placed to understand the history of the spiritual jurisdiction between 1559 and 1563 as were the commissioners who had resolved to erect the new system of commissary courts. In this respect there may be presumed to have been a shared view among this group of lawyers as to what the significance of the new commissary system was within the context of the Reformation crisis. The hallmarks of the new system appear to have reflected desires for order in a time of revolution, for the retention of Canon law, for the maintenance of the constitutional concept of the spiritual jurisdiction of the medieval Scottish Church and for the exclusion of the courts of the Church of Scotland from the consistorial jurisdiction. Taken as a whole, the new system appears to have been predicated on the view that the suppression of the courts spiritual had been too radical an action, and that the suppression should be effectively reversed in so far as religious, political and constitutional circumstances allowed.

THE INFERIOR COMMISSARIES

This sense of replicating the suppressed courts spiritual is pronounced when the judges of the inferior commissary courts are considered. In respect of the local jurisdiction of the Commissaries of Edinburgh, Balfour represented a direct continuity with the Official of Lothian, and he is known to have continued hearing cases as a Commissary of Edinburgh which had been pending before him as last Official of Lothian.[51] The situation in the local commissary courts has previously been discussed in the author's doctoral thesis, with supporting citation,[52] although various points of note may be recapitulated here. Many of the last Commissaries

---

[50] Shaw, *Acts and Proceedings*, i, 145 and 430–431.
[51] Green, *Consistorial Decisions*, xlii.
[52] For which see Green, 'Court of the Commissaries', 59 ff.

and Officials of the old courts spiritual continued as 'new' Commissaries within the new system, and in various instances continued to hold court in the same locations in which they had previously convened their Catholic church courts. The last Catholic Commissary of Dumfries, Archibald Menzies, became the first Commissary of Dumfries within the new system; and Hugh Craigie and James Duff replicated this continuity at Moray and Inverness respectively. The last Catholic Official of Glasgow, Archibald Beaton, became the first Commissary of Glasgow, and held his 'new' court in Glasgow cathedral, as he had done prior to the Reformation crisis. The last Official of Ross, Duncan Chalmer, took up office as the first new Commissary of Ross. One of the last Commissaries of Aberdeen, Nichol Hay, became the first 'new' Commissary of Aberdeen,[53] and continued to sit in judgement in 'the consistorie place of auld Aberdeen'. At Brechin continuity of judges cannot be confirmed, but Thomas Ramsay, the first commissary of the new system there, sat in Brechin cathedral. Evidence as to the actual appointment of 'old' Officials and Commissaries as 'new' Commissaries is often sparse, to the extant that Donaldson considered the possibility that on occasion pre-Reformation episcopal appointments may simply have held good.

Among this pronounced sense of direct continuity between the old system of courts spiritual and the new system of commissary courts, there was nevertheless a sense of change, no more so than at St Andrews. As has already been noted in Chapter 1, it is possible that the suppression of the old church courts occurred at St Andrews prior to the autumn of 1559, and it is probable that the kirk session there considered itself to have succeeded in its place. By 1564 St Andrews was the seat not only of a kirk session but of a superintendent's court, which courts appear to have carried on exercising aspects of the consistorial jurisdiction, albeit aspects often deeply entangled with their disciplinary jurisdictions, after the appointment of the Commissaries of Edinburgh, as is discussed at more length in Chapter 7. The appointment of the first new Commissary of St Andrews may therefore have been a particularly delicate matter. In any event neither the last Official of St Andrews, William Cranstoun, nor the last Commissary of St Andrews, James Rolland,[54] appears to have continued to act as judges there, with William Skene being appointed to the post of Commissary of St Andrews in 1564. Skene had been consulted in *Renton v. Gedde*, an action of Protestant divorce led before the kirk session of St Andrews during February and March 1559/60, which resulted in the first known pronouncement of a consistorial sentence in Scotland by a court of the Protestant Kirk, John Knox having publicly read out the sentence.[55] Skene was a member of the Protestant congregation of St Andrews, and may be presumed to have therefore been an acceptable choice as commissary within the burgh. Skene nevertheless 'retained strong links with

---

[53] A point not made quite clear in the author's doctoral thesis, but see Watt and Murray, *Fasti*, 33.
[54] Watt and Murray, *Fasti*, 421 and 426.
[55] *St Andrews*, i, 26. This case has already been noted in Chapter 3.

the old order, being a canonist at St Mary's College and sitting in judgement in the "college kirk of Sanctsaluatour".[56]

THE RESTORATION OF ORDER

As to the need for order to be restored in respect of the administration of the spiritual jurisdiction, the charter of constitution of the Commissaries of Edinburgh stated that the inaction of the old courts spiritual had occasioned a 'long delay of justice' whereby many spiritual actions had been postponed 'through a lack of order'.[57] This language was repeated in a letter from the queen presented to the Lords of Council and Session on 1 March 1563/4, in which it was narrated that the actions which used to be discussed in the courts spiritual 'hes takin sic lang delay, that the leiges of our realm hes bein greitlie indampnagit thaithrow'.[58] Evidence as to litigants' attempts to have their spiritual actions heard by the Court of Session and by the new church courts during the period 1559 to 1563/4 have already been discussed. Among the extant registers of acts and decreets of the Commissaries of Edinburgh are to be found various instances of non-matrimonial spiritual actions which further support the assertion that the administration of spiritual justice had been interrupted during that period.

In respect of actions for the payment of ecclesiastical revenues to titulars or tacksmen, for example, numerous actions were pursued before the Commissaries of Edinburgh, by virtue of their local jurisdiction, for the payment of ecclesiastical revenues variously falling within the period 1558 to 1564. Thus on 16 June 1564 the vicar of Stirling pursued for the payment of the teind wool of thirty sheep and the teind of twenty lambs for the years 1560 to 1564;[59] on 5 July 1564 the reforming bishop of Galloway pursued for the sum of 8 marks a year, being the fruits of the vicarage of Strageath, and that for the years 1559 to 1564;[60] and on 19 February 1564/5 the master and precentor of the hospital of Trinity collegiate church pursued for the payment of an annual rent of forty shillings, which had remained unpaid for the preceding six years.[61]

In respect of the administration of the laws governing succession in moveables, there is evidence that the years 1559–64 had witnessed considerable disruption. On 27 December 1560 the General Assembly had desired that Parliament 'take order with the confirmation of testaments, that pupils and orphans be not defrauded'.[62] Following the creation of the commissary system it appears to

---

[56] Green, 'Court of the Commissaries', 63.
[57] Ibid., 254 ff.
[58] *Acts of Sederunt of the Lords of Council and Session* (1790), 5–6.
[59] NRS, CC8/2/1, fos 61v–62r, 16 June 1564, *Auchmowlie v. Kynross*.
[60] NRS, CC8/2/1, fo. 90r, 5 July 1564, *Gordon v. Paterson*.
[61] NRS, CC8/2/1, fo. 352r–v, 19 February 1564/5, *Hendirson v. divers*.
[62] Shaw, *Acts and Proceedings*, i, 6.

have proved difficult to restore order. The most obvious problem faced in respect of the enforcing the executorial jurisdiction occurred because of the relative institutional dislocation which occurred between the structures of the Catholic Church and of the Church of Scotland. Prior to the Reformation, parish priests had been 'under obligation to report in writing the names of persons who died in their parishes each year'.[63] At the time of the creation of the commissary system, each Commissary had been directed to 'cause the Ministeris, or Reidaris, within everie parochin, [to] give in to him the namis of the parochineris deceissand thairin, ilk thre monethis',[64] being the only known reference to the Protestant Kirk among the constituting documents of the Court of the Commissaries of Edinburgh.

In respect of obtaining a knowledge of parochial deaths, the Commissaries of Edinburgh petitioned the General Assembly in 1565 requesting that every reader and minister should keep a register of the names of those who died in their parishes, so that the same could be conveyed to the procurator fiscal (presumably of each commissary court). The General Assembly declined to be burdened with such an undertaking on the ground that 'none or few of the ministry had manses and glebes to make residence in', yet accepted that, should this practical problem be remedied, they would conform to the Commissaries' request.[65] Yet as late as 1576 the General Assembly stated, in response to a petition received from the procurator fiscal of the Court of the Commissaries of Edinburgh, that an act it had made in this respect had not been 'put into execution for a lack of knowing the same'.[66] In this respect the judges of the new commissary system appear to have been lacking the intimate parochial knowledge of death necessary for the enforcement of their jurisdiction in executry business. A charge, known as a 'quot', was levied by the commissary courts on every testament they confirmed and these quots were centrally gathered and disbursed by a 'collector' at Edinburgh, being used in part to remunerate the senators of the College of Justice.[67] Hannay held that the apparent failure of the 'quot collectory' between 1564 and 1566 was occasioned by 'extreme difficulty in enforcing the submission and confirmation of testaments'.[68]

The restoration of order within the Scottish legal system by virtue of the creation of the commissary system was therefore not without its problems, either in respect of dealing with what appears to have been a backlog of cases in respect of ecclesiastical revenues, or in respect of reasserting the rule of law in respect of succession in moveables. The most delicate and complicated problem with which

---

[63] Donaldson, 'Church Courts', 366.
[64] Balfour's Practicks, ii, 660, item xxvii.
[65] Shaw, Acts and Proceedings, i, 85, 27 June 1565.
[66] Ibid., i, 441.
[67] Green, 'Court of the Commissaries', 47–50.
[68] MacQueen (ed.), College of Justice, 82–83.

the earliest Commissaries of Edinburgh were confronted, however, concerned the consistorial jurisdiction of the courts of the Church of Scotland.

THE COMMISSARIES OF EDINBURGH'S CONSISTORIAL JURISDICTION AND THE COURTS OF THE CHURCH OF SCOTLAND

As has already been noted in Chapter 4, the courts of the Church of Scotland had been active in regard of actions for the reduction of pre-Reformation sentences of heresy (an area of the spiritual jurisdiction not transmitted to the new commissary courts), and more notably in regard of consistorial actions. Yet despite the fact that the commissioners appointed by the Privy Council in December 1563, as well as the first Commissaries of Edinburgh, were in possession of a relatively detailed knowledge of the consistorial jurisdiction of the courts of the Church of Scotland, the charter of February 1563/4 passed over the subject of the courts of the Church of Scotland in silence. The most obvious explanation for this silence is that the constitutional basis upon which the appointment of the Commissaries of Edinburgh, and by extension the entire commissary system, had proceeded was one of an authorised temporary administration of the spiritual jurisdiction previously administered by the old Commissaries and Officials, which episcopal, or more generally prelatical, jurisdiction still remained part of the Scottish constitution. Such a view was obviously contradicted by the assumption of the consistorial jurisdiction by the courts of the Church of Scotland: this development had proceeded upon the basis that the courts of the Catholic Church and the jurisdiction which they had administered had been abolished, with the new church courts succeeding in their place and administering a new ecclesiastical jurisdiction, albeit one which retained aspects of the old spiritual jurisdiction as to function, if not as to law. In this respect, passing over the existence of the new church courts in silence appears to have been a sensible strategy: any direct mention of the courts of the Church of Scotland along with a simultaneous grant of the old spiritual jurisdiction to the Commissaries of Edinburgh would have necessitated a discussion and explanation as to the constitutional basis of the new church courts, together with an explanation as to why they were being denuded of their consistorial jurisdiction. This was fraught territory, since two contradictory understandings of what had befallen the old courts spiritual, with two potentially contradictory outcomes, were at play, and the policy of the moderates of the day was to avoid any detailed formal or public discussion of the events of the Reformation crisis.

Some consideration of the General Assembly's petition of 1562 to the Privy Council in respect of divorce actions within the legal context of the Proclamation of Leith has already been offered. If such a petition betokened the consent of the Protestant Kirk for some 'alteration in the state of religion' to occur in respect of the consistorial jurisdiction, it is conceivable that there was some risk in committing the consistorial jurisdiction entire to the Commissaries of Edinburgh, in that it went beyond the compass of the types of consistorial action specifically mentioned in the General Assembly's petition. That this was a potential difficulty appears, as already noted, to have been reflected in some of the underlying constitutional dynamics surrounding the appointment of the Commissaries of Edinburgh: the authoritative alliance of Lords of Secret Council and Lords of Council and Session, together with the latter's course of action in respect of the spiritual jurisdiction being consummated and superseded by a direct grant of full power from the person of the sovereign, following consultation with the Privy Council, in favour of the Commissaries of Edinburgh. In these respects, it is difficult to see how the General Assembly might have effectively resisted this development within the spiritual jurisdiction, or upon what constitutional grounds its objection could have rested. Yet within less than three years of the appointment of the Commissaries of Edinburgh, the General Assembly stated clearly that the spiritual jurisdiction of the Archbishop of St Andrews pertained 'to the true Kirk . . . howbeit, that, for hope of good things, the Kirk overlooked the queen's majesty's commission given thereto to such men, who for the most part were our bretheren'.[69] This indirect reference to the Commissaries of Edinburgh demonstrates that by 1566 the General Assembly believed the Commissaries to be exercising jurisdictions which properly pertained to the courts of the Church of Scotland, but that the Assembly had been prepared to let the matter go because the first Commissaries had been, for the most part, Protestants.

While this statement was made by the General Assembly at a particularly difficult juncture in the history of the spiritual jurisdiction, in that the temporary nature of the Commissaries' administration of the spiritual jurisdiction had just been demonstrated through the restoration of the same to the Archbishop of St Andrews, it is strongly suggestive that the Assembly was conscious of the fact that the courts of the Church of Scotland had been denuded of their consistorial jurisdiction through the appointment of the Commissaries of Edinburgh. Since neither the charter of constitution nor any of the ancillary instructions passed to the first Commissaries of Edinburgh made any mention of the actual courts of the Protestant Kirk, it would appear that the problem of the Kirk's consistorial jurisdiction was left to the Commissaries of Edinburgh to resolve through their judgements and decreets.

Yet notwithstanding this official silence, the charter of constitution granted the Commissaries of Edinburgh an exclusive national jurisdiction in all consistorial actions while it empowered them to inhibit any incompetent judge who presumed to hear such actions, and to reduce the sentences of the same, should they happen to be pronounced. While exclusive national jurisdictions and powers to inhibit were not a feature exclusive to the new Court of the Commissaries of Edinburgh, it is difficult to imagine that they were not aimed to some extent against those courts of the Church of Scotland which might decline to fully acknowledge the new order of the commissary courts.[70] As is discussed at length in Chapter 7, the complexities occasioned by trying to disentangle the consistorial jurisdiction of the Commissaries from the disciplinary jurisdiction of the new church courts led on occasion

---

[69] Shaw, *Acts and Proceedings*, i, 112–115.
[70] As was held to be the case by Joseph Robertson (*Concilia Scotiae*, i, clxxvi).

to the court of superintendent Winram at St Andrews apparently resisting a full transfer of the consistorial jurisdiction to the Commissaries of Edinburgh.

The Commissaries of Edinburgh appear to have charted a careful course through these potential difficulties, and developed a fairly consistent policy in respect of the courts of the Church of Scotland, on what appears to have been a case-by-case basis. There were two main problems with which the Commissaries were faced in this regard: on the one hand, how to deal with consistorial sentences pronounced by the courts of the Church of Scotland prior to the appointment of the Commissaries of Edinburgh; and, on the other hand, how to deal with any on-going exercises of the consistorial jurisdiction by the new church courts. The first problem is discussed immediately below, while the second problem is discussed in Chapter 7. What is clear, however, is that the Commissaries addressed this 'problem' within the consistorial jurisdiction only as and when processes and sentences led before and pronounced by courts of the Church of Scotland were produced in litigation before them. In this respect, neither the Commissaries of Edinburgh nor any other judicial body in Scotland appears to have had any intention of undertaking a full-scale review of the consistorial sentences of the courts of the Church of Scotland for the period 1559 to 1563/4, or indeed for the period following thereafter. Rather, the Commissaries were left to pass judgement on such matters as part of the ordinary exercise of their jurisdiction, and only in those instances when such matters were expressly raised in litigation before them.

THE PRE-1564 CONSISTORIAL JUDGEMENTS OF THE COURTS OF THE CHURCH OF SCOTLAND

Almost a year after the appointment of the Commissaries of Edinburgh, on 26 January 1564/5, two sentences of Protestant divorce on the ground of adultery pronounced by the kirk session of Edinburgh were subject to the judgement of the Commissaries as to validity, in two separate decreets pronounced on the same day. In the first case, *Weston v. Ewart*, the Commissaries accepted a sentence of Protestant divorce on the ground of adultery pronounced by the kirk session of Edinburgh. The precise basis upon which the Commissaries accepted this sentence as valid was not clear, there being no other explanation offered in their decreet other than that 'the said diuorcement' had been 'lauchfullie led'.[71] It does not appear from the decreet that the defender had entered any exception in respect of the competency of the kirk session's sentence. The phrase 'lawfully led' calls to mind proceedings before the kirk session of St Andrews in 1562, when the session held a sentence of annulment on the ground of impotence pronounced by the last Official of St Andrews to be valid, on the narrative that it had been 'ordorlie led accordyng to [the] law and practyk of Papistrie'.[72] This sense of litigation being

---

[71] Green, *Consistorial Decisions*, item 8.
[72] *St Andrews*, i, 146–147, 12 August 1562.

accepted because it has been 'lawfully' or 'orderly' led suggests a degree of scrutiny of the processes of superseded courts, both by the kirk session of St Andrews as it succeeded to the Official of St Andrews in consistorial actions, and by the Commissaries of Edinburgh as they succeeded to the consistorial jurisdictions both of the old courts spiritual and of the courts of the Church of Scotland.

In the second case, *Hamilton v. Sclater*, the defender was decerned by the Commissaries to have forfeited her tocher, or dowry, together with all other things given to her by the pursuer in respect of their marriage, on the ground that the couple had been divorced by the kirk session of Edinburgh on 25 July 1560. During the course of litigation before the Commissaries, it would appear that the defender had argued that some problem pertained in respect of the validity of the kirk session of Edinburgh's sentence of divorce, since the pursuer is known to have replied explicitly by way of an answer to an exception that 'the minister and eldaris of the said burgh of Edinburgh, in respect of the wechtines of the caus, had speciale licence gevin to thame be the Lordis of Secreit Counsale to proceid and do justice in the said mater', which reply had been admitted to probation by the Commissaries of Edinburgh and proven.[73]

Given the date of the sentence of the kirk session of Edinburgh, namely 25 July 1560, it follows that the 'special licence' had been granted by the Privy Council of the Lords of the Congregation between the deposition of Mary of Guise and the convening of the Reformation Parliament, that is to say, by the Privy Council which had issued ordinances against the courts spiritual during the autumn of 1559. Yet since the Law of Oblivion of 1563 must have precluded any distinction being made in respect of the legitimacy of the Privy Councils of October 1559 to August 1561 and that of Mary's personal reign, the Commissaries were most probably obliged to accept the sentence of the kirk session of Edinburgh as having been competently pronounced by virtue of a commission from the Privy Council. In this respect, the Commissaries may have been able to make a useful distinction: they were not accepting the sentence of the kirk session by virtue of an acknowledgement of the inherent authority of the courts of the Church of Scotland in consistorial actions, but were rather accepting the sentence of such a court by virtue of the supervening authority of the Privy Council.

The next two consistorial sentences of the courts of the Church of Scotland which came before the Commissaries of Edinburgh raised questions concerning the consistorial jurisdiction of the superintendents of the Church of Scotland, and of the reforming bishop of Orkney, together with the principle of the appellate jurisdiction of the General Assembly. These two sentences were considered by the Commissaries at the same time, within the context of two cases, *Hamilton v. Maxwell & Lindsay* and *Tulloch v. Sinclair*. The initial diet for *Hamilton v. Maxwell & Lindsay* occurred on 15 November 1564,[74] with the Commissaries' final judgement

---

[73] Green, *Consistorial Decisions*, item 9.
[74] For the initial diet see NRS, CC8/2/1, fos 222v–223r.

being pronounced on 16 March 1564/5.[75] The initial diet for *Tulloch v. Sinclair* occurred on 5 August 1564,[76] with the Commissaries' final judgement being pronounced on 31 March 1564/5.[77]

Hamilton v. Maxwell & Lindsay was an action for reduction of a sentence of Protestant divorce, *Maxwell v. Hamilton*, pronounced by John Willock, superintendent of Glasgow, or 'the West', together with the elders and deacons of the kirk of Glasgow, in August 1563. The details of the original case and of the Commissaries' subsequent reduction of the original sentence of divorce have already been discussed in the author's *Consistorial Decisions*: new evidence had come to light subsequent to the pronouncing of sentence in *Maxwell v. Hamilton* which meant that it should undoubtedly be reduced. The point of interest for the present discussion concerns arguments contained within the process led before the Commissaries as to which court enjoyed appellate jurisdiction in respect of a consistorial sentence pronounced by a superintendent's court.

Arguments as to the competence of the Commissaries of Edinburgh to reduce consistorial sentences pronounced by the courts of the Church of Scotland had already been raised before them in an incomplete action, *Forrester v. Rollock, Gilbert, Superintendent of Angus et al.* (1564). In that action, the pursuer sought the reduction of a Protestant sentence of divorce pronounced by Christopher Goodman, minister of St Andrews, superintendent Erskine of Dun and the kirk session of Dundee at an unknown date. At the only recorded diet in that action, one of the defender's procurators, Master John Shairp, argued that since 'the said sentence wes gevin be the saidis minister, eldaris, deaconis and superintendent as havand sufficient power to do the samyn for the tyme and, gif ony reductioun be persewit, the samyn aucht tobe persewit befoir the generale kirk and na vther juges', against which the pursuer's procurator, Henry Kinross, 'allegit that the samyn aucht tobe persewit befoir the said Commissaris as iuges competent thairto'. The Commissaries assigned *litteratorie* to pronounce their interlocutor in respect of these arguments, but no further diets for this action are known.[78]

During the course of *Hamilton v. Maxwell & Lindsay*, the defenders' procurator, Henry Kinross, in a departure from his earlier position, argued that the Commissaries 'aucht not to proceid as juges competent in this mater, being discussit be the kirk of befoir'. This was of course a cogent argument to put forward, in view of the fact that the General Assembly had explicitly stated the order of appellation within the courts of the Church of Scotland on 26 June 1563, with appeal lying from superintendents' courts to the General Assembly.[79] Against Kinross's argument, the pursuer's procurator, Richard Strang, argued that the Commissaries 'aucht to proceid as juges competent thairin, becaus he callis not for ony Iiniquitie [sic] committit be the kirk' but because new evidence had come to light in the

---

[75] Green, *Consistorial Decisions*, item 12.
[76] For the initial diet see NRS, CC8/2/1, fo. 140r–v.
[77] Green, *Consistorial Decisions*, item 13.
[78] Appendix, item 4.
[79] As already noted in Chapter 4.

case. It is particularly striking to find Strang in effect arguing for the appellate superiority of the Court of the Commissaries of Edinburgh and against that of the General Assembly: in 1563 he had been among those commissioned by the General Assembly, along with Clement Litill, to hear the appeal against the bishop and kirk session of Orkney's sentence of divorce, that is to say, against the 'first' *Tulloch v. Sinclair* action. In addition, Strang, again with Litill, had been among the elders and deacons of the kirk session of Edinburgh commissioned by the Privy Council to take cognisance of *Hamilton v. Eglinton* (1562). It is therefore yet more striking that Strang was putting forward arguments in favour of the appellate jurisdiction of the Commissaries of Edinburgh in respect of the consistorial sentences of a superintendent's court on a day when Litill was actually sitting in judgement as a Commissary of Edinburgh. Litill, together with his colleague on the bench, Edward Henryson, appear to have rejected Kinross's argument and accepted those of Strang, in so far as they took cognisance of the action of reduction, and, the new evidence having been proven, reduced the sentence of the superintendent and kirk session of Glasgow. From this it would appear that the Commissaries of Edinburgh held the appellate jurisdiction of the General Assembly, in respect of consistorial sentences pronounced by the courts of the Church of Scotland, to have been transferred to them. At the same time, no challenge appears to have been made as to the competence of the superintendent of Glasgow to have pronounced the original sentence of divorce in 1563, notwithstanding its subsequent reduction by the Commissaries of Edinburgh.

The date at which the appellate jurisdiction of the General Assembly had passed to the Commissaries of Edinburgh in this respect was being considered by the Commissaries in *Tulloch v. Sinclair*, being an action for tint of tocher *et donationes propter nuptias* on the ground of prior Protestant divorce for adultery. In the interests of clarity, some rehearsal of prior proceedings before the courts of the Church of Scotland is required. On 8 August 1562, the bishop and kirk session of Orkney had pronounced a sentence of Protestant divorce on the ground of adultery in the first action designated *Tulloch v. Sinclair*. The defender in that action had subsequently appealed to the General Assembly of the Church of Scotland, which appeal may be designated *Sinclair v. Tulloch*. As has already been discussed in Chapter 4, the General Assembly took cognisance of this appeal on 27 June 1563. The appeal was committed by the General Assembly to the 'ministers, deacons and elders of the kirks of Edinburgh',[80] together with various other specifically named persons, and was heard by, among others, John Knox and John Craig,[81] superintendent Spottiswoode, John Spens and James MacGill, together with Clement Litill and Richard Strang.[82] The appeal was still pending when the Commissaries of Edinburgh were appointed on 8 February 1563/4, and no attempt appears to have been made to transfer this appeal to the new judges. Rather, on 27 April 1564, those commissioned by the General

---

[80] The Commissaries' decreet refers only to the 'kirk', rather than 'kirks', of Edinburgh.
[81] That they were the 'ministers' referred to, see Shaw, *Acts and Proceedings*, i, 22; *Fasti*, I, 23, 49–50.
[82] Shaw, *Acts and Proceedings*, i, 44.

Assembly upheld the original sentence pronounced by the bishop and kirk session of Orkney. This original sentence of divorce therefore formed the basis of the action of tint of tocher heard by the Commissaries of Edinburgh, being the second action designated *Tulloch v. Sinclair*. The Commissaries accepted the original sentence of divorce and the outcome of the appeal to the General Assembly, and pronounced decreet accordingly, decerning the defender to have forfeited her dowry and all other things given to her in respect of her marriage.

The precise basis on which the Commissaries so proceeded is not clear. On the face of it, it would appear that the Commissaries held themselves to be the proper court of second instance in respect of consistorial sentences pronounced by the courts of the Church of Scotland prior to February 1563/4, except where an appeal was already pending before the General Assembly. In terms of the specific circumstances surrounding *Sinclair v. Tulloch*, the fact that sentence in the appeal was pronounced by, among others, Clement Litill may have been significant. Litill had been among those commissioned to hear the appeal by virtue of the fact that he was a member of the kirk session of Edinburgh, but by the time judgement was given in the appeal he was a Commissary of Edinburgh. In this respect, it may have been consistent for Litill and his fellow Commissaries – who all sat in judgement the day they pronounced decreet in the 'second' *Tulloch v. Sinclair* action – to accept a judgement in which Litill had been involved. Whatever the precise reasoning of the Commissaries in *Tulloch*, their acceptance of the validity of a consistorial appeal already pending before the General Assembly at the time of their appointment occurred within the context of their consideration of *Hamilton v. Maxwell & Lindsay*, wherein they asserted their appellate superiority over a superintendent's court in succession to the General Assembly in respect of consistorial actions.

While the appeal pending before the General Assembly in *Tulloch* was allowed to run its course, the principle of transferring consistorial cases which were pending before courts of the Church of Scotland to the Court of the Commissaries of Edinburgh upon their appointment was a pronounced feature of *Hardy v. Rutherford*, in which the Commissaries pronounced decreet on 11 April 1565, less than two weeks after *Tulloch v. Sinclair*. In *Hardy v. Rutherford* the kirk session of Jedburgh had been commissioned at some unknown date by the Privy Council to take cognisance of an action for Protestant divorce on the ground of adultery. The official narrative ran that the

> actioun of diuorce, being concludit befoir the saidis minister, eldaris and deaconis, reddy to the avysing thairwith and geving furth of thair decreit thairin, thai, in respect of the erecting of the jurisdiction of the said Commissarie, on na wyis will pronunce the samyn. And thairfoir the saidis Commissaris direct out thair precept to summound the said [defender] to compeir befoir thame at ane certane day bipast, to heir it be proceidit befoir thame in the said actioun quhair it left befoir the saidis minister, eldaris and deaconis. That is to say to heir sentence and decreit gevin and pronuncit in the said mater, *secundum allegata et probata* in the samyn: As the precept beris.[83]

---

[83] Green, *Consistorial Decisions*, item 15.

The Commissaries accepted the process previously led before the kirk session of Jedburgh, explicitly mentioning the Privy Council commission, and proceeded to pronounce decreet in conformity with the process already led. According to the official narrative contained in this decreet, the kirk session of Jedburgh held its jurisdiction in consistorial causes to have come to an end with the appointment of the Commissaries of Edinburgh.

From these cases it is clear that the Commissaries of Edinburgh were succeeding to the consistorial jurisdiction not only of the suppressed courts spiritual but also of the courts of the Church of Scotland. In respect of the courts spiritual, the Commissaries had been directly authorised so to act by their charter of constitution. In respect of the courts of the Church of Scotland, the same process of succession applied: this must have proceeded by virtue of the explicit granting of the consistorial jurisdiction exclusively to the Commissaries of Edinburgh, and possibly the general clauses both of appellate superiority in respect of judgements pronounced by 'other ecclesiastical judges whatsoever in times gone by' and of the power to inhibit incompetent judges. In the absence of any official guidance as to the constitutional basis upon which this latter succession ought to have proceeded, the Commissaries had to tread a careful line. In respect of the courts spiritual, the Commissaries administered their jurisdiction by virtue of the 'absence or inaction' of those courts. No such constitutional understanding could be applied to the courts of the Church of Scotland, and, as such, the Commissaries had to navigate the difficult constitutional problem as to how consistorial sentences pronounced by the new church courts between 1559/60 and 1563/4 could be regarded as valid, while subsequent similar sentences were no longer valid. Either the courts of the Church of Scotland enjoyed an inherent authority by which they could hear such actions, and yet had surrendered the same to the Commissaries of Edinburgh, or they had been authorised so to act by a supervening authority as a temporary expedient. Both theories could be thought to apply at the same time. The General Assembly's petition to the Privy Council suggested a surrendering of jurisdiction on account of practical difficulties in administering the same. As discussed in Chapter 7, the principle of an inherent jurisdiction surrendered appears also to have pertained at St Andrews following February 1563/4, although negatively so, in so far as the court of superintendent Winram resisted a full surrender of consistorial jurisdiction to the Commissaries of Edinburgh. Yet in so far as the courts of the Church of Scotland claimed an inherent authority to hear consistorial litigation, and in so far as they resisted a transfer of jurisdiction to the Commissaries, the Commissaries' succession to the consistorial jurisdiction of the courts of the Church of Scotland appears as a suppression of jurisdiction properly pertaining to the Reformed Church. Yet if at least some sections of the Protestant Kirk held their consistorial jurisdiction to have been a temporary expedient, perhaps proceeding upon a temporary extension of disciplinary jurisdiction in lieu of competent courts to hear certain matters, then the jurisdiction of the commissary courts was less problematic. From this perspective, or something like it, the temporary competences both of the Court of Session and of the courts of the Church of Scotland in respect of various spiritual causes had simply given way to the more ordered succession of the commissary courts to the suppressed courts spiritual.

In respect of the consistorial sentences of the courts of the Church of Scotland subject to the judgement of the Commissaries of Edinburgh, the possibly more palatable theory for the predominantly Protestant Commissaries, that of supervening authority, could be sustained in respect of the Privy Council commissions granted to kirk sessions in *Hardy v. Rutherford* and in *Hamilton v. Sclater*. Yet no such commission is known to have been granted in *Weston v. Ewart* – notwithstanding that the process was determined to have been 'lawfully led' – or in *Tulloch v. Sinclair*, or in *Maxwell v. Hamilton*. In those latter two cases, process had been led before a reforming bishop and kirk session, and before a superintendent and kirk session. Both had been the subject of a process of appeal, the former before the General Assembly, the latter before the Commissaries of Edinburgh, although a Commissary of Edinburgh, Clement Litill, had heard both appeals. In these respects, the theory of supervening authority just about holds good, with Privy Council commissions and the presence of Clement Litill providing a theory for the acceptance of such sentences on the basis that, while not pronounced by virtue of an innate or inherent authority on the part of the new church courts, they were nevertheless valid in law. It is possible that Clement Litill may have been central to this view: while *Hamilton v. Eglinton* (1562) was not produced in litigation before the Commissaries of Edinburgh, it was a sentence of Protestant divorce pronounced by a new church court by virtue of a Privy Council commission, which had appointed, among others, Clement Litill.

On balance, and while both theories could have been viewed as plausible and applicable at the time, a consideration of the development of the marriage law enforced by the Commissaries of Edinburgh suggests that they adhered to the theory of supervening authority whereby the temporary administration of the consistorial jurisdiction of the courts of the Church of Scotland had been authorised. From their appointment in February 1563/4 down to the Parliament of December 1567, during which period the Commissaries were left to their own devices in respect of formulating the marriage law of Scotland, they enforced the pre-Tridentine Canon law of marriage entire, with the sole exception that they accepted Scottish Protestant divorce on the ground of adultery and enforced the same. From this perspective the Commissaries' succession to the jurisdiction of the old courts spiritual brought with it an acceptance of the Canon law enforced by that jurisdiction; while the Commissaries' acceptance of several specific sentences of Protestant divorce on the ground of adultery pronounced by the courts of the Church of Scotland brought with it an acceptance of only this one aspect of the marriage law enforced in those courts. If the Commissaries had held that the courts of the Church of Scotland enjoyed an inherent consistorial jurisdiction to which the Commissaries had succeeded, it would have followed that a more wide-ranging acceptance of the laws of those courts would also have been in evidence.[84] Moreover, and as

---

[84] Green, 'Authority of the Sources'.

already noted in passing, one of the underlying intentions behind the commissary system appears to have been to salvage Canon law, and to limit the development and application of the marriage laws of the courts of the Church of Scotland: a conservative reaction against radical law reform. In these respects, the theory of supervening authority offers the more coherent explanation of the Commissaries' policy in respect of the consistorial sentences of the early Church of Scotland pronounced prior to February 1563/4.

The potential danger inherent in any appearance that the Commissaries were suppressing the consistorial jurisdiction of the Church of Scotland ought not to be underestimated. Although far more subtle and legitimate that the initial suppression of the old courts spiritual, it was still part of a policy which aimed at an almost full-scale resurrection of the suppressed system in respect of function, and cut across one of the principal developments of the jurisdiction of the Church of Scotland. While the careful construction of the Court of the Commissaries of Edinburgh, and the commissary system more generally, avoided the dangers of signalling a direct return to the old courts spiritual, it occupied a constitutionally undefined position between the old and new church courts. The strong Protestant presence on the bench of the Court of the Commissaries of Edinburgh appears to have helped various of the courts of the Church of Scotland to relinquish entire their consistorial jurisdictions into the hands of 'men of good lives'. Yet the precarious constitutional position of the new commissary system variously made itself apparent. On the one hand, the superintendent's court at St Andrews refused to yield entire its consistorial jurisdiction, as is discussed at more length in Chapter 7. On the other hand, the continued activity of Archbishop Hamilton in spiritual causes, which continued throughout Mary's personal reign, moved towards its logical culmination with the restoration of the archbishop to his 'ancient jurisdictions' in December 1566, by virtue of which the Commissaries of Edinburgh were expressly discharged from exercising their jurisdictions within the diocese of St Andrews (as has already been discussed in Chapter 3). The General Assembly, clearly incensed by Hamilton's restoration of jurisdiction, immediately petitioned the Privy Council, in which petition was to be found once more the radicalism of the revolution. In that petition the failing of Mary's personal reign was writ large: she had made an innovation to the state of religion without the consent of the Kirk, thereby violating her own Proclamation of Leith; she had restored once more to his ancient jurisdictions 'that Roman antiChrist', who had been stripped of his jurisdiction by the legislation of the Reformation Parliament; rather, his 'usurped authority' pertained to the 'true Kirk', which for hope of good things had 'overlooked' the queen's appointment of the Commissaries of Edinburgh.[85] By December 1566 both the Catholic Church and the Church of Scotland laid claim once more to the spiritual jurisdiction: the legal framework within which the revolution of 1559 to 1561 had been contained, and within which the new commissary courts had been created, was already coming to an end.

---

[85] Shaw, *Acts and Proceedings*, i, 112–115.

Chapter 7

The Commissary Courts and the Jurisdiction of the Courts of the Church of Scotland

During the course of the Reformation crisis and of the government of Scotland between the Reformation Parliament and Mary Stewart's return to Scotland, the courts of the Church of Scotland had become established throughout much of lowland Scotland. The development of the legal system of the Church of Scotland had occurred outwith the context of lawful government, and was therefore not formally acknowledged in law, although the reality of the existence of the General Assembly, superintendents and reforming bishops, and local kirk sessions was to some extent countenanced by Mary's Privy Council, the Commissaries of Edinburgh and the justiciary court at Edinburgh, although there appears to have been no direct acknowledgement of the same by the Court of Session. While the courts of the Church of Scotland were not explicitly mentioned in Mary's Proclamation of Leith in August 1561, the Proclamation offered protection to the state of religion as found universally standing in Scotland and thus by extension must have protected these courts against any threat of suppression by Mary's government. Yet during Mary's personal reign neither were the courts of the Church of Scotland acknowledged by statute nor was the jurisdiction of these courts expressly defined.

Notwithstanding these constitutional difficulties, the courts of the Church of Scotland continued to hear consistorial actions following Mary's return to Scotland. Upon the appointment of the Commissaries of Edinburgh in February 1563/4, the consistorial jurisdiction of the courts of the Church of Scotland was held by the Commissaries to have come to an end, to have been in effect an extraordinary and temporary jurisdiction. While the Commissaries accepted as valid any consistorial sentences pronounced by the new church courts down to February 1563/4, in so far as they were produced in litigation before them, they nevertheless considered themselves to have superseded the consistorial jurisdiction of the courts of the early Church of Scotland. This view was explicitly accepted by the kirk session of Jedburgh (*Hardy* v. *Rutherford*). The Commissaries proceeded to replace the General Assembly as final court of appeal in respect of consistorial sentences pronounced by the new church courts prior to their appointment, with the exception of *Sinclair v Tulloch*, which was pending before a commission appointed by the General Assembly prior to the appointment of the Commissaries, but in which sentence was pronounced on 27 April 1564. This development within the spiritual jurisdiction brought with it the problem of clearly defining the jurisdiction of the new church courts in view of the new commissary system.

Apparently aware of this difficulty, on 29 December 1564 the General Assembly 'anent the causes of the whole Kirk and jurisdiction thereof' appointed superintendents Erskine, Winram, Spottiswoode and Willock, together with various ministers, including John Row, George Hay, Robert Pont, Christopher Goodman, John Knox and John Craig, in addition to various others, including George Buchanan and Clement Litill 'to convene tomorrow after the sermon, and to reason and confer anent the said causes and jurisdiction pertaining to the Kirk, and to report their opinions again to the next convention'.[1] The outcome of this attempt to define the jurisdiction of the courts of the Church of Scotland is not known. Leading documents of the Scottish Reformation to which recourse might have been had in this respect appear to be relatively silent on the matter. Cameron has noted that while the *First Book of Discipline* expected principal churches to provide, 'through its ministry, an area or diocesan court for the assistance' of the superintendents, it made no mention of synods, and passed little comment in respect of the General Assembly in its capacity as a court 'or of its relation to the civil government. As will have been noticed the references to it are all of an incidental character.'[2] Yet notwithstanding this apparent brevity or silence concerning the higher courts of the Church of Scotland, the kirk session and its ecclesiastical jurisdiction were defined at length in the *First Book of Discipline*. The *Scots Confession of Faith* had held that one of the three hallmarks 'of the trew kirk', by which it might be differentiated from 'the kirk malignant', was 'ecclesiasticall discipline uprichtlie ministerit as Goddis words prescribis, quhairby vice is repressit and vertew nurischit'.[3] According to the *First Book of Discipline* this ecclesiastical or disciplinary jurisdiction consisted in the 'reproving and correcting' of various faults. On the one hand, blasphemy, adultery, murder, perjury and 'other crimes capital' were held to fall outwith the ecclesiastical jurisdiction, pertaining properly to the 'civil sword', while drunkenness, various forms of excess relative to apparel and eating, fornication, oppression of the poor through exactions, wanton words and licentious living, were held to 'openly appertaine to the kirk of God to punish ... as God's word commands'. Nevertheless, where the civil magistrate failed in its duty to take cognisance of those faults falling within its assigned jurisdiction, such matters could be dealt with by the courts of the Church. Those who committed such faults might be privately admonished if their fault were not common knowledge, but, where such faults were public, such persons were to be summoned before a kirk session. Three outcomes awaited those summoned before kirk sessions in such matters: exoneration; admission of fault and subsequent public repentance; excommunication.[4] The points of interest for this present study are those faults which came within the ecclesiastical jurisdiction of the Church

---

[1] Shaw, *Acts and Proceedings*, i, 68–69.
[2] *First Book of Discipline*, 69.
[3] *The Scots Confession of Faith* as per *RPS*, A1560/8/3, under the heading 'Of the notis by the quhilk the trew kirk is decernit fra the fals'.
[4] *First Book of Discipline*, 68, 165–173.

of Scotland which could nevertheless readily bring within the purview of kirk sessions and superintendents' courts what were in effect consistorial actions. In this respect, fornication and adultery are especially relevant. Adultery was held by the *First Book of Discipline* to fall outwith the disciplinary jurisdiction of the new church courts, unless its punishment be neglected by the civil sword. Adultery was not made a criminal offence in Scotland until the enactment of the Adultery Act on 4 June 1563, and then only 'notour' adultery fell within its compass: as a consequence the earliest courts of the Church of Scotland had dealt with the marital consequences of adultery prior to its criminalisation, treating the adulterous party as though dead, while the limited scope of the 1563 Act meant that adultery continued for a time to fall within the purview of the new church courts, albeit as a moral and consistorial, rather than criminal, matter.[5] In this respect, it is possible that the kirk sessions' earliest forays into consistorial litigation, that is to say into hearing actions for divorce on the ground of adultery, represented an initially temporary extension of disciplinary jurisdiction into an area properly falling outwith the Kirk's defined jurisdiction. Quite how all consistorial actions came to be heard by kirk sessions and superintendents' courts is less clear, although perhaps a wide interpretation of fornication and adultery could encompass not only the failures associated with breaking such commands but also the positive fulfilment of such commands, which would have brought within its purview the fulfilment of the obligations of marriage.[6]

As has already variously been noted, a detailed kirk session and superintendents' court register for the period of the Reformation remains extant only for St Andrews, but in considering its contents both as to 'disciplinary jurisdiction' and 'consistorial jurisdiction' the intertwined nature of both jurisdictions may be observed, and the difficulties, in respect of defining the Protestant Kirk's jurisdiction subsequent to its loss or otherwise of consistorial jurisdiction, may more fully be appreciated. With this in mind, some of the details of the consistorial and closely associated disciplinary decisions pronounced by the new church courts at St Andrews between Mary's return and the appointment of the Commissaries fall to be considered. As has already been noted in Chapter 4, during this period around twenty consistorial processes, that is to say processes involving litigation between parties, were led before the court of superintendent Winram at St Andrews, including actions for annulment, actions for divorce on the ground of adultery, actions for solemnisation of marriage on the grounds both of prior exchanges of promises of marriage and of deflowered virginity, actions for adherence, and an action probably arising out of the staying of banns.[7] The kirk session appears for the most part to have avoided taking

---

[5] See Green, *Consistorial Decisions*, lv ff.

[6] For example, this sort of interpretation of the Decalogue, as concerning not only the breaking of commandments but also their positive fulfilment, is found within the 1551/2 *Catechism set forth by Archbishop Hamilton* (1882).

[7] The specific citations in support of this have already been provided in Chapter 4.

cognisance of obviously consistorial actions at first instance during this period, although it did take cognisance of an action for declarator of legitimacy.[8] This apparent avoidance of consistorial litigation before the kirk session may be explained, if only in part, by an ordinance of the General Assembly made in December 1562, which reserved actions for Protestant divorce to superintendents' courts.[9]

THE INTERPLAY BETWEEN DISCIPLINARY AND CONSISTORIAL JURISDICTIONS

In addition to the more obviously consistorial processes, several processes falling within the disciplinary jurisdiction of the new church courts nevertheless resulted in what were effectively judgements which compelled the solemnisation of marriage. The disciplinary processes in this group were not examples of litigation between parties, as were the more obviously consistorial actions, but rather examples of couples being disciplined for moral faults at the instance of a new church court. The court in which this group of processes was heard, whether the kirk session or the superintendent's court, cannot always be determined from the extant sources. The records usually make clear when the superintendent was present, and, while references to 'the ministry' or 'the minister, elders and deacons' clearly indicate the kirk session, references to 'the seat' have been taken to refer to the kirk session;[10] in other instances there is a lack of internal evidence as to which court was hearing a process. While consistorial actions tended to be heard by the superintendents' court, it is not clear to what extent 'disciplinary' actions were assigned specifically to the kirk session.

The first such process within this group, *Anderson & Sym*, concerned a formal 'delation' of fornication made, presumably before the kirk session, against Robert Anderson and Euphemia Sim, who had procreated a child together. The couple confessed, and agreed, perhaps conditionally, to solemnise marriage; in addition, Anderson confessed that he was bound by the law of God to marry Sim, because he had deflowered her virginity, and obliged himself so to proceed, providing Sim did not have carnal relations with any other man.[11] A similar process, *Car & Sanderis*, proceeded upon a formal delation of fornication, this time certainly given in before the superintendent's court, against a couple who had procreated children together. The couple compeared before the superintendent, confessed their fault and stated that they were content to solemnise marriage together, for the avoidance of slander, mutual help and the well-being of their children. Winram ordained that they compear before their local congregation,

---

[8] I.e. *Colt*, 8 July 1562 (*St Andrews*, i, 147–148).
[9] Shaw, *Acts and Proceedings*, i, 38.
[10] Per *Dischington & Calland* (1569) 'the superintendent, wyth avis of the seat and ministerie' (*St Andrews*, i, 315).
[11] *Anderson & Sym*, 11 February 1561/2 (ibid., i, 142).

confess their fault and solemnise marriage within forty days, under the pain of excommunication.[12] In another similar process, *Oliphant & Morton*, this time certainly heard by the kirk session, a couple were 'delated' for 'keeping company in bed and board unmarried'. In their defence the couple alleged that they were 'contracted and [had] maid promise of marriage', by virtue of which they were ordained to make public satisfaction, to have their banns proclaimed and to solemnise marriage thereafter.[13] A similar remedy was ordained in another process, *Davidson & Stewart*, although the reasons, beyond 'transgressing the order of the kirk', are unclear.[14] The intermingling of what began as a matter of discipline, but which resulted in what was in effect a sentence of solemnisation, may be observed in other processes variously involving fornication, irregular marriage and deflowered virginity, such as *Morton & Brown*,[15] *Zeasteris & Bunche*,[16] and *Reid & Cuthbert*.[17] In all these processes, what could be considered to have been disciplinary matters resulted in the solemnisation of marriage, with the possible exception of *Reid & Cuthbert*. In all these processes, saving *Davidson & Stewart*, the details of which are unclear, these processes resulted in solemnisation because the parties either alleged promise of marriage, or consented and agreed to solemnise marriage, or because, as in *Reid & Cuthbert*, a virgin had been deflowered. This feature of these processes brings with it a suggestion of Protestants willingly submitting and consenting to the discipline of the kirk, and in this sense the spontaneous development of the Kirk's disciplinary jurisdiction and its direct bearing upon consistorial questions may well have been driven by the consent of Protestant congregations.

By the time the Commissaries of Edinburgh were appointed in February 1563/4, the kirk session and superintendent's courts at St Andrews were clearly exercising between them wide-ranging disciplinary and consistorial jurisdictions which were not always clearly differentiated. While disciplinary proceedings occurred within the context of formal delations being made against those accused of moral faults, with subsequent trial before the kirk session or superintendent's court, consistorial proceedings occurred within the context of litigation between parties. The intermingling of, and interplay between, the disciplinary and consistorial jurisdictions within the context of the courts of the early Church of Scotland may well have been the single most difficult issue faced by those commissioned by the General Assembly in 1564 to define the jurisdiction of the Kirk following the appointment of the Commissaries of Edinburgh.

The lack of any explicit mention of the courts of the Church of Scotland in the charter of constitution of the Commissaries of Edinburgh, together with the

---

[12] *Car & Sanderis*, 3 June 1562 (ibid., i, 146).
[13] *Oliphant & Morton*, 2 September 1562 (ibid., i, 149–150).
[14] *Davidson & Stewart*, 25 November 1562 (ibid., i, 174).
[15] *Morton & Brown*, 30 December 1562 (ibid., i, 175).
[16] *Zeasteris & Bunche*, 3 March 1562/3 (ibid., i, 180–181; Winram).
[17] *Reid & Cuthbert*, 1 September 1563 (ibid., i, 185–186; Winram).

apparent failure of those appointed by the General Assembly in 1564 to define the jurisdiction of the Kirk, meant that the difficult task of defining the jurisdiction of the Kirk in relation to the new commissary courts fell to be decided by the judges of those courts, as and when difficulties arose. Defining the spheres of jurisdiction of different courts within the legal system through judicial pronouncements was a common feature of the Scottish legal system during this period, and is often one of the only sources of evidence as to the precise limits of respective competent jurisdictions.

In respect of the judicial delineation of the boundaries of the consistorial jurisdiction of the Commissaries of Edinburgh and the disciplinary jurisdiction of the courts of the Church of Scotland, the principal extant sources of evidence to which recourse may be had are the registers of acts and decreets of the Commissaries of Edinburgh and the registers of the new church courts at St Andrews, the latter, as already noted, containing evidence of the proceedings of the court of the superintendent of Fife, Fotherick and Strathearn. From the multitude of processes, sentences and decreets contained in these two sources, a complex picture emerges of the jurisdiction of the Kirk relative to that of the Commissaries.

JURISDICTIONAL CO-OPERATION AND DIVERGENCE: THE STAYING OF BANNS

Beyond the kirk session of Jedburgh's explicit acceptance of the Commissaries' consistorial jurisdiction in *Hardy* v. *Rutherford*, further, less pronounced, examples of acceptance can be found among the extant evidence. This evidence is particularly clear in respect of litigation arising out of the staying of banns in parish kirks. The staying of banns provided the primary context within which allegations of impediments to marriage occurred, such impediments often involving prior promises of marriage and, though not always, *copula carnalis*. In such instances local ministers were manifestly, and the commissary courts potentially, involved. On a procedural level, banns were proclaimed by a minister in his parish subsequent either to a couple voluntarily giving up their names to be proclaimed, or as the result of a couple being compelled so to proceed, either by a decreet of solemnisation pronounced by the Commissaries of Edinburgh or as the result of proceedings before a court of the Church of Scotland. Once the banns were being proclaimed, they could variously be stayed by an allegation of prior betrothal, prior irregular marriage or indeed prior regular marriage. The basic jurisdictional question was whether the local ministers and kirk sessions ought to take cognisance of such allegations, or whether the determination of such allegations fell within the competence of the commissary courts.

Within the immediate environs of Edinburgh, local kirk sessions appear to have accepted and co-operated with the consistorial jurisdiction of the Commissaries of Edinburgh in this respect. In a rare survival among the fragmentary records of the early kirk session of the Canongate, it would appear that, at least in this close proximity to the Court of the Commissaries of Edinburgh, the latter's jurisdiction was acknowledged. Thus on 8 December 1565 one Christine Weddell appeared before the kirk session of the Canongate and alleged 'promis of marriaig of Thomas Russall, cordinar, desyring the said Thomas to be no ferder proclamit with nane uthair': 'The kirk avasing thairupon . . . remitti[t] bothe the perteis to the commissaris, requyring the said Cristane to intend actioun befoir thame quha wes juge competent'.[18] A decade or so later the kirk session of Musselburgh, which also lay within close proximity of Edinburgh, took the same course of action, declaring that they would not proceed to proclaim certain banns in the kirk of Inveresk which had been stayed by an allegation of prior promise of marriage, until 'the same wer first decydit befoir the saidis Commissaries, juge compitent in that behalf'.[19]

The principle that allegations of impediments by which banns had been stayed should be determined by the Commissaries of Edinburgh appears to have been widely accepted throughout south-east Scotland. Between 1564 and 1576/7 some fifteen cases are known to have been heard by the Commissaries of Edinburgh relating to impediments by which banns had been stayed, according to the evidence of their registers. Of these fifteen cases, the parish kirk in which the banns had been stayed is known in twelve instances, and a map of the locations of the kirks in question has been provided elsewhere.[20] To this evidence may now be added the additional example noted above for the kirk of the Canongate in 1565, bringing the total number of instances where the parish kirk was named to thirteen. The locations of all these named parish kirks are confined to south-east Scotland, although a few of them lie outwith the territorial bounds of the Commissaries of Edinburgh's local, or inferior, jurisdiction. Of those that lay within the bounds are to be found the kirks of Edinburgh (1569), Holyroodhouse (1576), St Cuthbert's (1569, 1574), the Canongate (1565, 1575), Leith (1576), Currie (1573), Musselburgh (1570/1, 1576), Inveresk (1576) and Kirknewton (1568); the exceptions to this pattern are the kirks of Fishwick (1573) and Foulden (1574) on the eastern Anglo-Scottish border, and Culross (1572) in southern Fife.[21] The predominant pattern, however, is that the determinations of such impediments were ordinarily dealt with by an exercise of the Commissaries of Edinburgh's local, or inferior, jurisdiction, rather than by an exercise of their national consistorial jurisdiction. The inference is that beyond the bounds of the Commissaries of Edinburgh's local jurisdiction, allegations of impediments by which banns were stayed fell to be heard by the inferior commissaries within the bounds of their local jurisdictions.

---

[18] *Buik of the Canagait*, ed. Calderwood, 30.
[19] Green, *Consistorial Decisions*, item 176, *Carrick v. Gibson*.
[20] For which see Green, 'Court of the Commissaries', 235 ff., and 237 for the map. The only new addition to these data concerns the evidence for the kirk of the Canongate in 1565, bringing the number of instances of stayed banns from that kirk to two, rather than the previously noted one.
[21] For which cases recourse may now be had to Green, *Consistorial Decisions*, items 18, 44, 55, 59, 88, 106, 123, 125, 146, 152, 176, 185, together with *Buik of the Canagait*, ed. Calderwood, 30.

On the one hand, this inference appears to be confirmed from an extant process in respect of the local commissary court of Hamilton and Campsie, for which court one early register is still extant, the only such survival for the earliest years of the local commissary courts beyond Edinburgh.[22] Yet, on the other hand, this inference is directly contradicted by the evidence from the new church courts at St Andrews. The Commissaries of Edinburgh were formally appointed 8 February 1563/4, and on the following day provision was made for the erection of a new commissary court at St Andrews,[23] of which the first commissary was William Skene.[24] On 22 March 1563/4 certain banns were stayed at the kirk of St Andrews. The kirk session there took cognisance of the alleged impediment by which the banns had been stayed, in the event determining the impediment to be of verity.[25] Similar proceedings occurred before the court of the superintendent at St Andrews between 19 December 1565 and 20 February 1565/6,[26] and again between 3 and 10 July 1566.[27] In the first example of the exercise of the superintendent's jurisdiction in this respect, the kirk in which the banns had been stayed was not mentioned, but in the second example the kirk in question was Lathrisk, which may suggest that the superintendent heard such proceedings in preference to the kirk session of St Andrews when the stayed banns in question had been proclaimed outwith St Andrews. This is possibly confirmed by similar proceedings concerning banns stayed at Kilconquhar on 22 June 1569, the 'trial and discussion' of the impediment being committed by the superintendent to the kirk session of St Andrews during his absence.[28] Further evidence of the kirk session of St Andrews determining the verity of an impediment by which banns had been stayed occurred in July 1570.[29] In these respects it would appear that neither the kirk session of St Andrews nor the superintendent's court felt under any procedural constraint to remit such matters to either the Commissaries of Edinburgh or the local Commissary of St Andrews. Nevertheless, the 'St Andrews' position in respect of the staying of banns could on occasion be challenged by litigants: the one known instance of this, *Kay v. Arnot* (1565), is discussed at length below within the context of the jurisdictional arguments and conflicts which arose between the Commissaries of Edinburgh and the church courts at St Andrews.

---

[22] NRS, CC10/1/1, fo. 123v, 9 February 1564/5, *Zoung v. Richie*; for a brief discussion of this case and some partial transcriptions of the same see Green, 'Court of the Commissaries', 241–242.
[23] Dunbar, *Reforming the Scottish Church*, 90, n.38.
[24] The earliest mention of Skene being in office is 11 August 1565 (Watt and Murray, *Fasti*, 427), although perhaps this date might be pushed back further by a reconsideration of the source cited by Dunbar immediately above.
[25] *Moffat v. Thomson* (St Andrews, i, 212–221).
[26] *Laing v. Flemming* (ibid., i, 255–257).
[27] *Beaton v. Arnot* (ibid., i, 279-281).
[28] *Dischington & Calland* (ibid., i, 321).
[29] *Dande & Dairny* (ibid., i, 340).

The general picture found among the extant cases, of the acceptance of the competence of the commissary courts in these matters by the courts of the Church of Scotland, is confirmed indirectly by another source.[30] Yet the exception of St Andrews is also confirmed by the extant records of a synod convened by superintendent Winram around 1570. Those records contain a statute which recognised the competence of local kirk sessions within Fife, or the superintendent's court at St Andrews, to take cognisance of impediments by which banns had been stayed, and to pronounce decreets accordingly.[31]

THE EXCEPTION OF ST ANDREWS

The apparent pattern of acceptance of the consistorial jurisdiction of the new commissary courts by the courts of the Church of Scotland does not appear to have applied at St Andrews, not only in respect of the staying of banns but in a wide range of other consistorial areas. Before entering into a detailed discussion of the relevant processes which illustrate the jurisdiction of the kirk session and, more pertinently, the superintendent's court at St Andrews, together with their jurisdictional relations with the Commissaries of Edinburgh, some thoughts may be offered as to the constitutional basis of the St Andrews church courts' divergent activities.

In respect of the authority by which superintendent Winram, sitting with the kirk session, held himself to administer a superintendal jurisdiction, the case of *Cunningham* v. *Wood* (1561) is instructive. In that action of adherence, which entered into a detailed discussion of the defence of prior annulment of marriage on the ground of the Canon law forbidden degrees, the defender was decerned to adhere to the pursuer by Winram and the kirk session 'according to the law of God, and owr autorite quhilk we have of the law of God to be thairto interponit'.[32] The suggestion here was that the court did not enjoy jurisdiction by virtue of the consent of the parties, but by virtue of an authority derived from the law of God. While the inherent authority of the new church courts in respect of disciplinary jurisdiction was not denied to the courts of the Church of Scotland, it has already been argued that the involvement of these courts in consistorial litigation prior to the appointment of the Commissaries of Edinburgh was held by the Commissaries to have been extra-ordinary and temporary, rather than inherent. Nevertheless, the suggestion from *Cunningham* was that prior to the appointment of the Commissaries of Edinburgh the superintendent at St Andrews considered himself to be in possession of an inherent authority vested in him by the law of God. Winram clearly held the jurisdiction emanating from this authority to encompass actions for adherence within the specific context of *Cunningham*, and the fact that he took cognisance of almost every other type of consistorial

---

[30] I.e. Shaw, *Acts and Proceedings*, i, 211.
[31] Dunbar, 'Early Record from the Synod of Fife', 234, item 19.
[32] *St Andrews*, i, 133, 10 December 1561.

action prior to the appointment of the Commissaries of Edinburgh brings with it the possibility that he believed such matters to fall within the competence of his office by virtue of an authority derived from the law of God. If this was Winram's position, it would help to explain why he proved resistant to a full acceptance of the consistorial jurisdiction of the Commissaries of Edinburgh, since he would not have viewed his consistorial jurisdiction as either extra-ordinary, nor its authority a result of some supervening cause. This theory would appear to fit with the evidence discussed below.

From the following it appears that Winram continued to take cognisance of actions for adherence and for solemnisation subsequent to the appointment of the Commissaries of Edinburgh, while the on-going activity of both Winram and the kirk session in respect of processes arising out of the staying of banns has already been noted. Yet at the same time Winram is not known to have heard any first or second instance actions for Protestant divorce on the ground of adultery subsequent to the appointment of the Commissaries of Edinburgh, notwithstanding the fact that the church courts at St Andrews were sometimes drawn into pronouncing sentences of divorce when adultery was proven before them within the context of other processes. The absence of first or second instance actions for Protestant divorce before Winram would have been a coherent position for him to have adopted following the appointment of the Commissaries of Edinburgh: as already discussed at the beginning of Chapter 6, it was Winram, together with John Spottiswoode, who gave in the General Assembly's July 1562 petition to Mary's Privy Council concerning the appointment of judges to hear actions of divorce. While it has been argued that the Privy Council took this as betokening consent of the General Assembly to an alteration of religion in respect of the creation of the commissary system, it is conceivable that Winram held that the General Assembly had consented only to the surrender of actions for divorce, and not actions for solemnisation and adherence, or processes arising out of the staying of banns. While this must remain a theory for want of further evidence, it does accord with the evidence provided by extant processes heard by the church courts at St Andrews following the appointment of the Commissaries of Edinburgh.

The last known disciplinary process with strong consistorial overtones to have been led before the superintendent's court at St Andrews prior to the appointment of the Commissaries of Edinburgh was *Sandelandis & Forbes*. This process was initiated by a delation alleging that one John Forbes would not adhere to his wife, Barbara Sandilands, and was as such an example not of litigation between parties but of an exercise of disciplinary jurisdiction. Forbes excepted that Sandilands had committed adultery with one William Hunter, and that as such he ought not to be compelled to adhere. Probation as to the adultery was led before the superintendent's court, to which end twenty witnesses were summoned and examined, their depositions still being extant. The alleged adultery with Hunter was duly proven, and the superintendent pronounced sentence on 8 December 1563, finding that Forbes would not be decerned to adhere and committing

Sandilands to the temporal magistrate, 'judge competent' in respect of the crime of adultery.[33]

Two months after this action, on 8 February 1563/4 the Commissaries of Edinburgh were appointed. On 8 March 1563/4 a cluster of disciplinary and consistorial processes were heard or commenced before the superintendent, and a week later further proceedings occurred with a direct bearing on *Sandelandis & Forbes*. Thus on 8 March 1563/4 a disciplinary action before the superintendent at St Andrews, *Bet & Anderson*, resulted in a couple accused of fornication confessing mutual promise of marriage, by virtue of which they were decerned to solemnise marriage.[34] On the same day a woman gave in a claim before the superintendent alleging irregular marriage with a man who had subsequently contracted marriage with a third party; the superintendent inhibited the man and his alleged second wife from cohabiting during the dependence of the action. Notwithstanding the fact that this process is incomplete, it arose out of actual litigation between parties before the superintendent.[35] And on the same day again, a couple were summoned before the superintendent to hear themselves decerned to adhere to one another (*Boswell & Wemyss*);[36] this exercise of disciplinary jurisdiction rapidly morphed into a consistorial action, and was the subject of subsequent litigation, *Boswell v. Wemyss*, before the Commissaries of Edinburgh, and further proceedings before the kirk session of St Andrews, as is discussed below at more length.

FORBES V. SANDILANDS

On 15 March 1563/4 superintendent Winram, with advice from the ministry, in a clear exercise of his disciplinary jurisdiction, decerned William Hunter – the adulterer in *Sandelandis & Forbes* – to compear before the congregation of the kirk of Kilconquhar on Sunday 11 April 1564, there to confess his offence of adultery upon his knees, to ask for God's mercy and to crave forgiveness of the congregation.[37] On 12 May 1564 John Forbes brought an action of Scottish Protestant divorce on the ground of Sandilands's adultery with Hunter before the Commissaries of Edinburgh, and in the event sentence was pronounced in Forbes's favour on 15 January 1564/5.[38] Forbes's allegation of adultery in *Forbes v. Sandilands* was admitted to his probation by interlocutor of the Commissaries of Edinburgh on 2 August 1564, at which diet were produced the 'sentence gevin be the superintendent and ministerie of Sanctandrois' in the process of adherence, together with

---

[33] *Sandelandis & Forbes*, 8 December 1563 (St Andrews, i, process from 156; depositions 160–167; sentence 167–168).

[34] *Bet & Anderson* (ibid., i, 188).

[35] *Tynchar v. Strang*, 8 to 22 March 1563/4 (ibid., i, 188–189; incomplete process).

[36] *Boswell & Wemyss*, 8 March 1563/4 to c.3 May 1564 (ibid., i, 207–212; incomplete process).

[37] *Huntar & Sandilands* (ibid., i, 190–191).

[38] For the diets in *Forbes v. Sandilands* see NRS, CC8/2/1, fos 18v–19r, 37r, 47v, 133v, 153v, 258v, 269r, 270v, 280r, 288r, 304v–305v (decreet). The decreet has been published in Green, *Consistorial Decisions*, item 6.

'the testificatioun of repentance maid be Williame Huntar in Balcarrois befoir the ministerie and congregatioun of Sanctandrois'.[39] Notwithstanding the production before the Commissaries of Edinburgh of two written pieces of evidence attesting to Barbara Sandilands's adultery with William Hunter, the Commissaries elected to admit the allegation of adultery to probation by witnesses, rather than by writ. Whether this was because Forbes insisted on being allowed to prove his libel by writ *and* deposition, or whether this was because the Commissaries declined to accept the written evidence as valid proof of adultery because it had arisen within the context of the disciplinary proceedings of a court of uncertain constitutional status, is not immediately clear.

Yet from the witnesses subsequently summoned and examined before the Commissaries of Edinburgh further insights may be gleaned. On the one hand, of those witnesses summoned before the Commissaries of Edinburgh who actually compeared and deponed on oath, four had already deponed before the superintendent's court in *Sandelandis & Forbes*. The depositions of those four witnesses are still extant in the registers of the church courts at St Andrews, from the tenor of which the adultery in question was clearly proven. Yet no attempt appears to have been made to have these depositions extracted from the registers kept by the new church courts at St Andrews and produced before the Commissaries. On the other hand, in addition to this process of re-examination of witnesses, several members of the superintendent's actual court, whose signatures had been appended to the superintendent's sentence in *Sandelandis & Forbes*, were summoned before the Commissaries of Edinburgh and examined as witnesses. These members of the superintendent's court, namely Master John Douglas, Rector of St Andrews, Master William Ramsay, Master of St Salvator's and elder in the kirk, and Master James Wilkie, elder and prominent member of the kirk of St Andrews, had not been witnesses in *Sandelandis & Forbes*.[40]

This process whereby witnesses in *Sandelandis & Forbes*, together with members of the superintendent's court before whom the process had been led, were summoned before the Commissaries of Edinburgh in *Forbes v. Sandilands* and examined on oath is suggestive. While it is not certain that the Commissaries were effectively declining to accept as valid disciplinary judgements of the new church courts, the examination of various members of the superintendent's court by the Commissaries of Edinburgh brings with it the suggestion that a jurisdictional point was being made. The presence of members of the superintendent's court in the actual Court of the Commissaries of Edinburgh, within the context of a consistorial action, must have impressed upon those members the fact that the Commissaries were now sitting in judgement in an action of Protestant divorce, which would formerly have been heard by the new church courts at St Andrews. At the same time, the summoning of the members of the superintendent's court

---

[39] NRS, CC8/2/1, fo. 133v; in respect of the delation mentioned in the MS, see *St Andrews*, i, 156.
[40] For the relevant citations in support of this paragraph, see Green, 'Court of the Commissaries', 87–88, where the case has already been discussed.

proceeded upon the apparent rejection of two disciplinary judgements of that court, which in turn suggests that the Commissaries may have entertained doubts as to the constitutional status of the new church courts. If they did entertain such doubts, it may help to explain why the three estates in Parliament deemed it necessary in December 1567 to enact the Church Jurisdiction Act. Be that as it may, if the Commissaries were trying to underscore the very fact of their appointment and their exclusive consistorial jurisdiction, it would appear that the lesson was heeded only in part, and that the on-going entanglement between disciplinary proceedings and consistorial judgements continued at St Andrews.

THE CONTINUED INTERPLAY OF DISCIPLINARY AND CONSISTORIAL JURISDICTIONS AT ST ANDREWS

During the dependence of *Forbes* v. *Sandilands* before the Commissaries of Edinburgh, various processes involving promises of marriage, solemnisation, adherence and adultery were heard by the church courts at St Andrews. During April and May 1564 the superintendent at St Andrews had taken cognisance of an action of adherence, *Bawerage* v. *Gylmore*. The defence of adultery was entered, together with an intimation that, should the same be proven, the remedy of divorce for adultery was desired. The pursuer confessed the adultery, yet was reconciled to the defender, and the litigants agreed to adhere. While there is a pastoral element in these proceedings, it had occurred as a result not of discipline but of litigation before the superintendent's court.[41] Adherence was again the outcome of proceedings before the superintendent's court in August 1564,[42] while in July 1564 the kirk session commanded a couple of solemnise marriage.[43] It is possible that both these last two processes arose out of an exercise of disciplinary jurisdiction, yet the outcomes were in effect consistorial sentences.

Subsequent to the proceedings found in *Forbes* v. *Sandilandis* before the Commissaries of Edinburgh, the intermingling of the disciplinary and consistorial jurisdictions appears to have continued at St Andrews. Thus several processes before the new church courts, which appear to have arisen out of an exercise of disciplinary jurisdiction, involved judgements involving irregular marriage,[44] solemnisation,[45] adherence[46] and licit non-adherence on the ground of adultery.[47]

The next three suchlike processes heard before the church courts of St Andrews, however, provide examples of more pronounced and at times convoluted

---

[41] *Bawerage* v. *Gylmore*, 19 April to 24 May 1564 (*St Andrews*, i, 192–193).
[42] *Nycholson & Efflek*, 2 August 1564 (ibid., i, 222; Winram); cf. Dunbar, *Reforming the Scottish Church*, 96.
[43] *Lyp & Scot*, 25 July to 2 August 1564 (*St Andrews*, i, 222–223).
[44] *Myllar & Lauder* (ibid., i, 244).
[45] *Smart & Scot* (ibid., i, 244; Winram).
[46] *Benns & Smyth* (ibid., i, 246; kirk session).
[47] *Scot & Wyliamson* (ibid., i, 246; Winram).

forays into consistorial matters. In June 1565 the superintendent's court decerned a couple to solemnise marriage on pain of excommunication, as the result of the pursuit of a claim of marriage;[48] so far as can be determined from the extant records, the proceedings appear to have been identical to the types of actions for solemnisation on the ground of *sponsalia per verba de futuro cum copula subsequente* then being heard by the Commissaries of Edinburgh.[49]

During the course of October 1565 the superintendent's court became entangled in a complex process involving two alleged irregular marriages contracted by the same woman. The original intention of the superintendent's proceedings had again been to consider an accusation of fornication made against a couple, that is to say, the process began as an exercise of disciplinary jurisdiction. The couple were in the event found to be irregularly married, yet the wife, presently with child, had subsequently contracted a second irregular marriage with a third party, which third party pleaded ignorance of the earlier marriage. This second marriage was held to be invalid, with the consequence that the wife to the first marriage had committed adultery. On the ground of this adultery, sentence of Scottish Protestant divorce was in effect pronounced in respect of the first marriage. After all three persons involved in the process had made public satisfaction for their faults, the original husband and wife, although divorced, were reconciled, and subsequently solemnised marriage together.[50] This process can be taken to highlight one of the potential dangers of failing to properly differentiate the disciplinary from the consistorial jurisdiction: whatever had motivated the court to reach these judgements, from the perspective of consistorial law they were convoluted and confused. In this, a simple attempt to punish fornicators had raised issues concerning irregular marriage, bigamy, annulment, divorce for adultery, licence to marry and, by extension, legitimacy. On 12 December 1565 a not dissimilar foray into matters consistorial occurred, again within the context of discipline. On that occasion a couple were delated for adultery before one of the church courts at St Andrews: the adultery was duly proven, as a result of which a sentence of Protestant divorce was also pronounced, in respect of the irregular marriage of the adulterer.[51] In both these cases, no attempt was made to remit any parts of these processes to the Commissaries of Edinburgh once disciplinary proceedings had in effect morphed into consistorial actions.

In the aftermath of these processes, it may well have been the case that the reputation of the church courts at St Andrews for defining the jurisdictional boundaries between disciplinary and consistorial actions in a manner not entirely in conformity with the appointment of the Commissaries of Edinburgh was becoming well known. At some point between July 1565 and April

---

[48] *Rynd v. Gardinar* (ibid., i, 247).
[49] E.g. Green, *Consistorial Decisions*, items 2, 5 etc.
[50] *Ledop, Russell & Kyninmouth*, 24 October 1565 (*St Andrews*, i, 252–254; Winram).
[51] *Duplyn & Angus; Smyth v. Duplyn?* (ibid., i, 254–255).

1566 the queen and her second husband, Lord Darnley, appear to have issued ordinances throughout the kingdom by which their lieges and subjects were expressly prohibited from usurping any jurisdiction previously exercised by spiritual judges;[52] and in the two subsequent, relevant processes brought before the new church courts at St Andrews, explicit arguments as to the jurisdiction of the Commissaries of Edinburgh were actually advanced within the context of litigation.

KAY V. ARNOT

The first such process, *Kay v. Arnot*, arose out of the staying of banns before the kirk of Crail. The stayer alleged prior promise of marriage with one of the parties whose banns had been proclaimed. The kirk session of Crail determined on 8 December 1565 that, for various technical reasons, the alleged promise of marriage by which the banns had been stayed could not be proven. The kirk session of Crail therefore determined that the stayed banns might continue to be proclaimed, and put the stayer to silence. The silenced stayer of the banns appealed to the superintendent's court at St Andrews. At a diet of the superintendent's court on 9 January 1565/6, representatives of the kirk session of Crail appeared before the court and alleged that 'bayth the contrackyng of mariaige and divorciment is provydit, be the King and Quenis Maieste and Secreit Consall, to be discussit and tried befoir the commissaris of Edinburgh, deput tharto, and tharfor the Superintendent nor his collegis, commissaris [depute be the General Kyrk][53] awcht nocht nor suld nocht sit nor proceid in this accion, nether concernyng the minister nor parteis'. The superintendent determined that the original sentence pronounced by the kirk session of Crail remained unreduced, but that he could not hear the case further, stating that the silenced stayer of the banns was free 'to apprev the said decreit or to perseu [sic] for reduccion tharof, as scho and hyr frendis sall think gud'.[54] This suggests that superintendent Winram thought that the sentence of the kirk session of Crail was capable of being reduced, but not by his court. The obvious court by which it could be reduced was that of the Commissaries of Edinburgh. Given the explicit argument made concerning the jurisdiction of the Commissaries of Edinburgh before the superintendent's court, it seems that Winram and his colleagues had been unwilling to repel that argument: perhaps it was one thing for the new church courts at St Andrews to delineate the bounds of their own jurisdictions, quite another to pass judgement on the jurisdiction of the Commissaries of Edinburgh.

---

[52] As is discussed more fully immediately below in respect of *Dalgleis & Wemyss*

[53] Literally *commissaris* in the text, but this was certainly a reference to "commissaris depute be the General Kyrk', who were among the members of the superintendent's court that day, rather than a reference to the Commissaries of Edinburgh.

[54] *Kay v. Arnot* (St Andrews, i, 257–260).

DALGLEIS & WEMYSS; BOSWELL V. WEMYSS

Nevertheless, as the second such process heard at St Andrews demonstrates, when a new church court at St Andrews was surer of its ground, it was prepared to repel arguments concerning the jurisdiction of the Commissaries of Edinburgh. During the winter of 1565–6 a process was led before the minister, elders and deacons of St Andrews against a couple delated before them for 'whoredom'. The couple in question, John Dalgleish and Janet Wemyss, had procreated a child without having solemnised marriage together, which left open the possibility that they were not necessarily fornicators, but perhaps rather irregularly married. The couple had also failed to present their child for baptism. While the second point concerning baptism was undoubtedly a matter for the kirk session, the first point concerning 'whoredom' actually had both disciplinary and consistorial overtones. The couple were summoned before the kirk session so that they might 'resave and underly disciplyn of the kirk' under the threat of excommunication.[55] The couple variously failed to appear before the kirk session, but prior to excommunication they entered defences, the first point of which sought to decline the jurisdiction of the kirk session, and to have the matter remitted to the Commissaries of Edinburgh. Both this declinatory exception and the kirk session's ground for repelling the same are still extant. It is remarkable that such a detailed level of argument about jurisdiction is still extant for any Scottish court during the era of the Reformation, let alone for the vexed question of the jurisdiction of the Church of Scotland over and against that of the old courts spiritual and the Commissaries of Edinburgh during those few short years between the appointment of the Commissaries of Edinburgh and the passage of the Church Jurisdiction Act of 1567.

In respect of these jurisdictional arguments, Dalgleish and Wemyss argued that the minister, elders and deacons of St Andrews were:

> na juge competent to cognosce in the said accione of delation, becaus thai ar mer layik and ignorant personis for the maist pairt, havand na commissione or power gevyn to thaim be our Sowerane Lord and Lady [i.e. Mary and Lord Darnley] or thar Session, nor ony other ordinary juge havand power to gyf the sammyn; bot gyf ony power thai have, the sammyn is ane usurpit power and autorite tane at thar awyne handis, makand dirogacion to other ordinarie jurisdiccione, in hie contempt of the King and Quenis Maiesties autorite, and expres aganis thar ordinancis and inhibicionis latyle mayd, statut, and publist, be oppyn proclamacion, at the marcat croces of all burrowis and citeis wythin the reallm: That nan thar lieges nor subjectis suld tak upon hand or usurp ony jurisdiccion of thais causis, quhilk wes wont to be tretit, cognoscit and decidit befoir be the spirituall jugis. Lyikas this pretendit caus and utheris siclyik war wont, in all tym bypast, to be treatit and decidit befoir tham, as ordinarie jugis, tharto havand sufficient power, bayth of the spirituall and civil magistrat to that effect and be tham apprevit, be the lawis of this realm and actis of Parliament maid thairupon, standand as yit unrevocat, reducit, or tane away be ony contrar statut or law, be ony havand

---

[55] *Dalgleis & Wemyss* (ibid., i, 260).

power to do the sammyn. And sua the saidis pretendit minister, eldaris and diaconis of this citie, being bot certan pryvay and ignorant personis for the maist part, ar na wyis jugis competent to cognosce in this caus, havand na power tharto, as said is, bot onlye usurpit in hie contempt of the King and Quenis Maiesties autorite and utheris mennis jurisdiccione, *mittentes falcem in messem alienam*. And tharfor the saidis M. Ihon and Jonat awcht and suld be remittit to thar jugis ordinar and competent in this caus, vidz., the commissaris of Edinburgh, quhai ar speciall deput to that effect . . .[56]

While the phrasing and organisation of this defence is not as clear as it might be, the general construct of the argument is clear: (i) the matter presently before the kirk session of St Andrews would previously have been heard by a pre-Reformation spiritual judge; (ii) nothing had been done in 'statute or law' to alter the ordinary jurisdiction of spiritual judges; (iii) the kirk session of St Andrews has received no authorisation to hear the present action, either from Mary and Darnley, or from their 'Session'; (iv) therefore the kirk session was attempting to exercise a usurped jurisdiction in contempt of the sovereign power; (v) the present action ought to be remitted forthwith to the Commissaries of Edinburgh, being judges 'specially depute' to that effect. The general construct of this argument accords with the explanation offered in Chapters 5 and 6 in respect of the response first of the Lords of Council and Session and second of the commissioners appointed in December 1563 in respect of the problem of the spiritual jurisdiction following the Reformation crisis.

From this evidence there also seems no reason to doubt that Mary and Darnley had recently issued ordinances and inhibitions forbidding any person from taking cognisance of any actions which used to be heard by spiritual judges: in this respect it would appear that, at some point between the queen's second marriage in July 1565 and the advancing of these argument in April 1566, Mary's government had thought it needful to publicly forbid any person in effect to usurp the spiritual jurisdiction. Such public proclamations may explain the appearance of jurisdictional arguments among the records of the church courts at St Andrews in respect of *Kay v. Arnot* and *Dalgleis & Wemyss*.

Despite the cogency of the argument advanced by Dalgleis and Wemyss, it was repelled by the kirk session of St Andrews '. . . in respect of the generall proclamacion of owr Soweran, set furth in approbacione of owr relegion fundyn at hyr Gracis arryvall to stand, the sam standing undischargit; and that disciplin is ane part of owr relegion, and we in possession tharof at our Soweranis arryvall, to quhom we ar obedient subjectis and na usurparis of autorete'.[57] The argument that the Kirk's disciplinary jurisdiction was protected by the Proclamation of Leith was undoubtedly a persuasive one: certainly there is no evidence that it was ever seriously challenged following the Reformation crisis. Whether the process before them was purely disciplinary in the event proved to be another

---

[56] *Dalgleis & Wemyss* (ibid., i, 267–270, 27 April 1566).
[57] *Dalgleis & Wemyss* (ibid., i, 270; kirk session).

matter. Nevertheless, in adopting this position, the kirk session prudently avoided engaging too closely with the contents of the declinatory exception, including addressing the argument concerning the on-going validity of 'the laws of this realm and Acts of Parliament made thereupon' in favour of pre-Reformation spiritual judges. McNeill has noted that James Balfour, in his *Practicks*, held pre-Reformation statutes concerning the Church still to be in force, 'subject to the abolition of the mass and papal jurisdiction',[58] and that he also retained the decisions which related 'to the spiritual judges and the jurisdiction of bishops', notwithstanding the fact that such decisions were all pre-Reformation.[59]

While the ancillary litigation and processes, both disciplinary and consistorial, surrounding this particular affair are highly complex, it proved to be the case that Dalgleish and Wemyss were eventually married, their banns being ordained to be proclaimed by the kirk session of St Andrews on 26 April 1570.[60] The main impediment to their marriage, that Wemyss was allegedly married to one Robert Boswell, was cleared following an action of adherence brought by Boswell against Wemyss before the Commissaries of Edinburgh. The Commissaries assoilzied Wemyss from this action on 26 March 1568, having determined that the litigants were not married. Probation in this action had been led in part before William Skene, Commissary of St Andrews, by virtue of a commission from the Commissaries of Edinburgh.[61] This decreet was subsequently produced before the kirk session of St Andrews, on the basis of which the aforementioned banns were ordained to be proclaimed. In this respect, notwithstanding the assertion of disciplinary jurisdiction by the kirk session over and against arguments advanced to the effect that the Commissaries of Edinburgh were judges competent in the vexed question of whether or not Dalgleish and Wemyss were living in 'whoredom', it was not until the Commissaries of Edinburgh pronounced judgement as to Wemyss's marital status that the matter was finally resolved before the kirk session. In this respect it would appear that while the kirk session had been correct in asserting that its disciplinary jurisdiction was protected by the Proclamation of Leith, it is not clear that the kirk session's attempt to discipline Dalgleish and Wemyss was a matter of discipline only, raising as it did consistorial questions eventually resolved by the Commissaries of Edinburgh. As such, this entire sequence of processes illustrates both the competence of a kirk session's disciplinary jurisdiction in respect of the Proclamation of Leith and the constitutional basis of the Commissaries' consistorial jurisdiction, together with the protracted difficulties involved in clearly differentiating the two.

While it might be supposed that the detailed jurisdictional arguments advanced in *Kay v. Arnot* and *Dalgleis & Wemyss* would have led to a renewed effort on the

---

[58] It will be noted that Balfour compiled his *Practicks* after the ratification of the Papal Jurisdiction Act and Mass Act in December 1567.
[59] *Balfour's Practicks*, i, xliv.
[60] *St Andrews*, i, 334.
[61] Green, *Consistorial Decisions*, item 33, *Boswell v. Wemyss*.

part of the church courts at St Andrews to more fully delineate their disciplinary jurisdiction over and against the consistorial jurisdiction of the Commissaries of Edinburgh, the at times bewildering interplay between the two jurisdictions continued. Thus delations for fornication continued to involve determinations as to marital status,[62] including what were in effect sentences of solemnisation being pronounced by the superintendent's court.[63] Determinations as to marital status also continued to be made in the superintendent's court within or outwith the context of the staying of banns,[64] and also before the kirk session,[65] with attendant sentences of solemnisation, or of absolvitor. On another occasion a process involving claims of marriage on the ground of deflowered virginity appears to have morphed into an exercise of disciplinary jurisdiction in the superintendent's court.[66] And on another occasion the superintendent, styled 'juge in the cause of adherence', decerned a couple to be married and therefore to adhere to one another, pronouncing sentence 'in our consistoriall place, wythin the parrochie kyrk of the cite of Sanctandrois'.[67]

At this point in proceedings there is a break in the extant register for St Andrews, which resumes once more only in respect of disciplinary and consistorial processes from March 1567/8, and then the extant register is considerable more fragmented as to its content. In the interim the Reformation had entered its more discernably magisterial phase and many of the legal considerations which had pertained during the personal reign of Mary where obviated by the overthrow of her personal reign and by the legislation of the 'second' Reformation Parliament. While Mary had effectively been deposed, she had technically abdicated and approved the appointment of her illegitimate half-brother, the leading Lord of the Congregation, Lord James Stewart, by then Earl of Moray, as regent during the minority of Mary's infant son James VI.[68] The three estates in Parliament were duly summoned, the principal legislation of the Reformation Parliament re-enacted,[69] Moray's regency confirmed[70] and new legislative provisions made in various respects, including the finances of the Protestant Kirk, litigation concerning benefices, the ecclesiastical jurisdiction of the new church courts, marriage law, fornication and the imposition of a religious test for public offices.[71]

---

[62] *Fayrfull & Cunnyne* (St Andrews, i, 276–277).
[63] *Skaythlok & Watson* (ibid., i, 277–278).
[64] *Beton v. Arnot* (ibid., i, 278–281); *Ogylwy v. Clark* (ibid., i, 283).
[65] *Gedde & Suntar* (ibid., i, 280–281).
[66] *Huntar v. Skyrling* (ibid., i, 278).
[67] *Cristeson & Lyndesay* (ibid., i, 284–293).
[68] Mary abdicated on 24 July 1567 and her son, James VI, was crowned at Stirling on 29 July 1567; James Stewart accepted the regency on 22 August 1567.
[69] RPS, 1567/12/1-4.
[70] RPS, 1567/12/105.
[71] I.e. RPS, 1567/12/6; 1567/12/9; 1567/12/35; 1567/12/11; 1567/12/15; 1567/12/13; 1567/12/8 respectively.

CHURCH JURISDICTION ACT 1567

Within the context of the second legal framework considered in Chapter 2, the disciplinary jurisdiction of the new church courts had clearly been held by the kirk session of St Andrews to be acknowledged and protected by the Proclamation of Leith (*Dalgleis & Wemyss*). Although the courts of the Church of Scotland laid claim to the consistorial jurisdiction of the old courts spiritual from 1559, the General Assembly appears to have in effect consented to the same to be transmitted to new commissary courts, again within the context of the second legal framework. Yet at the same time the Court of Session appears to have been content to continue to acknowledge papal jurisdiction in respect of appeals pending before papal judges delegate, while the Commissaries of Edinburgh appear to have countenanced as valid a sentence pronounced by a papal judge delegate in 1565. In addition, the archbishop of St Andrews continued to exercise his legatine jurisdiction in consistorial matters, and the events of the winter 1566–7 had demonstrated that the restoration of the spiritual jurisdiction to the old hierarchy was still a possibility. These 'uncertainties' were considerably lessened by the re-enactment of the Papal Jurisdiction Act on 15 December 1567 and by the enactment of the Church Jurisdiction Act on the same day. The latter Act expressly granted an ecclesiastical jurisdiction to the Church of Scotland and declared '. . . that thair is na uther face of kirk nor uther face of religioun than is presentlie, be the favour of God, establischeit within this realme; and that thair be na uther jurisdiction ecclesiasticall acknawlegeit within this realme uther than that quhilk is, and salbe, within the same kirk, or that quhilk flowis thairfra . . .'[72]

On the one hand, this clause of the 1567 Act decisively precluded any form of continued exercise of spiritual jurisdiction by the hierarchy of the Catholic Church, such as had occurred during Mary's personal reign, and also, by stressing the exclusivity of the ecclesiastical jurisdiction of the Kirk, this clause could be construed as having indirectly regularised the legal position in respect of the suppressed courts of the pre-Reformation Officials and Commissaries. Yet on the other hand, the statute does not appear to have intended to deny that the new commissary courts exercised the old spiritual jurisdiction. Thus in 1592 an Act of Parliament, whereby the original appointment of the Commissaries of Edinburgh and the inferior commissaries was ratified, narrated that at the time of the Reformation 'the jurisdictioun ecclesiasticall belanging to the officiallis of auld . . . wes divolvit in the commissaris chosin and nominat be oure soverane lordis darrest mother' which commissaries therefore administered a 'jurisdictioun in spirituall caus[es]' which was 'of the same force and auctoritie with the jurisdictioun of the saidis officiallis to quhome thai succedit'.[73] At around the same time as the passage of this 1592 Act, Thomas Craig of Riccarton, who procured before

---

[72] RPS, A1567/12/11.
[73] RPS, 1592/4/86.

the Court of the Commissaries of Edinburgh during the era of the Reformation, styled the Commissaries 'ecclesiastical judges' and 'judges of the Christianity' in his celebrated *Ius Feudale*.[74] In these respects, it would appear that the Church Jurisdiction Act stressed the exclusivity of the ecclesiastical jurisdiction of the Church of Scotland solely in respect of courts convened by the Church, and was not subsequently construed either by Parliament, or by so celebrated a lawyer as Craig, as defining the nature and constitutional provenance of the jurisdiction of the commissary courts.[75]

The problem of defining and delineating the ecclesiastical jurisdiction of the courts of the Church of Scotland was clearly understood by the three estates in 1567 to be a problem of sufficient complexity to warrant further consideration. While the 1567 Act stated that the Kirk's ecclesiastical jurisdiction '. . . consistis and standis in preicheing of the trew word of Jesus Christ, correctioune of maneris and administratioun of haly sacramentis . . .',[76] the task of actually defining the Kirk's ecclesiastical jurisdiction, presumably in respect of the rest of the Scottish legal system, and in particular the new commissary courts, was entrusted to a group of commissioners appointed by the Act. The first-named parliamentary commissioner was Sir James Balfour of Pittendreich, last Official of Lothian, and former 'chief' Commissary of Edinburgh, who just nine days prior to the passage of the Act had been appointed Lord President of the Court of Session.[77] Among the officers of state appointed to the commission were to be found the ubiquitous James MacGill of Nether Rankeillour and Sir John Bellenden of Auchnoul, together with William Maitland of Lethington. In this there was a strong continuity with the December 1563 commission which had proposed the new commissary system: in fact, only Sir Richard Maitland and Henry Sinclair were absent, and, while Maitland was still alive, Sinclair had died in 1565. The ministry of the Church of Scotland, so conspicuously absent from the December 1563 commission, was well represented on the 1567 parliamentary commission, among whose number were the ministers of Edinburgh, John Knox and John Craig, together with superintendents Spottiswoode and Erskine of Dun, and David Lindsay, minister of Leith. The conspicuous absence from this parliamentary commission, whether by design or otherwise, was superintendent Winram. These commissioners were expressly enjoined by the 1567 Act 'to seirche furth mair speciallie and to considder quhat uther speciall pointis or clausis sould appertene to the jurisdictioun, privilege and authoritie of the said kirk, and to declair thair myndis thairanentis to my lord regent and thre estatis of this realme at the nixt parliament, swa that thay may

---

[74] Craig, *Ius Feudale*, trans. and ed. Dodd, 82–85.

[75] This view is further confirmed by Sir Thomas Hope's consideration of the jurisdiction of the commissary courts within the context of the Jacobean episcopate (*Hope's Major Practicks*, ed. Clyde, ii, 49).

[76] RPS, A1567/12/11.

[77] The Church Jurisdiction Act passed on 15 December 1567, Balfour having been appointed Lord President on 6 December (Brunton and Haig, *Historical Account*, 112).

tak ordour thairintill and authoreis the samin be act of parliament, as salbe fund aggreabill to the word of God'.[78]

Within less than two weeks of the appointment of this parliamentary commission, on 26 December 1567, the General Assembly appointed various 'brethren . . . to concur at all time with such persons of parliament or secret council as my lord regent's grace has nominated for such affairs as pertain to the Kirk and the jurisdiction thereof'. Those accordingly appointed included Knox, Craig, Erskine of Dun and Spottiswoode, together with 'Mr David Lindsay, minister of Leith; George Hay, minister of Rathven; and John Row, minister of St Johnston'.[79] While many of those appointed out of the ministry were already on the parliamentary commission, and, moreover, had been active within the consistorial jurisdiction prior to the appointment of the Commissaries of Edinburgh, John Winram was again conspicuous by his absence. Little progress appears to have been made by the parliamentary commission, with various articles being presented by the General Assembly to Regent Moray in 1568 and 1569 to the effect that progress should be made by the commission.[80] It would appear that little or no progress was ever made: several years later the General Assembly appointed various persons 'for making an overture on the policy and jurisdiction of the Kirk',[81] while in 1579 Parliament effectively re-enacted the Church Jurisdiction Act and thereby appointed another parliamentary commission concerning the jurisdiction of the Kirk.[82]

If the parliamentary commission of 1567 ever met to deliberate on these questions, there appears to be no record of it, and it is much to be regretted that no recommendations appear to have been made to the three estates. The apparent failure of the 1567 commission could conceivably have been a matter of policy in and of itself, in that in the absence of any statutory guidance on the precise delineation of the ecclesiastical jurisdiction of the courts of the Church of Scotland, the matter was left to the discretion of Scottish judges. Given the fact that jurisdictional relations between the commissary courts and the courts of the Church of Scotland had passed without mention in the charter of constitution of the Commissaries of Edinburgh, with the result that such matters were left to the discretion of the first Commissaries to determine on a case-by-case basis, the 1567 commission may have deemed it advisable to allow such an approach to continue to be adopted. In this respect the parliamentary commission would have avoided direct engagement with the problem of delineating the 'exclusive' ecclesiastical jurisdiction of the new church courts and the jurisdiction of the new Commissaries, 'ecclesiastical judges' administering the spiritual jurisdiction of the old Catholic Commissaries and Officials. Whether intended or not on the part of

---

[78] RPS, A1567/12/11.
[79] Shaw, *Acts and Proceedings*, i, 145.
[80] Ibid., i, 161, 184–185.
[81] Ibid., i, 430–431, April 1576.
[82] RPS, 1579/10/22.

the 1567 commission, in the event the jurisdiction of the courts of the Church of Scotland was further defined through a series of cases involving the Commissaries of Edinburgh, and, although the process was not without conflict, such conflict was limited to relations between courts and judges, rather than being a broader conflict involving debates about the future of the commissary courts and internal debates within the Church of Scotland concerning its initial assumption of the consistorial jurisdiction.

ST ANDREWS AND THE COMMISSARIES OF EDINBURGH POST-1567

Within the context of the legislation of the second Reformation Parliament, the Church Jurisdiction Act may be viewed as part of the legislative programme of the magisterial Reformation in Scotland, whereby the Catholic ascendancy was brought decisively to an end, and the Protestant ascendancy was put on an enduring constitutional and legal footing. With the re-enactment of the principal legislation of August 1560 by the 1567 Parliament, the manifest problems which had attended the legislation of the Reformation Parliament were resolved, and the remarkable set of constitutional and legal contexts which had applied during Mary's personal reign were brought to an end: from the time of that Parliament, no exercises of papal jurisdiction may be found among the extant evidence. Within the context of the Court of the Commissaries of Edinburgh, the final abrogation of papal authority appears to have had a subtle effect as to Canon law. While the law of the Commissaries remained pre-Tridentine Canon law – with the exception of divorce for adultery, and the reduction of the forbidden degrees of consanguinity and affinity by statute in 1567 – the pre-December 1567 practice of citing directly the Decretals of Gregory IX in litigation appears to have fallen out of favour.[83] Yet although the conditions experienced during Mary's personal reign no longer applied, the post-1567 Protestant ascendancy in Scotland fell heir to various provisions made within the context of those conditions, most obviously the new commissary system and the vexed question of the jurisdictional consequences of the existence of those courts for the jurisdiction of the courts of the Church of Scotland.

As to the specific consequences of the Church Jurisdiction Act 1567 in respect of relations between the new commissary system and the new church courts, little discernible effect may be observed. Rather, those patterns of jurisdictional definition, co-operation and conflict observed prior to December 1567 were allowed to continue to develop. The evidence for the co-ordination of the procedures and jurisdictions of the Protestant Kirk and Commissaries in respect of the staying of banns has already been discussed for the pre- and post-December 1567 periods: while the proclamation of banns and the solemnisation of marriage pertained to the Kirk, actions arising out of the staying of banns fell to be determined by the

---

[83] Green, *Consistorial Decisions*, xliv–xlv; at some as yet undetermined point prior to the second half of the seventeenth century such citations came back into fashion (for which see *Lord Hermand's Consistorial Decisions*, ed. Walton, xv ff.),

commissary courts, yet within this context the church courts at St Andrews continued to be the exception to the rule.

While there is perhaps an inherent danger that the unique survival of evidence from St Andrews has a tendency to create a skewed vision of the extent of this 'St Andrews exceptionalism', several factors tend to mitigate this danger. Within the context of the staying of banns, for which there is tolerable evidence for a range of kirk sessions, St Andrews is the exception; the extant evidence from St Andrews demonstrates that the approach taken by the kirk session of Jedburgh in *Hardy v. Rutherford* (1565) was not widely followed at St Andrews; the unique approach of the Commissaries of Edinburgh in *Forbes v. Sandilands* (1564/5) concerned St Andrews; and, at the end of the period under consideration in this chapter, a consistorial sentence pronounced by the court of the superintendent at St Andrews became the only consistorial sentence pronounced by a new church court following the appointment of the Commissaries of Edinburgh to be reduced on the ground of incompetence. In the light of these unique features, the church courts at St Andrews do appear to have consistently sought to define and defend their own jurisdictions, rather than to have allowed the bounds of the same to be defined solely by the Commissaries of Edinburgh.

The evidence from St Andrews for the post-1567 period contains various features already noted for the preceding period. There continued to be a lack of clarity within the registers both as to whether processes were initially an exercise of discipline following a delation, or actual litigation following the giving in of a complaint or libel, and as to the court by which such processes were being heard. Yet notwithstanding these problems, the interplay between disciplinary and consistorial matters continued to be a pronounced feature of the record. All the processes of note for this period appear to concern adherence or solemnisation, with the usual attendant issues of promises of marriage, deflowered virginity and fornication, and arose either out of actual pursuit of one party by another before a church court at St Andrews, or out of disciplinary proceedings, or on account of the staying of banns. In various instances it is unclear as to whether processes occurred because of litigation between parties or because of exercises of discipline,[84] yet on occasion litigation certainly took place: thus on 6 July 1569 a couple were litigating before one of the church courts at St Andrews, and on that occasion the defender was held to pay the pursuer a tochir, or dowry, since he had deflowered her virginity.[85] Litigation before the court of the superintendent on the ground of deflowered virginity is also known to have occurred.[86]

---

[84] *Wallace & Hakstoun*, 10 March 1567/8 (*St Andrews*, i, 294; Winram); *Walcar & Dayis* (ibid., i, 295; kirk session).
[85] *Walcar v. Dayis* (*St Andrews*, i, 322); similar litigation, with distinct disciplinary aspects, concerning solemnisation on the ground of deflowered virginity appears to have occurred before the kirk session in December 1571 to January 1571/2 (*Gibsoun & Kenlowly* (ibid., i, 357–359)).
[86] *Wallace v. Rymour* (*St Andrews*, i, 308) and *Bruce & Geddie* (ibid., i, 337–338); cf. *Rauff v. Nicholsoun* (ibid., i, 313) and *Jamesoun v. Staig* (ibid., i, 316–317), although in neither of these last two cases is litigation certain.

The subsequent activity of the church courts at St Andrews was particularly pronounced in respect of disciplinary proceedings or litigation which resulted in couples being decerned to adhere to one another,[87] or to solemnise marriage,[88] with the majority of these processes falling to the superintendent's court. In January 1569/70 the superintendent brought two separate actions by virtue 'of his office' against two specific couples for adherence, although neither process is complete.[89] While these processes proceeded by virtue of exercises of disciplinary jurisdiction, they are not dissimilar to processes brought by the procurator fiscal of the Court of the Commissaries of Edinburgh.[90] The second process, *Winram v. Beton & Leslye*, dragged on for at least several months, during the course of which Beatrix Leslie alleged that she ought not to adhere to her husband, David Beaton of Creich, because she had an action of divorce on the ground of adultery in dependence before the Commissaries of Edinburgh.[91] At the next diet assigned Winram was absent, by reason of which it was noted in the register that 'the cause slepis'.[92]

Processes before the new church courts involving divorce on the ground of adultery are conspicuous by their absence during the post-1567 period. While no actions for divorce on the ground of adultery are known to have been pursued before the church courts at St Andrews following the appointment of the Commissaries of Edinburgh, it was the case that, between the appointment of the Commissaries of Edinburgh and the passage of the Church Jurisdiction Act, the church courts at St Andrews did deal with divorce for adultery, but apparently only as an indirect consequence of processes commenced before them for other reasons. That even such indirect forays into this aspect of the consistorial jurisdiction ceased to occur at St Andrews after 1567 may reflect some conscious decision on the part of the church courts there, or may represent nothing more than the fact that no processes at St Andrews indirectly raised the matter of adultery, and thus by extension divorce.

As has already been noted above, the absence of actions for divorce for adultery at St Andrews, yet the continued occurrence of processes involving adherence and solemnisation, might be explained in so far as Winram may have taken the view that the erection of the commissary courts had overstepped the limits of the consent of the General Assembly granted in 1562. This line of thought provides an at least plausible explanation for the activity of the new church courts at St Andrews. In any event, after 1567 Winram clearly continued to hold himself competent to repeatedly decern couples to solemnise marriage,

---

[87] *Galbraitht & Brown* (ibid., i, 308); *Rait & Inglis* (ibid., i, 311–313, 345–346, 347; 308–309).
[88] *Wilson v. Gourlay* (St Andrews, i, 298–301); *Alexander & Wischart* (ibid., i, 299–300); *Gairdnar & Scott* (ibid., i, 307); *Smytht v. Thomson* (ibid., i, 315, 315–316, 321–322); *Dischingtoun & Calland* (ibid., i, 318–319 and 321); *Skirling & Lamb* (ibid., i, 318); *Schewes & Dikesoun* (ibid., i, 361).
[89] *Winram v. Wemis & Trail*; *Winram v. Beton & Leslye* (ibid., i, 327–328, 340).
[90] Green, *Consistorial Decisions*, items 1, 137, 163; Green, 'Court of the Commissaries', 45–46.
[91] Leslie successfully pursued Beaton for divorce before the Commissaries of Edinburgh, although decreet was not pronounced until June 1575 (Green, *Consistorial Decisions*, item 158); the initial diet in that action has not been located.
[92] *Winram v. Beton & Leslye* (St Andrews, i, 331–332, 340, 341).

including as a result of litigation before his court. Whatever efforts had been made by the Commissaries of Edinburgh to assert their consistorial jurisdiction in respect of St Andrews, the records of a synod convened by Winram around 1570 further confirm that the superintendent still held firm to his own understanding of his jurisdiction. In addition to synodal statutes concerning matters falling within the compass of the ordinary parochial functions of kirks, or of the disciplinary jurisdiction, are to be found statutes concerning matters falling within the compass of the consistorial jurisdiction. Among this group of statutes are to be found synodal provisions concerning: the necessity of obtaining from 'the kirk' what was in effect a declarator of freedom from a prior promise of marriage within the context of the proclamation of banns; procedures concerning the probation of secret promises of marriage upon which were predicated irregular marriages; and a fragmentary act concerning the solemnisation of marriage or the provision of a dowry on the ground of deflowered virginity.[93] In addition, and as already noted towards the beginning of this chapter, the same synod maintained that objections by which the proclamation of banns were stayed in any given parish kirk within their jurisdiction might competently be resolved either by the kirk session of the parish in question or by the 'superintendent and ministry of St Andrews'. The conception of the jurisdiction of the Kirk underpinning these synodal statutes may have enjoyed support beyond Fife: on 6 March 1571/2 the General Assembly framed certain articles concerning the jurisdiction of the Kirk to be submitted to the regent and Privy Council, article six stating that 'because the conjunction of marriages pertains to the ministry, the causes of adherences and divorcements ought also to pertain to them, as naturally annexed thereto'.[94]

JOHNSTON V. MORRIS; MORRIS V. JOHNSTON & WINRAM

In addition to such instances already noted, one final example of Winram pronouncing a sentence of solemnisation as a result of litigation is known, not from the extant records of the church courts of St Andrews, but from its reduction by the Commissaries of Edinburgh. The sentence in question, *Johnston v. Morris*, is in fact the last known sentence of solemnisation pronounced by the court of the superintendent of Fife, Fotherick and Strathearn, being pronounced at St Andrews on 8 February 1571/2. The superintendent's court at St Andrews is though to have officially come to an end with the consecration of John Douglas as Archbishop of St Andrews,[95] which occurred on 10 February 1571/2.[96]

Clearly discontent with the sentence pronounced by Winram in *Johnston v. Morris*, the defender in that action, Morris, pursued Johnston and Winram before the Commissaries of Edinburgh for reduction of the original sentence of

---

[93] Dunbar, 'Early Record from the Synod of Fife', 228, item 2; 232, item 14; 227, item N.
[94] Shaw, *Acts and Proceedings*, i, 231.
[95] Dunbar, *Reforming the Scottish Church*, 83.
[96] Watt and Murray, *Fasti*, 387.

solemnisation. This action, *Morris v. Johnston & Winram*, was not one of reduction on the ground of the appellate superiority of the Commissaries of Edinburgh over the superintendent at St Andrews, but rather one of reduction on the ground of the superintendent's incompetence to have pronounced the same. Specifically, Morris argued relevantly:

> that the said decreit is pronuncit & gevin be the said superintendent wranguslie, he na wayis being judge to cognosce or decerne thairintill, or ony sik actioun. In respect, mony zeris of befoir the pronunceing of the said pretendit decreit, thair was ane commissioun gevin be oure Soverane for that tyme, with the advis of the Lordis of Secreit Counsale, to the saidis Commissaris to cognosce in all sik actionis as solemnizatioun of mariage, adherence & dissolutioun of mariage, lik as thai have bene in vse continewalie sensyne to cognosce thairintill and all vther consistoriall causes, as only judge competent thairto. Quhair foir the said decreit, being pronuncit and gevin, as said is, be the said superintendent *cumque per non suum judicem*, aucht tobe reducit . . .[97]

The Commissaries of Edinburgh accepted this argument and accordingly reduced Winram's original sentence of solemnisation on 16 June 1572. While it may well have been that the opportunity afforded to the Commissaries by this case had been presented to them only because of Morris's desire to have the original sentence reduced, the opportunity was clearly taken. The period of exceptionalism at St Andrews therefore appears to have been brought to a close within less than a three-month period in 1572, both with the cessation of the superintendent's court, and with the explicit assertion by the Commissaries of Edinburgh in *Morris v. Johnston & Winram*, with the superintendent's court in full view, that the Commissaries were sole judges competent 'in all sik actionis as solemnizatioun of mariage, adherence & dissolutioun of mariage . . . and all vther consistoriall causes'.

CONCLUSION

The extent to which St Andrews was the exception to the rule of acceptance of the jurisdiction of the commissary courts must ultimately remain an open question. Nevertheless, it is clear from the example of St Andrews that defining the jurisdiction of the new church courts relative to the commissary courts was a vexed problem during the era of the Reformation. The creation of the commissary system had cut across the independent development of the jurisdiction of the courts of the Church of Scotland, and, while the jurisdiction of the Commissaries of Edinburgh in actions for divorce appears to have been fully accepted at St Andrews by the end of 1567, other aspects of the consistorial jurisdiction continued to be exercised by the new church courts there. On a practical level there

---

[97] Green, *Consistorial Decisions*, item 102, *Morris v. Johnston & Winram*.

was a simple and long-established procedure by which such jurisdictional conflicts could easily have been resolved. On the one hand, when the new church courts at St Andrews had been petitioned by a litigant seeking a remedy of adherence or solemnisation, such litigants could simply have been directed to the Commissaries of Edinburgh as judges competent in such causes. On the other hand, when consistorial questions arose within the context of an exercise of disciplinary jurisdiction, such disciplinary proceedings could simply have been sisted (i.e. paused), and the relevant questions remitted to the commissary courts for determination, following which determinations the sisted disciplinary processes could have been resumed. These were the normal procedures by which courts avoided jurisdictional conflicts, and both from the example of the remitting of questions concerning impediments to marriage alleged during the proclamation of banns from kirk sessions to the commissary courts, and from the parallel example of sheriffs remitting questions concerning legitimacy to the Commissaries of Edinburgh within the context of serving brieves of inquest,[98] it is clear that such procedures were well known to both the new church courts and the new commissary courts.

The fact that the church courts at St Andrews proved resistant to availing themselves of such procedures brings with it a suggestion that the consistorial jurisdiction of the Commissaries of Edinburgh was itself resisted by these courts. This in turn would indicate that the problem faced by those appointed by the General Assembly in 1564, or by Parliament in 1567, in respect of defining the jurisdiction of the courts of the Church of Scotland, failed to report because they were faced with the problem of contending conceptions of that jurisdiction, which ranged from being delineated by a full acceptance of the jurisdiction of the commissary courts, through to a limited acceptance of that jurisdiction in respect of actions for Protestant divorce arising outwith the context of disciplinary proceedings. Such an impasse appears to have been resolved only with time, with a slow and at times circumspect assertion of consistorial jurisdiction by the Commissaries of Edinburgh in respect of the church courts at St Andrews, culminating in 1572 with a direct rebuttal of the competence of the court of the superintendent at St Andrews in consistorial causes.

Within the context of the fact of the creation of the new commissary system, the decline of the consistorial jurisdiction of the courts of the Church of Scotland was logical, if not entirely inevitable. To what extent the limitation of the jurisdiction of the new church courts by the commissary courts continued to be a source of contention within the Kirk after 1572 has fallen beyond the scope of this present work to determine. From time to time there appear to have been murmurings within the Kirk concerning the jurisdiction of the commissary courts. In the *Second Book of Discipline* of 1578, among various items listed as abuses requiring reform, it was argued that 'the dependences also of this papisticall jurisdictioun ar to be abolishid of quhilk sort is the mingled jurisdictioun

---

[98] For which see ibid., lxiv.

of the commissaris in safar as thay mell with ecclesiasticall materis and have no commissioun of the kirk thairto, bot war erectit in tyme of our soveranis mother quhen thingis war out of order'.[99] While in 1581 the General Assembly commissioned some of the last men standing from the various commissions who had deliberated upon the jurisdiction of the courts of the Church of Scotland during the 1560s to confer 'anent the jurisdiction of the commissary of Edinburgh and wherein they meddle with the jurisdiction of the Kirk',[100] there is no evidence that any serious challenge was ever made to the jurisdictions of the commissary courts during the sixteenth century.

---

[99] *Second Book of Discipline*, ed. Kirk, 228; although this appears to have taken aim at the Commissaries of Edinburgh's beneficial, rather than consistorial, jurisdiction.
[100] Shaw, *Acts and Proceedings*, i, 638.

Conclusion

The history of the spiritual jurisdiction in Reformation Scotland can be considered as two histories often running in parallel to one another, particularly during the period 1559 to 1567. One history was driven and generated by the Protestant nobility and the Scottish reformers during the Reformation crisis. The other history was driven by a group of leading judges and officers of state who were often, although not invariably, judges of the Court of Session. While these two histories were not entirely mutually exclusive, they were to an extent contradictory.

The more 'radical' history had its genesis in the midst of the revolution of 1559 and its principal features were the wholesale abolition of the legal system of the Catholic Church in Scotland and the spiritual jurisdiction it administered, and the rapid development of a new system of Protestant church courts. This history was more driven by actual deeds and events than regulated by law. Not that legal provisions were absent for the process, as the 1559 ordinance of the 'Privy Council' against the Catholic church courts and the legislation of the Reformation Parliament demonstrate. However, within this history law and legal provision were not driving change, but rather seeking to give expression to alterations within the religion of the kingdom which were already occurring. Thus it would appear that the old church courts at St Andrews were suppressed during the summer of 1559 prior to the issuing of any ordinance against the same. By the same measure the process by which the celebration of Mass was widely suppressed was clearly in motion before given statutory expression in August 1560. Papal jurisdiction also must self-evidently have been rejected within the Protestant Kirk prior to the legislation of the Reformation Parliament. And clearly the courts of the Church of Scotland were in an advanced state of development long before their acknowledgement in statute law by virtue of the Church Jurisdiction Act.

In these respects, the use of law as a governor and regulator of reform was of secondary importance during the first phase of the Reformation: what really mattered was actual religious change. Once the primacy of religious change is recognised, the apocalyptic struggle of Protestants against the power of the Antichrist can be seen to have aimed at a radical overthrow of all aspects of medieval Catholicism and the establishment of a new Reformed Church in Scotland. In respect of spiritual jurisdictions and church courts, even where legal expression had been given to the revolution, it appears not to have been binding in respect of the actions of the Scottish reformers. While the 'Privy Council' ordinance of 1559 and the legislation of the Reformation Parliament appear to have envisaged the transfer of jurisdiction both from the native Catholic courts spiritual and from Rome to the Scottish temporal courts, this did not preclude the widespread development of a matrimonial jurisdiction, in addition to a disciplinary jurisdiction, within the courts of the Church of Scotland. This spontaneous development within the religious and legal life of the kingdom was quite simply something which was happening. While it might in part be described by law, and in part acknowledged and augmented by the Privy Councils active during the years encompassed by the 1563 Act of Oblivion, such recognition in law or by authority was of secondary importance.

In contrast, the other history of the spiritual jurisdiction in Reformation Scotland was dominated by considerations of law, since it proceeded out of the reactions and actions of judges. From the perspective of these judges, the deeper significance of the Reformation crisis was that it was a revolution by which the Scottish constitution and legal system had been thrown into confusion. The restoration of order within the legal system was, therefore, their principal concern.

This history of the restoration of order within the Scottish legal system has two discernible stages. The first stage concerned the assumption of the spiritual jurisdiction of the old church courts by the Court of Session in December 1560. The deliberations of the judges of the Court of Session in this respect were occasioned by and predicated upon an acceptance that the old church had 'ceased, or had been stopped by civil war, or by some other cause'. This acceptance did not proceed upon the basis of an acceptance by these judges of some provision contained in valid law. Neither the 1559 ordinance against the courts spiritual nor the legislation of the Reformation Parliament was regarded as law, and as such had no direct bearing upon the deliberations of the judges of the Court of Session. Such ordinances and statutes, though bereft of the force of law, were not, however, without significance for these judges, for they contained within them an indication of what the Protestant nobles and reformers would and would not accept in respect of the spiritual jurisdiction. One thing it appears that would be acceptable was some sort of transfer to, or assumption of, the spiritual jurisdiction by the temporal courts.

Although the actual armed conflict witnessed during the Wars of the Congregation had come to an end during the summer of 1560, and although an at least provisional government had been appointed in August 1560, the legal framework contained in the 'Concessions' had not come to pass. In this respect the Lords of Council and Session were in uncharted territory during the period August 1560 to August 1561, with no obvious framework within which to work. As far as these judges were concerned, nothing had been done in law by which the Scottish constitution had been altered, in respect both of the Catholic Church and royal government. There was therefore no basis in law to assert that the legal system of the Catholic Church had been abolished and its jurisdictions transferred to the Court of Session and other temporal courts. Yet, at the same time, Scotland had experienced a revolution, which by the winter of 1560 had proved successful. Within this context the judges of the Court of Session determined that they could, as a temporary expedient, hear such spiritual causes as ordinarily fell to be heard by the old Commissaries and Officials. In apparent contrast, appeals pending before papal judges delegate were to be allowed to run their course, except where practical problems attended such appeals continuing to be heard.

The second stage concerned the lawful transfer of all causes formerly decided by ordinary spiritual judges appointed by the prelates of the Scottish Church to a new system of commissary courts. This lawful transfer proceeded upon the recommendation of a group of judges of the Court of Session who had been commissioned to that end by Mary's Privy Council in December 1563. Within the context of Mary's personal reign these commissioners enjoyed the benefit of a legal framework created in response to the Reformation crisis within which they could make decisions. In this respect, the Proclamation of Leith of August 1561 and the Act of Oblivion of June 1563 provided a legal context in which to act. The consequences of the revolution were accepted in law, although the revolution itself had not been sanctioned by law. Judicial consideration of the details of the actions of those by whom the revolution had been effected had been consigned in law to oblivion and extinguished for ever. Within this legally valid framework, the earlier reasoning of the judges of the Court of Session in December 1560 essentially held good, in that the December 1563 commissioners were obliged to accept as given the consequences of the revolution in respect of the suppression of the old church courts. Yet, at the same time, their reasoning that nothing had been done in law whereby the ordinary spiritual jurisdiction of the Scottish episcopate and other prelates of the kingdom had been abolished also held good. As to the 1559 ordinance concerning the old church courts and the 1560 legislation concerning the spiritual jurisdiction, these were still invalid in law, although they could be used to determine what the Protestant nobility and reformers would and would not find acceptable in respect of the future constitution of the Scottish legal system. Within the context of the Proclamation of Leith, it would also appear that the consent of the General Assembly had been given to the establishment of some more cogent order in respect of the consequences of the overthrow of the legal system of the Catholic Church. Taken together, the 1563 commissioners appear to have reached the view that the Protestant party might at least tolerate a system of courts which both continued to administer the jurisdictions and laws of the old church courts and relieved the courts of the Church of Scotland of their matrimonial jurisdiction.

Through the creation of the commissary system, and in particular through the appointment of the Commissaries of Edinburgh, the jurisdictional consequences of the Reformation crisis in respect both of the courts of the Church of Scotland and of the Court of Session began to converge. While for a time the archbishop of St Andrews continued to hold out against the consequences of the Reformation crisis, and even sought to effect a restoration of spiritual jurisdiction within the diocese of St Andrews at the expense of the new commissary courts, such actions proved futile within the context of a successful revolution. The religious beliefs by which the revolution had been driven lost none of their potency following 1560 and, while order was for a time restored, the potential for renewed revolutionary endeavour remained a hallmark of Scottish Protestantism. Within this context the Commissaries of Edinburgh proceeded with the greatest of caution and circumspection both in salvaging from the wreckage of revolution much of the old Canon law and the jurisdiction by which it had been enforced and in quietly asserting their exclusive jurisdiction in matrimonial causes throughout the kingdom of Scotland.

Appendix

These transcriptions of manuscript source materials have been included here on the grounds that they represent important, albeit miscellaneous, sources of evidence for the history of the spiritual jurisdiction in Reformation Scotland not previously available in print.

1. NRS, GD1/371/1, fo. 98r, 19 March 1560/1, *Commission from the Protestant 'Secret Council' to John Spottiswoode, superintendent of Lothian, to hear all actions of divorce within the 'diocese' of Lothian.*

Apud Edinburgh xix° Martij anno 1560

The Lordis of Secreit Consale, vndestanding that Maister Jhonne Spottiswod, persoun of Calder, be thare specialle nominatioun and admissioun is appoynttit to the office of Superintendentorie within the diocesye of Lautheane, quha for dischargeing of his office and conscience aucht to discus', discerne and decyde vpoun' all actionis of divorce to be intentit afor him, of personis duelland within the said diocesye, for the cryme of adultre. And vnderstanding that thai ar daylie trublit and cummerit to grant commissionis to proceid in sik causes, and that thai ar no(ch)t to continew and be of sufficient numer, quhill the parliament, to grant the samin commissionis, quhar throw the saidis actiones, to the greit hurt of the persones quhilkis ar offendit, salbe vndecidite, without sufficient remeid be providit thareffor: heirffor the saidis Lordis gevis, grantis and committis full power to the said Maister Jhone Spottiswod, to proceid, discus' and di(s)c[e]r[ne]¹ vpoun all actionis of diuorce intentit or to be intentit befor him at the instance of quhatsumeuir persones duelland within the boundis of the said diocesye quhill the nixt parliament, that forther ordour be takin thairin; and requiris him to do the samyn as he will anser to God heirupoun. And that the said superintendent adione to him the ministeris, elderis and deaconis of the burgh of Hadingtoun to decide vpoun the saidis diuorcementis gif the crymes be committit within the constabularie of Hathingtoun; the ministeris elderis and deaconis of the burgh of Edinburgh, gif the offences be committit within the schirefdome of Edinburgh principallie; the ministeris, elderis and deacones of the burgh of Linlithgw, gif crymes be committit within the schirefdome thairof; and the ministeris, elderis & deacones of the burgh of Striviling, gif the wickitnes be committit within that schirefdome, sua that wickitnes' may ceis' and vertew increis' etc.

[no signatures]

---

¹ MS damaged at this point, due to having been folded.

2. NRS, GD1/371/1, fo. 95r, December 1561, *Commission to John Spottiswoode, superintendent of Lothian, from Mary, Queen of Scots.*

Regina
Superintendent of Lowthiane: It is oure will and we desire zow to do iustice in the actioun' and cause tobe intentit befoir zow, at the instance of Margaret Dorbell (sic) aganis Johnne Fras(er) hir pretendit spous, conforme to the supplicatioun' tobe gevin in befoir zow thaiupoun', with all expeditioun' according to Godis word, as ze will anser to God and us thairupoun. Subs(cr)iuit with oure hand, At Edinburgh the [blank] day of December 1561
  Marie R

3. NRS, CS7/20, fo. 219r–v, 19 December 1560, *Chalmer v. Lumisdene.*

This action for adherence is mentioned twice in *Balfour's Practicks*. Regarding jurisdiction, the case was held to illustrate the principle that 'The Lordis of counsall hes powar to cognosce and decide upon spiritual causis, gif the consistorie, or ecclesiastical jurisdictioun ceissis, or be stopt be civil wars or utherwayis'.[2] In terms of law, the case was held as demonstrating that an allegation of adultery was a valid defence against an action for adherence, 'albeit the committar thairof be not convict befoir a Judge as ane adulterar, or adulteress'.[3]

Decimo nono Decembris anno etc sexagesimo
Sederunt D(o)m(ini) Sessionis ut in die preciden(ti)[4]

Anent oure Soveranis lettres purchest at the instance of John Chalmer in Fintray, aganis Agnes Lummisden';

---

[2] *Balfour's Practicks*, i, 269.
[3] Ibid., i, 99.
[4] Which Lords of Session sat in judgement on this day is not entirely clear. The sederunt for the preceding day occurs on 16 December (fo. 211r), which likewise gives the names of the Lords as 'ut in die precidentj'. The sederunt before this (14 December, fo. 209v) gives no sederunt whatsoever, which is also the case for the sederunt before that (11 December, fo. 207r). The sederunts for the next two sederunts before those already noted are for 9 and 10 December 1560. The sederunt for 9 December (fo. 198r) is good, and lists: Gavin Hamilton, Abbot of Kilwinning; John Sinclair, dean of Restalrig; Abraham Crichton, provost of Dunglass; John Stevenson, precentor of Glasgow; James Scott, provost of Corstorphine; John Spens of Condie, Queen's Advocate; James MacGill of Nether Rankeillour, Clerk Register; Sir Robert Carnegie of Kinnaird; and Master John Gledstanes. The sederunt for 10 December (fo. 201r) gives the judges 'as in the preceding day', but with the absence of the Abbot of Kilwinning. While the record keeping for sederunts seems quite poor, the plain reading of the record creates the presumption that the judges listed as present on 9 December 1560 were also present on 19 December 1560, with the exception of Kilwinning. If this is the case then two of those appointed to the commission charged with the erection of the commissary courts from 1563 were present on 19 December, namely John Spens and James MacGill.

Makand mentioun' That quhair, be the space of nyne zeir syne or thairby, he wes lauchfullie mariit with Agnes Lummisidane his spous and thai haue continewalie sensyne remanit to gidder as mariit personis. Nochttheles sche, laitlie in the moneth of October last bipast, hes, be instigatioun' of sum evill sprete or ellis be seductioun' of sum evill disposit personis and vnhappy counsalouris, diuertit and past away fra the said John Chalmer, tending nocht to returne agane and adheir to him as hir lauchfull mariit spous, and will on' na wis(e) do the samin without sche be compellit.

And becaus thair is na consistoreis instant and the office of the spirituale juge, quhilkis of befoir wes wont to cognosche in siclike causes, now ceises, thairfoir necessar it is that the Lordis of C(oun)sale put remeid thairto.

And anent the charge gevin to the said Agnes Lummisdane, to returne agane to the said Johne Chalmer and to remane and adheir with him in house and cumpany and to obey to him as hir lauchfull spous in all sortis and effaris, according to the ordinance of God and his haly kyrk, within sex dayis nixt eftir, scho wer chargeit thairto; or ellis to haue comperit befoir the Lordis of Counsale at ane certane day bipast and schew[i]n ane ressonable' cause' quhy the samin suld nocht haue bene done; with certificatioun' and sche failzeit, that lettres wald be direct' chargeing hir thairto simpl(icite)r: As at mair lenth is contenit in the saidis lettres.

The said Johne Chalmer being parsonalie present and the said Agnes Lummisdane comperand be Maister Alexander Skene hir procu(ratou)r, quha allegit that she aucht nocht tobe compellit to adheir to the said Johne according to the desyre of the saidis lettres: Because the said Johne hes committit manifest & oppin advltre with thre sundry wemen, in the zeris of God jai vc Lviij, lix and lx zeris. That is to say: ane ne'mit Elizabeth Chalmer; ane vthair callit Elizabeth Nicole; and hes instantlie the thrid with barne, quha is callit [blank], instantlie dwelland with the said Johnis brothir in Balbuchane;[5] quhilk manifest adultre is notourlie knawin in the cuntre and sua reput and haldin; quhilk allegeance the said Maister Alexander offerit him to preif sufficientlie.

Thairfoir the Lordis of Counsale assignis to the said Agnes Lummisdane the xxiiij day of Januar nixtt[oc(um)] with continewa(tiou)n of dayis fer preving of the said allegeance sufficientl[i]e'; and to that effect ordanis hir to haue lettres to summond sik witnes(es) and probatioun' and to produce sic writtis, [ry(cht)is], ressonis & documentis as sche hes or will vse fer preving thairof agane the said day; and siclike ordanis the said John[n]e Chalmer to haue lettres to charge the said Agnes to compeir personalie befoir the saidis Lordis the d[ay] foirsaid to geif hir *iuramentum calu[m]pni[e]* vpon' the poynttis of the said[6] exceptioun', with certificatioun to hir & sche failze thairin ∧ ane decrete condampnit(ou)r salbe gevin aganis hir according to the desyre of the said Johnis lettres ∧;[7] and inlykemaner ordanis the said Maister Alexander procu(ratou)r foirsaid to schaw the speciale name and surname' of the thrid woman', quha is now tobe with barne' with the said Johne, the day foirsaid, to the effect' that the witnes(es) may be exeminit thairupoun'. And in

---

[5] I.e. Balbithan.
[6] *su[d]mondis* scored out in MS.
[7] *sche salbe haldin pro confess[o]* scored out in MS.

the menetyme contin[e]wis the said principale mater in the same form', force and effect' as it is now, but preiudice of party, vnto the day foirsaid. And the part[ei]s, comperand as said is, ar warnit heirof *apud acta*.[8]

4. NRS, CC8/2/1, fo. 46v, 6 July 1564, *Forrester v. Rollock, Gilbert, superintendent of Angus et al.*

In this case the defender had married a third party, having been divorced from the pursuer by the superintendent of Angus, with the minister of St Andrews, sitting with the kirk session of Dundee. The pursuer desired the sentence of the kirk to be reduced by the Commissaries of Edinburgh, and by extension for the subsequent marriage of the defender to be annulled. The case does not appear again in the registers of acts and decreets, but the arguments of the procurators concerning the appellate jurisdiction of the General Assembly are of particular interest.

John Forrester aganis
Margaret Rollok etc

Anent the actioun' and caus intentit and persewit be Johne Forrester aganis Margaret Rollok, relict of vmquhile George Lovell, burges of Dunde, lauchfull spous to the said Johne, now being in cumpany with Maister Gilbert Gardin as his spouse putatiue, and the said Maister Gilbert, Cristofer Gudman minister, James Luvell, Robert Kid, Alexander Weddirburne, and the remanent eldaris and deaconis of the burgh of Dunde, and Johne [9] Erskin of Dvn, superintendent of Angus. [10] To heir and se certane pretendit sentences or declaratouris gevin and pronunceit be thame aganis the said Johne Forrester be reducit reducit [sic] and [infirmit][11] for diuers causes specif[i]it and contenit in the precept' rasit thairupone: As the samyn beris.

The said Johne Forrester comperand be Maister Henrie Kinross his p(rocuratou)r, and the said and the said [sic] Gilbert Gardin being personalie present, and the said Margaret Rollok comperand be Maister Johne Scharpe hir p(rocuratou)r; quha allegit that the said sentence we[s] gevin be the saidis minister, eldaris, deaconis and superintendent as havand sufficient power to do the samyn for the tyme and, gif ony reductioun' be persewit, the samyn aucht tobe persewit befoir the generale kirk and na vther juges. The said Maister Henrie allegit that the samyn aucht tobe persewit befoir the said [sic] Commissaris as iuges competent thairto and reducit in res[p]ect' of his libellit precept' and causes specifiit thairin. The Juges continewis the said mater to avys[e]ment, and assignis l(itte)ra(to)rie to pronunce thair interlocutour anent the allegeances foirsaidis proponit thairin.

---

[8] The outcome of the case was that Lumisden was ordained to adhere to her spouse (NRS, CS7/20, fo. 282r–v, 31 January 1560/1).
[9] [lord] scored out in MS.
[10] *gevaris and pronuncearis* scored out in MS.
[11] This is an unusual form, and some minor doubts remain as to the transcription.

Outline Chronology, 1558–1567

29 November 1558	Crown matrimonial granted to Queen Mary's husband, Francis Valois, Dauphin of France
1 March 1558/9	The last Provincial Council of the Catholic Church in Scotland convenes at Edinburgh
6 March 1558/9	The Reformation crisis begins in law according to the Act of Oblivion (1563)
10 April 1559	The last Provincial Council of Scotland ends
11 May 1559	Knox preaches at Perth, sparking an iconoclastic riot
c.28 June 1559	The Protestant Lords of the Congregation occupy Edinburgh for the first time
10 July 1559	Henry II, King of France, dies, shortly after which Francis and Mary are crowned King and Queen of France
23 July 1559	Regent Guise re-enters Edinburgh, following an agreement with the Lords of the Congregation
18 October 1559	The Lords of the Congregation re-take Edinburgh
21 October 1559	The Lords of the Congregation depose Mary of Guise from the regency
c.1 November 1559	The Lords of the Congregation commission an Edinburgh goldsmith to make a counterfeit signet for the issuing of Privy Council ordinances
early November 1559	Counterfeit signet delivered to James Hamilton, Duke of Chatelherault
6 November 1559	The regent's forces drive the Lords of the Congregation out of Edinburgh
8 November 1559	The Lords of the Congregation reach Stirling
10 November 1559	Mary and Francis commission La Brosse and Cleutin to hold an Inquiry at Holyrood
c.November 1559	The Lords of the Congregation issue a Privy Council ordinance suppressing the courts of the Catholic Church in Scotland

14 December 1559	A further ordinance is issued at Dundee against the Commissary of Brechin, for contravention of the earlier ordinance
24 January 1559/60	An English fleet arrives in the Firth of Forth
1 February–21 March 1559/60	The first extant process of Protestant divorce on the ground of adultery is led before the kirk session of St Andrews (*Renton v. Gedde*)
5 February 1559/60	La Brosse and Cleutin's Inquiry begins to examine witnesses at Holyrood Palace
27 February 1559/60	Treaty of Berwick entered into with England by the Lords of the Congregation
30 March 1560	An English army arrives in Scotland
May 1560	The Lords of the Congregation summon Parliament
11 June 1560	Mary of Guise dies
5 July 1560	The English and French conclude the Treaty of Leith
6 July 1560	The bilateral Treaty of Edinburgh between Elizabeth I and Mary and Francis is agreed by their respective commissioners
6 July 1560	A series of 'Concessions to the Nobility and People of Scotland' are offered by Mary and Francis's commissioners
10 July 1560	The three estates convene in Parliament at Edinburgh
25 July 1560	The kirk session of Edinburgh pronounces a sentence of Protestant divorce (*Hamilton v. Sclater*), by virtue of a 'special commission' from the 'Lords of Secret Council'
1 August 1560	The Reformation Parliament reconvenes
August 1560	The Reformation Parliament passes an Act of Oblivion
c.8–9 August 1560	The Reformation Parliament purportedly ratifies the 'Concessions'
18 August 1560	The Archbishop of St Andrews writes that 'the elderis callit of every town takis all the causis of our ecclesiasticall jurisdiction'
24 August 1560	The Reformation Parliament abrogates papal authority in Scotland, outlaws the Mass, and ratifies the Scots Confession of Faith. The three estates also appoint a *de facto* government

Outline Chronology

2 September 1560	Elizabeth I ratifies the Treaty of Edinburgh
15 September 1560	Francis and Mary decline to ratify the Treaty of Edinburgh
30 September 1560	The kirk session of Edinburgh pronounces a sentence of Protestant divorce (*Hamilton v. Semple*)
2 December 1560	The 'Lords of Secret Council' commission the kirk session of St Andrews to take cognisance of an action of Protestant divorce (*Lathrisk v. Symsoun*)
5 December 1560	Francis II dies, presaging Mary's return to Scotland
19 December 1560	The Lords of Council and Session take cognisance of their first spiritual action (*Chalmer v. Lumisdene*)
9 March 1560/1	John Spottiswoode elected superintendent of Lothian, shortly after which John Willock pronounces a sentence of divorce as superintendent-nominate of Glasgow (*Paterson v. Stevenson*)
19 March 1560/1	The 'Lords of Secret Council' commission the superintendent of Lothian to take cognisance of all actions for divorce within his 'diocesye'
13 April 1561	John Winram formally admitted to the superintendency of Fife, Fotherick and Strathearn
2 July 1561	Superintendent Winram takes cognisance of his first consistorial action at St Andrews (*Forret v. Leslie*)
19 August 1561	Mary Stewart returns to Scotland, landing at Leith
25 August 1561	Mary issues the Proclamation of Leith
1 September 1561	The Reformation crisis ends in law, according to the Act of Oblivion (1563)
5 September 1561	Superintendent Winram and the kirk session of St Andrews reduce a pre-Reformation sentence of heresy
6 September 1561	Mary appoints her Privy Council
14 September 1561	John Willock formally admitted to the superintendency of Glasgow
November 1561	Archbishop Hamilton issues a marriage dispensation by virtue of his legatine authority
1 April 1562	Archbishop Hamilton commissions judges delegate to hear an action of annulment between the Earl and Countess of Eglinton (*Eglinton v. Hamilton*)
2 April 1562	The kirk session of Edinburgh pronounces a sentence of Protestant divorce by virtue of a Privy Council commission (*Weston v. Ewart*)

25 June 1562	Superintendent Spottiswoode and the kirk session of Edinburgh pronounced a sentence of Protestant divorce (*Hamilton* v. *Eglinton*)
4 July 1562	The General Assembly apparently consents to some further order being taken in respect of consistorial actions
8 August 1562	The 'reforming' bishop and kirk session of Orkney pronounce a sentence of Protestant divorce (*Tulloch* v. *Sinclair*)
19 August 1562	Archbishop Hamilton grants a dispensation from the impediment of affinity in favour of the Earl of Eglinton
28 November 1562	The kirk session of Gamrie pronounces a sentence of annulment on the ground of impotence (*Mowat* v. *Craig*)
7 March 1562/3	The Lords of Council and Session defer to an appeal pending before papal judges delegate (*Crichton of Anstruther* v. *Melville*)
c.1563	Superintendent Erskine of Dun pronounces a sentence of Protestant divorce at Dundee (*Rollock* v. *Forrester*)
5 or 6 April 1563	Superintendent Willock pronounces a sentence of Protestant divorce at Glasgow (*Maxwell* v. *Hamilton*)
4 June 1563	The three estates enact the Act of Oblivion
28 December 1563	The Privy Council appoints a commission to consider the erection of jurisdictions throughout the realm in respect of 'the caussis quhilkis the prelattis of this realme had decidit in the consistories of befoir'
8 February 1563/4	Mary appoints the first four Commissaries of Edinburgh
21 February 1563/4	The Lords of Council and Session again defer to an appeal pending before papal judges delegate (*Sempil & Campbell* v. *Sempil*)
27 April 1564	Superintendent Spottiswoode and the kirk session of Edinburgh confirm a sentence of Protestant divorce pronounced by the bishop and kirk session of Orkney
7 June 1564	First consistorial sentence pronounced by the Commissaries of Edinburgh (*Procurator Fiscal* v. *Loch & Weland*)

15 January 1564/5	Commissaries of Edinburgh pronounce sentence in *Forbes* v. *Sandilands*
29 July 1565	Marriage of Mary Stewart and Henry Stewart, Lord Darnley
9 January 1565/6	Superintendent Winram pronounces judgement in *Kay* v. *Arnot*
17 February 1565/6	Archbishop Hamilton grants a dispensation from the impediment of consanguinity standing between James Hepburn, fourth Earl of Bothwell, and Jane Gordon
27 April 1566	Kirk session of St Andrews holds its disciplinary jurisdiction to be acknowledged by the Proclamation of Leith (*Dalgleis & Wemyss*)
19 June 1566	Birth of James Stewart, the future James VI of Scotland
17 December 1566	James Stewart baptised at Stirling in Catholic ceremony
23 December 1566	Archbishop Hamilton formally restored to his spiritual jurisdictions within the diocese of St Andrews
c.9 January 1566/7	Hamilton's restoration revoked
9 February 1566/7	Lord Darnley murdered
26 April 1567	Action of Protestant divorce on the ground of adultery (*Gordon* v. *Hepburn*) brought before the Commissaries of Edinburgh
27 April 1567	Action of divorce on the ground of consanguinity (*Hepburn* v. *Gordon*) brought before a judge commissioned by the Archbishop of St Andrews
3 May 1567	Decreet of divorce (*Gordon* v. *Hepburn*) pronounced in favour of Jane Gordon by the Commissaries of Edinburgh
7 May 1567	Sentence of annulment pronounced in *Hepburn* v. *Gordon*
15 May 1567	Mary, Queen of Scots, marries James Hepburn, fourth Earl of Bothwell, in a Protestant ceremony at Holyrood
15 June 1567	Mary surrenders to the confederate Lords at Carberry Hill
24 July 1567	Mary forced to abdicate the Scottish Crown in favour of her infant son; names her natural brother James Stewart, Earl of Moray, as regent

29 July 1567	James VI crowned at Stirling
22 August 1567	The Earl of Moray, sometime leading Lord of the Congregation, declared regent of Scotland
December 1567	The three estates in Parliament ratify the principal legislation of the Reformation Parliament
15 December 1567	Church Jurisdiction Act (1567) declares there to be no other ecclesiastical jurisdiction within the Church other than that exercised by the Church of Scotland

Select Bibliography

MANUSCRIPT SOURCES

National Records of Scotland:
CC8/2, *Registers of Acts and Decreets, Edinburgh Commissary Court.*
CC10/1/1, *Acts and Decreets, Hamilton and Campsie Commissary Court.*
CH2/448/1, *Aberdeen, St Nicholas Kirk Session (Minutes), Records of Church of Scotland synods, presbyteries and kirk sessions.*
CS7, *Registers of Acts and Decrees, 1st series, Lords of Council and Session.*
JC1, *Court Books (old series), Court of the Lord Justice General.*
GD1/371/1, *Warrender Papers.*
GD16/10/9, *Transumpt of an Instrument of Sasine, Papers of the Earls of Airlie, Lands and Barony of Craig.*
PA9/1, *Acts of the Lords Interpreters of the Act of Oblivion.*

PRINTED PRIMARY SOURCES AND REFERENCE WORKS

The Acts and Constitutions of the Realm of Scotland (Glashütten/Taunus: Verlag Detlev Auvermann, 1971), being a facsimile edition of *The Actis and Constitutiounis of the Realme of Scotland* (Edinburgh: Robert Lekprevik, 1566).
The Acts and Proceedings of the General Assemblies of the Church of Scotland, 1560–1618, ed. Duncan Shaw (Edinburgh: Scottish Record Society, 2004), 3 volumes.
The Acts of Sederunt of the Lords of Council and Session, from the 15th January 1553, to the 11th of July 1790 (Edinburgh: Elphinston Balfour, 1790).
Acts of the Lords of Council in Public Affairs 1501–1554, ed. R. K. Hannay (Edinburgh: HMSO, 1932).
Acts of the Parliaments of Scotland 1124–1707, ed. T. Thomson and C. Innes (Edinburgh: 1814–1875), 12 volumes.
Atlas of Scottish History to 1707, ed. P. G. B. McNeill and H. L. MacQueen (Edinburgh: The Scottish Medievalists and Department of Geography, University of Edinburgh, 1996).
Brunton, George and David Haig (eds), *An Historical Account of the Senators of the College of Justice from Its Institution in 1532* (Edinburgh: Thomas Clark, 1832).

The Buik of the Kirk of the Canagait, 1564–1567, ed. A. B. Calderwood (Edinburgh: Scottish Record Society, 1961).
The Byble in Englyshe (Printed at London by Rychard Grafton and Edward Whitchurch, 1539).
Calendar of the Manuscripts of the Marquis of Salisbury preserved at Hatfield House, Hertfordshire (London: HMSO, 1883–1976), 24 volumes.
Calendar of State Papers, foreign series, of the reign of Elizabeth, ed. Joseph Stephenson et al. (London: Longman, Roberts and Green, 1863–1950), 23 volumes.
Calendar of the State Papers Relating to Scotland and Mary, Queen of Scots, 1547–1603, ed. J. Bain et al. (Edinburgh: H. M. General Register House, 1898–1969), 13 volumes.
The Catechism set forth by Archbishop Hamilton, printed at St Andrews 1551 (Edinburgh: William Paterson, 1882).
Charters and Documents relating to the Burgh of Peebles, ed. William Chambers (Edinburgh: Scottish Burgh Records Society, 1872).
Cheney, C. R. (ed.), *Handbook of Dates for Students of English History* (London: The Royal Historical Society, 1978).
Correspondence of Sir Patrick Waus of Barnbarroch, Knight, ed. Robert Vans Agnew (Edinburgh: Ayr and Galloway Archaeological Association, 1887), 2 volumes.
Craig, Thomas, of Riccarton, *Ius Feudale Tribus Libris Comprehensum, Book I*, trans. and ed. Leslie Dodd (Edinburgh: The Stair Society, 2017).
Decrees of the Ecumenical Councils, ed. Norman P. Tanner SJ (London: Sheed & Ward; and Washington, DC: Georgetown University Press, 1990), 2 volumes.
A Diurnal of Remarkable Occurents that have passed within the country of Scotland since the death of King James the Fourth till the year 1575, ed. T. Thomson (Edinburgh: Bannatyne Club, 1833).
Extracts from the Records of the Burgh of Edinburgh, ed. J. D. Marwick (Edinburgh: Scottish Burgh Records Society, 1869–1882), 4 volumes.
Fasti Ecclesiae Scoticanae Medii Aevi ad annum 1638, ed. D. E. R. Watt and A. L. Murray (Edinburgh: Scottish Record Society, 2003).
Fasti Ecclesiae Scoticanae: The Succession of Ministers in the Church of Scotland from the Reformation, ed. Hew Scott (Edinburgh: Oliver & Boyd, 1915–28), 8 volumes.
The First Book of Discipline, ed. J. K. Cameron (Edinburgh: Saint Andrew Press, 1972).
Fraser, Sir William, *Memorials of the Montgomeries, Earls of Eglinton* (Edinburgh: 1859), 2 volumes.
Green, Thomas M. (ed.), *The Consistorial Decisions of the Commissaries of Edinburgh 1564 to 1576/7* (Edinburgh: The Stair Society, 2014).
Hope's Major Practicks 1608–1633, ed. The Rt Hon. James Avon Clyde (Edinburgh: The Stair Society, 1937–38), 2 volumes.
John Knox's History of the Reformation in Scotland, ed. W. C. Dickinson (London: Thomas Nelson, 1949), 2 volumes.

The Lag Charters, 1400–1720: Sir Philip J. Hamilton-Grierson Calendar, ed. Athol L. Murray (Edinburgh, Scottish Record Society, 1958).
Lord Hermand's Consistorial Decisions 1684–1777, ed. F. P. Walton (Edinburgh: The Stair Society, 1940).
Mason, Roger (ed.), *John Knox on Rebellion* (Cambridge: Cambridge University Press, 1994).
Oxford Dictionary of National Biography, ed. H. C. G. Matthew and B. Harrison (Oxford: Oxford University Press, 2004), 60 volumes; www.oxforddnb.com.
Pitcairn, Robert (ed.), *Ancient Criminal Trials in Scotland* (Edinburgh: Maitland Club, 1833), 3 volumes.
The Practicks of Sir James Balfour of Pittendreich, ed. Peter G. B. McNeill (Edinburgh: The Stair Society, 1962–3), 2 volumes.
The Records of the Parliament of Scotland, ed. Keith Brown et al. (St Andrews, 2007); www.rps.ac.uk.
The Register of the Great Seal of Scotland (Registrum Magni Sigilli Regum Scotorum), ed. J. M. Thomson et al. (Edinburgh, 1882–1914), 11 volumes.
The Register of the Minister, Elders and Deacons of the Christian Congregation of St Andrews, ed. D. H. Fleming (Edinburgh: Scottish History Society, 1889–90), 2 volumes.
The Register of the Privy Council of Scotland, ed. J. H. Burton et al. (Edinburgh, 1877–), 37 volumes.
The Register of the Privy Seal in Scotland (Registrum Secreti Sigilli Regum Scotorum), ed. M. Livingstone et al. (Edinburgh, 1908–), 8 volumes.
Robertson, Joseph, *Concilia Scotiae Ecclesiae Scoticanae Statuta tam Provincialia quam Synodalia quae Supersunt* (Edinburgh: Bannatyne Club, 1866), 2 volumes.
The Second Book of Discipline, ed. James Kirk (Edinburgh: Saint Andrew Press, 1980).
Selections from the Records of the Kirk Session, Presbytery, and Synod of Aberdeen, ed. J. Stuart (Aberdeen: The Spalding Club, 1846).
Shetland Documents 1195–1579, ed. J. Ballantine and B. Smith (Lerwick, 1999).
Statutes of the Scottish Church, 1225–1559, trans. and ed. D. Patrick (Edinburgh: Scottish History Society, 1907).
Teulet, Alexandre (ed.), *Relations Politiques de la France et de l'Espagne avec l'Écosse au XVIe siècle* (Paris: 1862), 5 volumes.

SECONDARY SOURCES: BOOKS

Cameron, A. I., *The Apostolic Camera and Scottish Benefices 1418–1488* (London: Oxford University Press for St Andrews University, 1934).
Dawson, Jane E. A., *John Knox* (New Haven and London: Yale University Press, 2016).
Dawson, Jane E. A., *Scotland Re-formed, 1488–1587* (Edinburgh: Edinburgh University Press, 2007).

Donaldson, Gordon, *Reformed by Bishops: Galloway, Orkney and Caithness* (Edinburgh: The Edina Press, 1987).
Donaldson, Gordon, *Scotland: James V to James VII* (Edinburgh: Oliver & Boyd, 1971).
Donaldson, Gordon, *The Scottish Reformation* (Cambridge: Cambridge University Press, 1960).
Dunbar, Linda J., *Reforming the Scottish Church: John Winram and the Example of Fife* (Aldershot: Ashgate, 2002).
Godfrey, A. M., *Civil Justice in Renaissance Scotland: The Origins of a Central Court* (Leiden: Brill, 2009).
Herkless, John, and Robert Kerr Hannay, *The Archbishops of St Andrews* (Edinburgh and London: W. Blackwood, 1907–15), 5 volumes.
Keith, Robert, *History of the Affairs of the Church and State in Scotland* (Edinburgh: Spottiswoode Society, 1844–50), 3 volumes.
Kingdon, Robert M., *Adultery and Divorce in Calvin's Geneva* (Cambridge, Massachusetts: Harvard University Press, 1995).
Kellar, Clare, *Scotland, England, and the Reformation, 1534–61* (Oxford: Oxford University Press, 2003).
Kirk, James, *Patterns of Reform: Change and Continuity in the Reformation Kirk* (Edinburgh: T. & T. Clark, 1989).
Leslie [Lesley], John, *The History of Scotland, from the death of King James I in the year 1436 to the year 1561*, ed. Thomas Thomson (Edinburgh: Bannatyne Club, 1830).
MacQueen, Hector L. (ed.), *The College of Justice: Essays by R. K. Hannay* (Edinburgh: The Stair Society, 1990).
Ollivant, Simon, *The Court of the Official in Pre-Reformation Scotland* (Edinburgh: The Stair Society, 1982).
Petrie, Alexander, *A Compendious History of the Catholick Church from the year 600 untill the year 1600* (The Hague: Printed by Adrian Vlack, 1657).
Riddell, John, *Inquiry into the Law and Practice in Scottish Peerages* (Edinburgh: Thomas Clark, 1842), 2 volumes.
Sanderson, Margaret H. B., *Ayrshire and the Reformation: People and Change 1490–1600* (East Linton: Tuckwell Press, 1997).
Shaw, Duncan, *The General Assemblies of the Church of Scotland 1560–1600* (Edinburgh: Saint Andrew Press, 1964).
Spottiswoode, John, *The History of the Church of Scotland* (Edinburgh: The Spottiswoode Society, 1847–51), 3 volumes.
Stuart, John, *A Lost Chapter in the History of Mary Queen of Scots Recovered* (Edinburgh: Edmonston and Douglas, 1874).
Witte, Jr, John, *Law and Protestantism: The Legal Teachings of the Lutheran Reformation* (Cambridge: Cambridge University Press, 2002).
Witte, Jr, John, and Robert M. Kingdon, *Sex, Marriage and Family in John Calvin's Geneva: Courtship, Engagement and Marriage* (Grand Rapids: William B. Eerdmans, 2005).

SECONDARY SOURCES: BOOK CHAPTERS AND ARTICLES

Cameron, James, 'The Office of Superintendent in the First Book of Discipline', in Bernard Vogler (ed.), *Miscellanea Historiae Ecclesiasticae VIII* (Brussels and Louvain: Revue D'Histoire Ecclesiastique, 1987), 239–250.

Dawson, Jane E. A., 'The Face of Ane Perfyt Reformed Kyrk: St Andrews and the Early Scottish Reformation', in James Kirk (ed.), *Humanism and Reform: The Church in Europe, England and Scotland, 1400–1643* (Oxford: Blackwell, 1991), 413–435.

Dawson, Jane E. A., 'The Scottish Reformation and the Theatre of Martyrdom', *Studies in Church History*, 30 (1993), 259–270.

Dawson, Jane E. A., 'The Two John Knoxes: England, Scotland and the 1558 Tracts', *Journal of Ecclesiastical History*, 42:4 (1991), 555–576.

Dickinson, G., 'Report by de la Brosse and D'Oysel on Conditions in Scotland, 1559–1560', in *Miscellany of the Scottish History Society IX* (Edinburgh: Scottish History Society, 1958), 85–125.

Dolezalek, Gero, 'The Court of Session as a Ius Commune Court – Witnessed by "Sinclair's Practicks", 1540–1549', in Hector L. MacQueen (ed.), *Miscellany IV* (Edinburgh: The Stair Society, 2002), 51–84.

Donaldson, Gordon, 'The Church Courts', in *An Introduction to Scottish Legal History* (Edinburgh: The Stair Society, 1958), 363–373.

Dunbar, Linda J., 'An Early Record from the Synod of Fife, c. 1570', *Records of the Scottish Church History Society* 28 (1998), 217–238.

Goodare, Julian, 'The First Parliament of Mary, Queen of Scots', *The Sixteenth Century Journal*, 36 (2005), 55–75.

Goodare, Julian, 'The Scottish Parliamentary Records, 1560–1603', *Historical Research*, 72 (1999), 244–267.

Green, Thomas M., 'The Authority of the Sources of Early Scots Consistorial Law: Reflections on Law, Authority and Jurisdiction during the Scottish Reformation', in Mark Godfrey (ed.), *Law and Authority in British Legal History* (Cambridge: Cambridge University Press, 2016), 120–139.

Green, Thomas M., 'Romano-canonical Procedure in Reformation Scotland: The Example of the Court of the Commissaries of Edinburgh', *The Journal of Legal History*, 36:3 (2015), 217–235.

Green, Thomas M., 'Scottish Benefices and the Commissary Court of Edinburgh: The Example of McGibbon v. Struthers', in Hector L. MacQueen (ed.), *Miscellany VI* (Edinburgh: The Stair Society, 2009), 45–61.

Hannay, R. K., 'The Early History of the Scottish Signet', in Hector L. MacQueen (ed.), *The College of Justice: Essays by R. K. Hannay* (Edinburgh: The Stair Society, 1990), 273–323.

MacQueen, Hector L., 'Two Visitors in the Session, 1629 and 1636', in Hector L. MacQueen (ed.), *Miscellany IV* (Edinburgh: The Stair Society, 2002), 155–168.

McNeill, Peter G. B., 'Discours Particulier D'Escosse', in David Sellar (ed.), *Miscellany II* (Edinburgh: The Stair Society, 1984), 86–131.

McNeill, Peter G. B., 'Interference with the Court of Session by the Privy Council', *Juridical Review* (1961), 253–255.

McNeill, Peter G. B., 'The Legal Aspects of the Scottish Reformation' in *Scots Law Times (News)* (1962), 84.

McNeill, Peter G. B., '"Our Religion, Established Neither by Law or Parliament": Was the Reformation Legislation of 1560 Valid?', *Records of the Scottish Church History Society*, 35 (2005), 68–89.

McRoberts, David, 'Material Destruction Caused by the Scottish Reformation', in David McRoberts (ed.), *Essays on the Scottish Reformation, 1513–1625* (Glasgow: Burns, 1962), 415–462.

Shaw, Duncan, 'John Willock', in Duncan Shaw (ed.), *Reformation and Revolution: Essays Presented to The Very Reverend Principal Emeritus Hugh Watt* (Edinburgh: Saint Andrew Press, 1967), 42–69.

Smith, David Baird, 'The Reformers and Divorce: A Study in Consistorial Jurisdiction', *Scottish Historical Review*, 9 (1912), 10–36.

Smith, David B., 'The Spiritual Jurisdiction 1560–64', *Records of the Scottish Church History Society*, 25 (1995), 1–18.

Winning, Thomas, 'Church Councils in Sixteenth-Century Scotland', in David McRoberts (ed.), *Essays on the Scottish Reformation, 1513–1625* (Glasgow: Burns, 1962), 332–358.

SECONDARY SOURCES: DOCTORAL THESES

Green, Thomas M., 'The Court of the Commissaries of Edinburgh: Consistorial Law and Litigation, 1559–1576' (PhD thesis, University of Edinburgh, 2010).

McNeill, Peter G. B., 'The Jurisdiction of the Scottish Privy Council, 1532–1708' (PhD thesis, University of Glasgow, 1960).

Index

Abbot, 57, 61
  Crossraguel, 66
  Glenluce, 66
  Kilwinning, 115
Abercromby (Abircrumby), John, 123–4
Abercromby, John, Commissary of the Chapel Royal at Stirling, 26
Aberdeen, 27, 47, 83, 90, 97, 103–4, 106
Act Concerning Religion, 73
Act of Oblivion, 13, 37–9, 42, 45, 49, 50–2, 58, 61, 70, 79, 81, 95, 109, 112, 131–2, 139, 188–9; see also Law of Oblivion
Acts of Parliament, 4, 11, 30, 34, 38–44, 46, 48, 50–65, 72, 77, 81, 86, 89–90, 95, 110, 112, 116–17, 119–22, 128, 131–2, 134, 157–8, 173–6, 179–80, 187–9; see also Act Concerning Religion; Act of Oblivion; Adultery Act; Black Acts of 1566; Church Jurisdiction Act; Commissariot Act; Divorce for Malicious Desertion Act; Jurisdiction of Rome Act; Lords Interpreters of the Law of Oblivion; Marriage Act; Mass Act; Papal Jurisdiction Act
Adultery Act, 132, 160
Aidman, Margaret, 90
Anderson, Robert, 161
Angus and the Mearns, 14
Archbishop, 61, 77, of
  Canterbury, 107
  Glasgow, 19, 31, 87
  St Andrews, 4, 8, 15, 28, 31, 41, 49, 54, 56, 58, 60–1, 63–4, 66, 68–74, 76, 80, 93, 108, 138, 149, 177, 189
  York, 107
Archdeaconry of Lothian, 71, 140
Argyll, 7, 31
Argyll, Earl of see Campbell, Archibald
Arran, Earl of see Hamilton, James
Ayrshire, 14

Bain, Joseph, 17
Balbithan (Balbuchane), 193

Balfour of Pittendreich, James, parson of Flisk, Official of Lothian, senator of the College of Justice, Commissary of Edinburgh, Lord President of the Court of Session 3, 26, 30, 62, 65, 115–16, 118, 124–5, 141–4, 175, 178
Balfour's Practicks, 65, 116, 118, 175, 192
Ballie, William, 62
Baron, John, minister of Galston, 107
Barratry, 54
Beaton (Betoun), Archibald, Official of Glasgow, Commissary of Glasgow, 28, 145
Beaton, David, Cardinal Archbishop of St Andrews, 93
Beaton, James, Archbishop of Glasgow, 19, 53; see also Archbishop
Beaton, James, Archbishop of St Andrews, 15, 108; see also Archbishop
Beaton of Creich, David, 182
Bellenden of Auchnoul, Sir John, Lord Justice Clerk, 3, 18, 20, 62, 115, 117, 129, 132–4, 178
Berwick-upon-Tweed, 35, 41, 73
Birnie, James, 104
Bishop, 3, 24, 54, 57, 61, 65, 75–9, 106–9, 156, 158, 175
  Aberdeen, 27
  Brechin, 25, 59, 61
  Caithness, 31, 76, 78
  Dunblane, 19, 74, 122, 129
  Dunkeld, 74, 76–7, 79
  Galloway, 31, 62, 75–6, 78–9, 146
  Orkney, 31, 62, 76, 78, 106–7, 142, 151, 153–4, 156
  Rome, 8, 54, 56, 61, 85
  Ross, 49–50, 59–62, 68, 133
  Valence, 35
Black Acts of 1566, 61–2, 64n
Borthwick, Sir John, 93, 108
Boswell, Robert, 173, 175
Bothwell, Adam, Bishop of Orkney, 78, 106; see also Bishop
Bothwell, Earl of see Hepburn, James

Boyd, Robert, fifth Lord Boyd, 14, 46–7, 91, 96
Brechin, 23, 27, 30–1, 72, 86, 145
Broun, William, Commissary of Brechin, 27–8
Buchanan, George, 159

Cairncross, John, canon of Ross, 140–1
Calton Hill, Edinburgh, 18
Calvinist, 2–3, 11–12, 94, 143
Cameron, James, 17, 47, 97, 104, 159
Campbell, Archibald, fifth Earl of Argyll, Lord Justice General of Scotland, 13–14, 17, 22, 29, 46, 49, 132–3
Canon
  Dunbar, 74
  Dunkeld, 74
  Glasgow, 67, 74
  Ross, 140–1
Canon Law, 3–4, 9, 24–5, 56, 66, 68–9, 73, 75, 83–5, 87, 94, 135–7, 141–4, 150, 156–7, 166, 180, 190
Carnegie of Kinnaird, Sir Robert, 115
Carswell, John, superintendent of Argyll, 92, 96; *see also* Superintendent(s)
Cassilis, Earl of, 66
Cecil, Sir William, 35, 40–1, 43, 73, 88, 96
Chalmer, Duncan, Official of Ross, Commissary of Ross, 145
Chalmer, Elizabeth, 193
Chalmer of Fintry, John, 115, 192, 193
Chisholm, Malcolm, Commissary of Dunblane, 26
Chisholm, William, Bishop of Dunblane, 19; *see also* Bishop
Christison, Thomas, minister of Gamrie, 105
Christison, William, minister of Dundee, 101
Church Jurisdiction Act, 80, 170, 173, 177–80, 182, 187
Clerk Register *see* MacGill of Nether Rankeillour
Cleutin, Henri, 17, 20, 115, 134; *see also* Inquiry
Cockie, James, goldsmith, 18–19, 21, 23
Collation, 76–9
College of Justice, 71, 110, 114–15, 125–6, 128, 133, 136, 142–4, 147
Commissaries, 7–8, 26, 55–7, 63, 65, 67, 71, 74–5, 78, 85, 87, 98, 103, 117, 125, 137–9, 142, 144–7, 149, 165, 177–9, 189
  Aberdeen, 26, 145
  Brechin, 22–5, 27, 30–1, 72, 122, 145
  Bute and Arran, 26
  Caithness, 26
  Campsie, 31, 165
  Chapel Royal, Stirling, 26
  Dumfries, 145

Dunblane, 26–7, 30–1, 118, 122
Edinburgh, 2–5, 30, 45, 55, 58, 62–3, 67–76, 78, 81–2, 85, 87–8, 91–2, 98, 100–4, 106–7, 109, 115, 117, 119, 121, 123–6, 128–86, 189, 190, 194
Glasgow, 28, 145
Hamilton, 26, 31, 165
Inverness, 145
Kilbride, 26
Moray, 145
Ross, 145
St Andrews, 26, 29–30, 71, 90, 145, 165, 175
Shetland, 28n
Stirling, 26
Wigtown, 28
see also Commissary system; Courts spiritual
Commissariot Act, 177
Commissary system, 3–5, 25, 45, 52, 69, 117, 124–7, 132–42, 144, 146–8, 157–8, 167, 178, 180, 184–5, 189
Commissioners
  for concluding the Wars of the Congregation, 35–9, 41, 49
  for creating the new commissary system, 25, 132–8, 144, 148, 174, 189
  for the correction of the laws of Scotland, 61
  of the General Assembly, 77–8, 136
Concessions to the Nobility and People of Scotland, 33, 35–45, 49–50, 58, 61, 95, 134, 188
Cook, George, canon of Dunkeld, 74
Council of State, 38, 39; *see also* Council of the Realm
Council of the Realm, 14, 17, 22, 24, 32–3, 40, 44–9, 52, 59, 80–1, 89, 93, 95, 114, 122, 128, 133, 188; *see also* Council of State
Court of Session, 3, 7, 9, 26, 28, 55, 59, 62–3, 69, 75, 79, 81, 110–30, 134, 136, 138–9, 141–4, 146, 155, 158, 173–4, 177, 187–9; *see also* Lord President of the Court of Session; Lords of Council and Session; Senators of the College of Justice
Court of the Lord Justice General, 7, 49, 105, 158
Court of the Official *see* Official(s)
Court of the Official Principal *see* Official(s) Principal
Courts of the Catholic Church, suppression of, 7–32, 45, 53, 56, 80, 81, 109, 121–3, 131, 138, 148, 173

Courts of the Church of Scotland 1, 3–5, 25, 45, 47, 56, 67, 75, 78, 80–112, 125–31, 135–8, 141, 143–5, 148–86; *see also* General Assembly; Kirk session(s); Superintendent's court

Courts of the Commissaries *see* Commissaries

Courts spiritual, 8–9, 15, 17, 21, 23–8, 30–2, 44, 47, 52–7, 62, 69, 70, 75–6, 79–80, 82–6, 106, 111–17, 121–9, 131–2, 134–40, 142, 144–6, 148, 151, 155–7, 173, 177, 188; *see also* Courts of the Catholic Church, suppression of

Craig, John, minister of the Canongate, minister of Edinburgh, 99, 107, 153, 159, 178, 179

Craig, John, parson of Kincardine, 105

Craig of Craig Fintray, John, 105

Craig of Riccarton, Thomas, 177–8

Craigie, Hugh, Commissary of Moray, 145

Cranston (Cranstoun), William, Official of St Andrews, 26, 145

Crawford, Archibald, canon of Glasgow, 67, 74

Crawford, Bessy, 74

Crawfurd, Earl of, 42

Crichton, Abraham, provost of Dunglass, Lord of Council and Session, 115, 142

Crichton, Alexander, canon of Dunkeld, 74

Crichton (Creytoun), Robert, 123

Crossraguel, Abbey of, 76

Culross, kirk of, 164

Cunningham, Alexander, fourth Earl of Glencairn, 13–14, 17–18, 22, 46–7, 96, 132–3

Cunningham of Cunninghamhead, William, 91

Cupar-Fife, 19

Currie, kirk of, 164

Dalgleish, John, 173–5

Darnley, Henry, Lord, king-consort, 70, 73, 172–4

Deacon(s), 87, 100, 106, 111, 152, 161, 194
  Argyll, 92
  Ayr, 86
  Dundee, 86, 101, 194
  Edinburgh, 68, 85, 87, 99–100, 107, 135, 142, 153, 191
  Fife, 92
  Gamrie, 105
  Glasgow, 92, 152
  Haddington, 191
  Jedburgh, 103, 154
  Kirkcaldy, 91
  Linlithgow, 191
  Lothian, 92
  Mearns, 92
  Montrose, 86
  Orkney, 78, 106
  St Andrews, 86–7, 92–3, 173
  Stirling, 191–2

Divorce for Malicious Desertion Act, 51

Donaldson, Gordon, 2, 17, 40, 50–1, 54, 63, 76, 79, 81, 83, 145

(Dorbell), Margaret, 192

Douglas, 31

Douglas, James, fourth Earl of Morton, Regent of Scotland, 14n, 46, 47, 133, 138

Douglas, John, Rector of St Andrews, Archbishop of St Andrews, 78, 85, 90, 169, 183; *see also* Archbishop

Drummond, Agnes, 66, 69

Duff, James, Commissary of Inverness, 145

Duncanson, Thomas, schoolmaster and reader in Stirling, 107

Dundee, 19, 21–3, 86, 97, 101–3, 106

Edinburgh, 16, 18–19, 21, 23–4, 29, 30–1, 36–7, 40, 49, 53, 68–9, 73–4, 80, 83, 85–91, 93–4, 97, 99–100, 103, 105–6, 113–14, 123–5, 128, 134, 139, 142, 147, 151, 158, 163–5, 191–2

Eglinton, Earl of *see* Montgomerie, Hugh

Elder(s), 31, 86–7, 91–3, 100, 106, 111, 152, 154, 161, 194
  Argyll, 92
  Ayr, 86
  Dundee, 86, 101, 194
  Edinburgh, 68, 85, 87, 99–100, 107, 135, 142, 151, 153, 191
  Fife, 92
  Gamrie, 105
  Glasgow, 68, 87, 92, 152
  Haddington, 191
  Jedburgh, 103
  Kirkcaldy, 91
  Linlithgow, 191
  Lothian, 92
  Mearns, 92
  Montrose, 86
  Orkney, 78, 106
  St Andrews, 82–3, 86–7, 90–3, 136, 169, 173–4
  Stirling, 191–2

Elizabeth I, 11, 35–6, 39, 43–4, 48, 111

Erskine of Dun, John, superintendent of Angus and the Mearns, 13–14, 17, 20–2, 46, 91–2, 96, 100–1, 105–6, 122, 152, 178, 179, 194; *see also* Superintendent(s)

Ewart, Katherine, 99

Fife, 14, 97, 106, 136, 164, 166, 183
Firth of Forth, 34, 71
Fishwick, kirk of, 164
Fleming, David Hay, 81–2, 84
Forbes, John, 167–9
Forrester, John, 194
Forret of that Ilk, John, 102
Foulden, kirk of, 164
Francis II *see* Valois, Francis
Frankfurt, 24
Fraser, John, 192

(Gardin), Gilbert, 194
Geddes, Elizabeth, 82, 90
General Assembly, 47–9, 57, 59, 63–4, 71–2, 77–8, 80, 83, 92, 94, 97, 101, 104, 106–9, 130–2, 142–4, 146–9, 151–9, 161–3, 167, 177, 179, 182–3, 185–6, 189, 194
Geneva, 10, 24, 94
  Consistory of, 84
  Genevan discipline, 39, 131
Glasgow, 19, 21–3, 28, 31, 54, 60, 67–8, 87–8, 92, 94, 97, 99–100, 105–6, 145
Gledstanes, Master John, 115
Glencairn, Earl of *see* Cunningham, Alexander
Goodacre, Anne, 107
Goodare, Julian, 53
Goodman, Christopher, minister of St Andrews, 83, 90–4, 101–2, 106, 152, 159, 194
Gordon, Alexander, Bishop of Galloway, 76, 78; *see also* Bishop
Gordon, George, fourth Earl of Huntly, 22, 67, 69
Gordon, Jane, 66–7, 70, 73–5
Gordon, William, Bishop of Aberdeen, 27
Guise, Mary of, Regent, 7, 9–10, 13–18, 20, 22, 34–5, 37n, 46, 52, 62, 85–6, 89, 110, 113–14, 128, 132, 134, 151

Haddington, 88, 99
Hamilton, 18, 22
Hamilton, Andrew, Commissary of Bute and Arran, 26
Hamilton, Gavin, Abbot of Kilwinning, 115
Hamilton, James, second Earl of Arran, Duke of Chatelherault, 10, 17–22, 46–7, 67, 91, 132–3
Hamilton, James, third Earl of Arran, 16–19, 22, 46–7, 96
Hamilton, Jane, 67, 100
Hamilton, Jerome, 85

Hamilton, John, Archbishop of St Andrews, 28, 41, 53, 64–7, 69–73, 79, 86, 129, 135–6, 140, 157; *see also* Archbishop
Hamilton, John, canon of Glasgow, 67
Hamilton, John, Commissary of Hamilton, 26
Hamilton, John, Commissary of Kilbride, 26
Hay, Edmund, procurator, 75
Hay, George, minister of Rathven, 101, 159, 179
Hay, Nichol, Commissary of Aberdeen, 26, 145
Henry II, 10, 42
Henryson, Edward, Commissary of Edinburgh, senator of the College of Justice, 62, 123–5, 142, 144, 153
Hepburn, James, fourth Earl of Bothwell, 66–7, 70, 73–5
Herbertson (Herbisoune), Robert, Commissary of Glasgow, 28, 67–8
Heresy, 9, 24–5, 72–3, 80–1, 93–4, 108, 148
Heriot, Adam, minister of St Andrews, minister of Aberdeen, 82–3, 90, 94, 97, 104–6
Holyroodhouse, kirk of, 164
Holyrood Palace, 17–18, 31, 52, 62, 75, 113
Holy Trinity kirk, St Andrews, 29, 92
Houston, John, canon of Glasgow, 67–8
Hume, Sir John, 122
Hunter, William, 167–9
Huntly, Earl of *see* Gordon, George

Innes, Thomas, 53
Inquiry of La Brosse and Cleutin, 17–21, 31, 33, 41, 62, 115, 134
Inveresk, kirk of, 164
Inverness, 145
ius commune, 9, 143

James I, 14
James V, 10, 19
James VI, 65, 70, 176
Jedburgh, 97, 103–4, 106
Johnston, Barbara, 183
Johnstone, Andrew, 108
Johnstone, William, advocate, 94, 108
Jurisdiction of Rome Act, 53–5, 63, 120
Justiciary Court *see* Court of the Lord Justice General

Keith, Robert, 17, 21, 53, 61
Keith, William, third Earl Marischal, 42n, 133n
Kidd (Kid), Robert, 101, 194
Kilconquhar, kirk of, 165, 168
Kincaid, Steven, sacristan of the collegiate church of Tain, 140–1

Index

King's Council, 110–11
Kinross, Henry, procurator, procurator fiscal, 75, 124, 152–3, 194
Kirk, James, 12, 17
Kirknewton, kirk of, 164
Kirk o' Fields, 73
Kirk session(s), 29, 45, 67, 82–95, 97, 98–109, 111–12, 142–3, 145, 156, 158–63, 165–7, 170, 175–6, 183, 185
  Aberdeen, 104–6
  Argyll, 92
  Ayr, 86
  Brechin, 86
  Canongate, 163–4
  Crail, 172
  Dundee, 86, 101, 106, 152, 194
  Edinburgh, 67–8, 80, 85–6, 89, 93–4, 100–1, 106–8, 135–6, 150–1, 153–4, 191
  Fife, 92, 106, 166
  Gamrie, 105–6
  Glasgow, 68, 87, 92, 99, 106, 152–3
  Haddington, 93, 191
  Jedburgh, 103–4, 106, 154–5, 158, 163, 181
  Kirkcaldy, 91
  Linlithgow, 93, 191
  Lothian, 92, 106
  Mearns, 92
  Montrose, 86
  Musselburgh, 164
  Orkney, 78, 106–7, 153–4
  Perth, 86
  St Andrews, 48, 80, 82–6, 89, 91–4, 98, 102–3, 106, 108–9, 136, 145, 150–1, 160, 162, 165–6, 168, 173–7, 181
  Stirling, 86, 93, 107, 191–2
Knox, John, minister of St Andrews, minister of Edinburgh, 10–12, 14, 24, 29, 59–61, 63, 68, 72–3, 80, 82–3, 85–90, 94, 96, 99–101, 103–4, 106–7, 135, 143, 145, 153, 159, 178–9

La Brosse, Jacques de, 17, 20, 115, 134; *see also* Inquiry
Lathrisk, Alexander, 91
Lathrisk, kirk of, 165
Law of God, 3, 68–9, 83, 85, 87, 90, 93–4, 98, 100, 102, 118n, 159, 161, 166–7, 179, 192–3
Law of Oblivion, 34, 42, 51–2, 64, 95, 116, 129, 151; *see also* Act of Oblivion
Legates, Papal *see* Papal legatine authority in Scotland

Legislation *see* Acts of Parliament
Leith, 16–18, 21, 35, 48–9, 93–4, 113, 164
Leslie, Andrew, fifth Earl of Rothes, 22, 46, 47
Leslie, Beatrix, 182
Leslie, Elizabeth, 102
Leslie, John, Bishop of Ross, 27, 39, 47, 50–1, 62; *see also* Bishop
Lindsay, David, minister of Leith, 178–9
Lindsay, Patrick, 19
Linlithgow, 19, 21, 29, 31, 88, 93, 99
Litill, Clement, advocate, Commissary of Edinburgh, 68, 100, 107, 123–4, 142, 144, 153–4, 156, 159
Livingston, Beatrix, 101
Lord Clerk Register *see* MacGill of Nether Rankeillour
Lord Justice Clerk, 18, 133; *see also* Bellenden of Auchnoul
Lord Justice General, 49; *see also* Campbell, Archibald
Lord President of the Court of Session, 30, 35, 59, 60, 62, 114–15, 125, 133–6, 143, 178; *see also* Court of Session
Lords Interpreters of the Law of Oblivion, 51–2
Lords of Council, 17, 20–5, 30, 37, 39, 41, 46, 52–3, 72, 86, 89, 91–3, 95, 99–100, 110–11, 122, 130, 132–3, 136, 138–9, 149, 151, 172, 179, 184, 191; *see also* Privy Council
Lords of Council and Session, 2, 7, 25–7, 55, 58–9, 62–3, 72, 75, 104, 110–30, 134–40, 142–3, 146, 149, 174, 188, 192–4; *see also* Court of Session
Lords of Secret Council *see* Lords of Council
Lords of the Congregation, 7, 9, 13–29, 31, 34–5, 37n, 38, 46–7, 49, 56, 81–2, 85–6, 96, 109–14, 122, 128, 132–4, 151, 176
Lothians, 14, 31, 93–4, 97–9, 106
Lovell, George, burgess of Dundee, 194
Lovell (Luvell), James, 101, 194
Lumsden (Lumisdene, Lummisden), Agnes, 192–3

MacCulloch of Ardwell, Golfride, 78
McGibbon, Thomas, 77
MacGill of Nether Rankeillour, James, Lord Clerk Register, 3, 18, 20, 35, 42, 58, 62, 68, 100, 107, 115–17, 128–9, 132–6, 142, 153, 178
McNeill, Peter, Sheriff, 2, 20, 36, 44, 50, 65, 175
Magistrate, civil, 10, 159, 168, 173
Maitland, Robert, Commissary of Edinburgh, senator of the College of Justice, 125, 142, 144

Maitland of Lethington, Sir Richard, senator of the College of Justice, 49, 62, 133, 134–5, 144, 178
Maitland of Lethington, William, Secretary, 19, 22, 24, 41, 43, 46–8, 70, 133–5, 178
Manderstoun, John, canon of Dunbar collegiate church, 74–5
Marischal, Earl *see* Keith, William
Marjoribanks, John, 123–4
Marriage Act, 51, 66, 69n
Martin, James, 93
Mary I *see* Tudor, Mary
Mary, Queen of Scots *see* Stewart, Mary
Mass Act, 28, 40, 46n, 49, 89, 187
Mauchan, Alexander, 123–4
Maxwell, John, Master of Maxwell, 17, 22, 46
Menteith, Earl of, 46, 47
Menzies, Archibald, Commissary of Dumfries, 145
Methven, Paul, minister of Dundee, minister of Jedburgh, 103, 106
Minister(s) 12, 39, 77, 82, 87–8, 91–7, 99–101, 103–4, 106, 109, 111, 136, 147, 152, 154, 159, 161, 163, 172, 194
  Aberdeen, 104–6
  Aberdour, 105
  Argyll, 92
  Ayr, 86
  Brechin, 86
  Dunblane, 136
  Dundee, 86, 101, 103, 106
  Edinburgh, 68, 85–6, 88, 99–100, 106–7, 136, 151, 153, 178, 191
  Elgin, 136
  Fife, 92, 106
  Galston, 107
  Gamrie, 105–6
  Geneva, 94
  Glasgow, 68, 87, 92, 99, 106
  Haddington, 191
  Jedburgh, 103, 106
  Kennoway, 136
  Kirkcaldy, 91
  Leith, 178–9
  Linlithgow, 191
  Lothian, 92, 106
  Mearns, 92
  Montrose, 86
  Orkney, 78, 106
  Perth, 86
  Rathven, 101, 179
  St Andrews, 82–3, 86, 90–3, 101–2, 106, 152, 168–9, 173–4, 194
  St Johnston, 179
  Stirling, 86, 191–2
Moneydie, parsonage and prebend of, 76–7
Monluc, John de, Bishop of Valence, 35
Montgomerie, Hugh, Earl of Eglinton, 28, 66–70
Moray, 145
Moray, Earl of *see* Stewart, Lord James
Morris, Robert, 183–4
Morton, Earl of *see* Douglas, James
Mowat, Margaret, 105
Murray, Margaret, 78
Murray of Tullibardine, Sir William, 17

Nicol (Nicole), Elizabeth, 193

Ochiltree, Lord *see* Stewart, Andrew
Official(s), 7, 26, 55–7, 62, 65, 75, 117–18, 125, 128, 137–9, 142, 145, 148, 177, 179, 189
  Aberdeen, 27
  Glasgow, 8, 28, 119, 145
  Lothian, 26, 30, 74, 114–15, 118, 124, 142–4, 178
  Orkney, 26
  Ross, 145
  St Andrews, 8, 26, 82, 119, 145, 150–1
  see also Courts spiritual
Official(s) Principal, 7, 55, 57
  Glasgow, 8, 54–5
  St Andrews, 8, 29–30, 54–5, 119
  see also Courts spiritual
Ogilvy, Janet, 104
Ollivant, Simon, 8, 56, 114, 125
Ordinance, of the Privy Council
  against the courts of the Catholic Church, 11, 15, 17–25, 27–8, 30–2, 52–3, 56, 72, 81, 89–90, 95, 112, 115–17, 120–2, 131, 134, 151, 187–9
  concerning usurping the spiritual jurisdiction, 172–4

Papal bulls, 59, 63; *see also* Papal provision
Papal judges, 4, 8, 54–6, 62–3, 66, 67–9, 115, 117–23, 128, 135, 140–1, 177, 189; *see also* Papal legatine authority in Scotland
Papal Jurisdiction Act, 40–1, 53–5, 57, 59–61, 63, 65–6, 140–1, 177, 187
Papal legatine authority in Scotland, 4, 8, 28, 54–6, 61, 63–4, 66–9, 71, 73–4, 76, 79, 136, 140, 177; *see also* Papal judges

Papal provision, 41, 59–61, 63; *see also* Papal bulls
Parliament, 1–2, 4, 7, 11–13, 17, 25–6, 28, 32–65, 68, 72, 77, 79–83, 86–91, 95, 99, 109–10, 112–14, 116–17, 120–3, 128, 131–4, 137, 151, 157–8, 170, 176, 179–80, 185, 187–8; *see also* Acts of Parliament
Perth, 13–14, 19, 22, 29, 31, 78, 86
Petrie, Alexander, minister of Rotterdam, 20–3
Pont, Robert, elder of St Andrews, minister of Dunblane and Elgin, commissioner of Moray, senator of the College of Justice, 136, 159
Privy Council, 7, 11–12, 17, 20, 22, 33, 45–7, 52, 56–7, 59–61, 63, 67–9, 71, 80–1, 86, 88–91, 93–100, 103–6, 108–12, 114–15, 121–2, 126, 129–36, 138–9, 142, 148–9, 151, 153–8, 167, 172, 179, 183, 187–9; *see also* Lords of Council; Ordinance, of the Privy Council
Proclamation of Leith, 34, 48–9, 52, 59–60, 64, 68, 70, 72, 95–7, 117, 129–31, 148, 157–8, 174–5, 177, 189
Procurator fiscal, 75, 124, 147, 182; *see also* Kinross, Henry
Provincial Council of the Catholic Church in Scotland, 50–1
Provision, papal *see* Papal provision

Queen's Advocate, 17, 115, 133; *see also* Spens of Condie

Ramsay, John, minister of Aberdour, 105
Ramsay, Thomas, Commissary of Brechin, 145
Ramsay, William, master of St Salvator's college, elder, 169
Randolph, Thomas, 40–3, 88, 96
Reader, 107, 147
Rector of St Andrews, 169; *see also* Douglas, John
Regalia of Scotland, 58
Regent of Scotland *see* Douglas, James; *see also* Guise, Mary of; Stewart, Lord James
Reid, Malcolm, Commissary of Caithness, 26
Renton, William, 82, 85, 90
Riddell, John, 81–2
Robertson, Joseph, 76, 81–2
Rochefoucauld, Charles de la, Comte de Randan, 35
Rolland, James, Commissary of St Andrews, 26, 145
Rollock (Rollok), Margaret, 194
Rothes, Earl of *see* Leslie, Andrew

Row, John, minister of Kennoway, minister of St Johnston, 136, 159, 179
Russell (Russall), Thomas, 164
Ruthven, Lord, 17–18, 22, 46–7, 96, 133

St Andrews, 7–8, 19, 22–3, 29–31, 54, 78, 82–3, 85–7, 90–4, 97–8, 101–4, 106, 145, 155, 160, 165–73, 176, 180–4
St Cuthbert's, kirk of, 164
St Giles' collegiate church, Edinburgh, 30, 74–5, 123–4
St John's church, Perth, 14
St Mary's college, St Andrews 146
St Paul, on obedience, 11–12
St Salvator's collegiate church, St Andrews, 146
Sandilands, Barbara, 167–9
Sandilands, James, Lord St John of Jerusalem, 40–5
Sclater, Elizabeth, 85
Scots College, Paris, 53
Scott, James, provost of Corstorphine collegiate church, 115
Senators of the College of Justice, 110, 114–15, 125–6, 133, 136, 142–4, 147; *see also* Court of Session
Shairp (Scharpe), John, procurator 124, 152, 194
Shaw, Duncan, 131
Sheriff(s), 7, 27, 118, 122, 185
Shetland, 7
Signet, Scottish, 18–21, 23, 95, 115, 131, 134
Sim (Sym), Alexander, Commissary of Edinburgh, 123–4, 144
Sim, Euphemia, 161
Sinclair, Henry, parson of Glasgow, Bishop of Ross, Lord President of the Court of Session, 3, 35, 49–50, 59–62, 68, 70, 115, 117, 129, 133–5, 142, 155, 178
Sinclair, John, dean of Restalrig, Bishop of Brechin, Lord President of the Court of Session, 3, 59, 61–3, 70, 115–16, 128–9
Skene, Alexander, procurator, 193
Skene, William, Commissary of St Andrews, 90, 145–6, 165, 175
Smith, David Baird, 124
Smith, David, Sheriff, 2, 81–2, 84, 117–19, 122–4
Spens of Condie, John, Queen's Advocate, 3, 17, 20, 62, 68, 100, 107, 115–17, 128–9, 133–5, 142, 153
Spottiswoode, John, Archbishop of St Andrews, 58, 61; *see also* Archbishop

Spottiswoode, John, superintendent of Lothian, 58, 68, 88–9, 92–4, 96, 98–100, 106–7, 130, 135–6, 153, 159, 167, 178–9, 191–2; *see also* Superintendent(s)
Stevenson, Constantine, 87
Stevenson, John, precentor of Glasgow, provost of Biggar collegiate church, 115, 120
Stevenson, Joseph, 21
Stewart, Alan, 76
Stewart, Andrew, second Lord Ochiltree, 14, 46–7, 91, 96
Stewart, Lord James, Prior of St Andrews, Earl of Moray, Regent of Scotland, 14, 17–18, 22, 29, 46–8, 65, 73, 91, 132–3, 176, 179
Stewart, Mary, Queen of Scots, 2, 10–13, 16–19, 22–3, 26, 28, 32–49, 52, 55, 57–61, 63–77, 79, 81, 89, 91–102, 106, 109, 111, 114, 128–30, 132–6, 138–9, 141, 146, 149, 151, 157–8, 172–4, 176–7, 180, 189, 192
Stewart, Robert, Bishop of Caithness, 78; *see also* Bishop
Stirling, 13–14, 18, 21–4, 26, 29, 31, 86, 88, 93, 99, 107, 146
Strageath, vicarage of, 146
Strang, George, Commissary of Shetland, 28n
Strang, George, Official of Orkney, 26
Strang, Richard, 124, 152–3
Struthers, Sir William, 76
Superintendent(s), 14, 45, 81, 88, 92, 94–7, 104, 106, 135, 151, 158
  Aberdeen, 97, 104–5
  Angus, 96, 101, 194; *see also* Erskine of Dun
  Angus and the Mearns, 94, 97, 100, 102, 122, 129, 194; *see also* Erskine of Dun
  Argyll, 92, 94, 96; *see also* Carswell, John
  Brechin, 92; *see also* Erskine of Dun
  Fife, Fotherick and Strathearn, 4, 29, 69, 77–8, 92–4, 97, 163, 183; *see also* Winram, John
  Glasgow and 'the West', 87–8, 94–7, 99–102, 152–3; *see also* Willock, John
  Jedburgh, 97, 104
  Lothian, 58, 88, 92, 97, 100–1, 107–8, 130, 136, 191–2; *see also* Spottiswoode, John, superintendent of Lothian
  St Andrews, 92, 168; *see also* Winram, John

Superintendent's court, 45, 69, 78, 83, 87–94, 98–106, 109, 142–3, 145, 152–4, 156–7, 160–3, 165–72, 176, 181–5; *see also* Superintendent(s)

Teulet, Alexandre, 40
Thacker, Elizabeth, 93
Throckmorton, Nicholas, 43–4
Tolbooth, Edinburgh, 16, 18, 75, 125
Torphichen, 41
Treaty of
  Berwick, 20, 35, 37, 40–3, 58, 116
  'Cambray', 35
  Edinburgh, 35–7, 39–44, 114, 134
  Leith, 35, 53, 114
Tudor, Mary, 10, 11

Valois, Francis, Dauphin of France, King of Scots, King of France, 10–11, 16–19, 22–3, 35–44, 46, 49, 58, 95, 114, 115

Wars of the Congregation, 7, 9, 13–16, 20, 25, 28, 31, 34, 42, 44, 47–50, 52, 57, 103, 113–16, 123, 131, 133, 142, 188
Weddell, Christine, 164
Wedderburn (Weddirburne), Alexander, 101, 194
Wemyss, Janet, 173–5
Weston, John, 99
Whithorn, 7
Wilkie, James, elder of St Andrews, 169
Willock, John, minister of Edinburgh, minister of Glasgow, superintendent of Glasgow, 14, 85–9, 92, 94–6, 99–101, 105–6, 130, 152, 159
Winram, John, subprior of St Andrews, superintendent of Fife, Fotherick and Strathearn, 78, 85, 90, 92–4, 96, 100, 102, 105–6, 130, 136, 150, 155, 159, 160–1, 166–8, 172, 178–9, 182–4; *see also* Superintendent(s)
Wishart of Pittarrow, John, 14, 17, 22, 46, 91, 133
Wotton, Nicholas, 35

EU representative:
Easy Access System Europe
Mustamäe tee 50, 10621 Tallinn, Estonia
Gpsr.requests@easproject.com

www.ingramcontent.com/pod-product-compliance
Lightning Source LLC
Chambersburg PA
CBHW070353240426
43671CB00013BA/2486